TO BEAR ~~THE~~

THE WAR *was a lot of things*
to Morgan Preston

It was the flag and honor and the promise of
adventure. It was buddies who became
closer than brothers.

It was a Saigon barmaid named Tam who
came to his bed for cash and stayed with him
for love. It was waiting in the jungle, the fire
fights that exploded like eruptions from Hell.

It was fighting to the limits of courage for
nothing more than the men around him and
his own survival. It was nights of drugs and
sex in search of forgetfulness.

It was coming home and finding the war
could not be left behind.

To Bear the Mark of Wounds

Ed Dodge

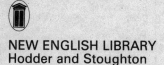

NEW ENGLISH LIBRARY
Hodder and Stoughton

Copyright © 1984 by Ed Dodge

The characters and situations in this book are entirely imaginary and bear no relation to any real person or actual happening.

First published in the United States by Macmillan Publishing Company

First New English Library Paperback edition, 1988

TO BEAR THE MARK OF WOUNDS was previously published under the title DAU

British Library C.I.P.

Dodge, Ed
  [Dau]. To bear the mark of wounds.
  I. [Dau]   II. Title
  813'.54[F]   PS3554.0334

ISBN 0 450 06122 1

Printed and bound in Great Britain for Hodder and Stoughton Paperbacks, a division of Hodder and Stoughton Ltd., Mill Road, Dunton Green, Sevenoaks, Kent TN13 2YA.
(Editorial Office: 47 Bedford Square, London WC1B 3DP) by Cox & Wyman Ltd., Reading.

For:

DAVE BRUNING, KIA

PETE COLLINS, KIA

THICH QUANG DUC

Seven hundred thousand Vietnam veterans who suffer from Post Traumatic Stress Disorder

JOE COCKER, *for a song of sustenance*

DON CRAIN, *who met the Buddha on the road*

NANA, *the Phantom of the RTD*

JAMIE DIANNE, *my sister, for her endless encouragement*
My "pup," SHANNON

And especially for my wife, ROSE DOYLE DODGE, *who always knew there was light at the end of the tunnel*

With special gratitude to ALICE FRIED MARTELL, HILLEL BLACK, ARLENE FRIEDMAN, *and* ANDREA RAAB *for taking a chance*

9 October 1983

Ed Dodge

Author's Note   The word "dau" in
Vietnamese means "pain." "Cô dầu bi
danh" means "to bear the mark of wounds."

*The soldier, above all other people,
prays for peace, for he must suffer
and bear the deepest wounds and scars
of war.*

—DOUGLAS MACARTHUR

— 1 —

July 1965. Fighting the oppressive heat of the sultry summer night, Morgan Preston and two friends piled into a maroon Chevy Malibu 396 and headed for the Music Box, a teen dance spot at Houghton Lake, Michigan. Harper was behind the wheel, Bartlett rode shotgun, and Morgan sat in back.

Speeding up U.S. 27 at seventy miles an hour, chain-smoking cigarets and swigging from ice-cold bottles of Pabst Blue Ribbon beer, they chattered inanely among themselves: random thoughts, dirty jokes, and other senseless maunderings. Their voices struggled to be heard above the radio music from WLS, Chicago, which rocked and rolled out of front and rear speakers, the bass music competing with the dual exhaust thunder of the Chevy's perfectly tuned engine.

After about an hour on the road the trio's adrenaline rush subsided, and they grew quiet. Harper and Bartlett slipped into individual but identical reveries in which everything, real or imagined, seemed good and right and true; both young men, oblivious to everything except their own lives, locked into dreams and hopes and possibilities that their futures promised to fulfill. And in so doing they deluded themselves, not only into believing themselves invincible but also immortal. The world, they both knew, was theirs for the taking.

Finally, the super Chevy turned right and followed the curves of the highway paralleling Houghton Lake's southern shoreline. Harper double-clutched and down-shifted in a screech of burnt tire rubber as they tacked onto the tail of an idled line of traffic: forty or fifty cars whose drivers revved the engines and honked horns while a wedge of teenagers staggered and stomped their way across all four lanes, heading for the beach, lugging with them two ponies of beer. Borne aloft in the arms of a hulking football player from Michigan State University, an underaged teenybopper cupped her small breasts with both hands, as though she were offering her tender buds to the stars which benignly shone down upon her.

Morgan and his friends followed the now-moving procession of bumper-to-bumper traffic, then lurched to a halt as the brake lights of the car ahead blazed red in response to the wail of an urgent siren which preceded a police car—its red and blue lights flashing as its state trooper driver fought for control on the shoulder of the road, the tires throwing up sand and gravel as he sped toward some unseen mishap further ahead.

Exhaust fumes polluted the lakeside air as the line of cars moved once more, past a hamburger stand and its parking lot filled with cars and moving bodies. Tanned kids with wide white smiles stood in line to order food, most of them in their mid- to late teens, all of them dressed identically in denim cut-offs and T-shirts and sporting sunglasses on top of their sun-bleached hair: midwestern boys who wore their hair in imitation Beatle-style and midwestern girls whose hairstyles were more diverse: some pigtailed and parted in the middle, others long and ironed straight, still others short and pixied. They stood in line, money in hand, laughing, talking, flirting—famished from a day spent waterski-ing, swimming, or simply tanning on the beach—and waited to gorge themselves on hamburgers, fries, and Cokes.

At the rear of the parking lot, a group of bikers—each individual as hirsute and grizzled looking as a Sierra Nevadan Silvertip—lounged against their chop-pers after their nonstop, Benzedrine-assisted run from Gary, Indiana. Grease from their piled pompadours dripped down behind their ears to their necks and mingled there with the dried sweat and grime accumu-lated on their long journey. Faded tattoos—crosses, devils, girls' names, hearts emblazoned with Mom or

Dad, or the words Born to Love, Born to Raise Hell,
Born to Die—were crudely etched into the skin of their
shoulders, biceps, forearms, backs of hands. Their
sleeveless denim jackets were unbuttoned and revealed
fish-white, beer-flabbed bellies. Their jackets themselves were festooned with metal swastikas and wings
enameled red or black, testimony to each biker's personal sexual proclivities. Sullenly out of place and
knowing it, the bikers—pallid caricatures of the Wild
Ones—preferred to remain in the long shadows thrown
across the parking lot by the hamburger stand's glaring,
bug-sizzling, neon lights.

Harper guided them through the town of Pruden-
ville. Pizza parlors and coffee shops emitted the steady,
happy sounds of the young—the binging, buzzing
sounds of pinball machines, the grinding of malted milk
mixers. The air was redolent with the smell of vented
grill grease.

The Chevy was parked in a huge parking lot, and the
three young men walked across the dewy grass to the
Music Box. They paid for their tickets and walked inside, where their ears were assaulted with the sound of
music coming from four-foot-tall speakers. Their eyes
took in the packed crowd of eight hundred teenagers,
most of whom were engrossed in dancing the Jerk, the
Frug, the Pony, the Swim.

Morgan and his friends found girls to dance with and
enjoyed themselves for the next two hours. At closing
time they found their car in the empty parking lot and
reversed their course, heading back to U.S. 27 for the
trip back home. None of the three youths knew at that
time that in the space of the next four years two of them
would be killed in Vietnam and one of them would go
insane. How could they have known? After all, being
only seventeen and eighteen, having the world by the
ass, and believing themselves immortal, they hadn't
understood the implications of the Gulf of Tonkin clash
between the destroyer *Maddox* and North Vietnamese
PT boats. They did not know nor did they care who

General Lewis Hershey was or what he symbolized.

For Morgan there had been early intimations of what was happening in Vietnam. In 1960, he had been leafing through a magazine and had come across a picture of a helmeted man seated behind a machine gun in a helicopter. The caption had said: American Advisor in Vietnam. And when he had been waiting to get his hair cut prior to graduating from eighth grade, he had picked up a comic book and read it. It told the story of a group of Vietnamese villagers sequestered behind the mud and bamboo walls of a New Life hamlet who had to fight off nightly attacks by the Viet Cong. In the end the villagers prevailed over their black-clad attackers.

In June of 1963 a Buddhist monk in Saigon had immolated himself in full view of television cameras, and Morgan had watched it on the nightly news, had watched the flames consume the bonze, had watched him topple sideways and lie burning on the pavement.

In November of the same year South Vietnam's president Diem had been assassinated following a coup by ARVN soldiers. Morgan thought this event rather significant but forgot it quickly later that month when President Kennedy had been gunned down in Dallas. Morgan had cried unabashedly as he watched the horses pull the casket-laden caisson through the streets of Washington to the final resting place in Arlington National Cemetery.

In August 1964 the North Vietnamese had launched PT boat attacks against an American destroyer in the Gulf of Tonkin, and American air strikes against North Vietnam had been launched less than twelve hours later.

In February 1965, during Morgan's senior year in high school, United States Army personnel at Pleiku were killed in a guerilla attack, and the United States once again bombed North Vietnam.

In March of the same year the first official United States combat troops, marines, landed at Danang and by August had mounted their initial combat operations.

Morgan was aware that the Vietnam ''thing'' was

growing every week, judging by the television and news-paper reports, but it did not bother him. It was too far away, too insignificant to his life.

He was drifting, and he knew it. He was not going to college in the fall, and he was too young to apply for work in the auto factories. The thought of spending a whole summer pumping gas for his grandfather depressed him. He knew he had to make some kind of move, any kind of a move.

— 2 —

Morgan's divorced parents stood with him inside the Lansing train depot. Outside, a thunderstorm lashed the dry Michigan countryside.

Morgan's father kept clearing his throat, as if preparing to say something, but he didn't. His face was red.

Morgan looked out a rain-washed window and remembered the separate conversations he had had two weeks earlier with his parents. His father had been playing golf when Morgan approached him near a sandtrap.

"Dad?"

"Wait a minute, Morg." His father chipped onto the green; the ball rolled to a halt several inches from the cup.

"Good shot, huh, son?" he said, sliding a seven iron back into the bag. "What's up?"

"I just wanted to tell you that I want to join the service."

The older man's features stiffened. "Jesus Christ, do you want to wind up at the University of Saigon?"

In response to his father's sarcasm, Morgan put his hands in his pockets and hung his head momentarily. Then he said, "I'm tired of pumping gas. I'm not old enough to get into the factories, and I'm not going on to college. I figured I'd do four years in the service and—"

"Four years? You want to join the navy?"

"No. I can't swim. I was thinking of the air force."

"You can't fly, can you?"

Morgan laughed uncertainly. "No, but I've always had a thing for the air force. When I was a kid I used to read about it in the encyclopedia."

"Are you sure about this, Morgan? Vietnam is going to get a hell of a lot worse before it gets better."

"Dad, there's nothing that says I'm automatically going to Vietnam just because I join the air force. I could wind up anywhere. Besides, you took your chances in World War Two."

"That was different."

"Why?"

"We knew who we were fighting, and why. But this Vietnam thing, nobody seems to know."

"The papers say we're fighting for a democracy and trying to stop the communists," said Morgan.

"That's all fine and good," said his father, "but it's so far away. It doesn't really affect us. It's not like they're going to attack us, like the Japs did at Pearl Harbor."

"I still want to join," Morgan said adamantly.

"Your mother's your legal guardian. I'm not going to sign for you, but if she does, then I guess you're on your way."

"Dad?"

"What?"

"How old were you when you joined the navy?"

"Eighteen."

"I'm almost eighteen, so what's the big deal?"

Morgan's father sighed. "The big deal is that you're my son. And I don't want to see you hurt."

Morgan's father turned away and walked toward the green. Reaching it, he lit a cigaret and watched his son walk back to the clubhouse. When he had disappeared, Morgan's father lined up the nine-inch putt carefully and putted. His hands were shaking so badly that he missed.

When Morgan had approached his mother with the request to sign the enlistment papers, her reaction was much the same as her ex-husband's had been. But Morgan had been persistent.

"Mom, just listen. I'm only seventeen, but if I wait a couple of years, I'll be drafted into the army. And if you're drafted, that's like getting a one-way ticket to Vietnam. At least in the air force I'll have a choice of where I get stationed, and I can learn a trade. In the army all I'd learn is how to fight."

After several days of being worn down by his insistence, Morgan's mother gave in and reluctantly signed the papers.

The PA system announcing that the train was ready to board brought Morgan back to the present. He picked up his overnight bag and walked through the double doors to the platform, flanked by his parents.

Morgan's father coughed nervously and shook Morgan's hand. "Good luck, son," he said. Morgan's mother hugged him, her eyes filled with tears. "Pray every night, and God will protect you." Morgan stepped back from the embrace then turned and boarded the train.

A half hour out of Lansing, the thunderstorm abated; the sun shone brightly in the blue sky. Morgan, growing accustomed to the rhythmical clacking of the train's wheels as he was carried southeast through Michigan farm land, sat in his seat and watched fields of wheat and corn receding. He heard the warning whistle as the train approached crossings in small towns and watched the lines of cars waiting behind the wooden crossing guards. He got up and, bracing himself against the train's rollicking motion, walked back to the dining car. He ordered a hamburger and a beer. The waiter, a white-haired black man, studied him. "How old you be, boy?"

Morgan didn't even try to lie. "Seventeen," he said.

"You a little under age."

"But I'm going into the service. I'm joining the air force."

"That so? I was in the air force, a long time ago. Brown shoe air force in them days. You gonna be a pilot?"

"No. You have to have a college degree to become a pilot."

"I was a cook, myself. Never had no use for pilots." The waiter lowered his voice to a conspiratorial level and said, "What kind of beer you want to go along with that hamburger, boy? I got Bud and Pabst and Schlitz."

"Pabst will be fine." The waiter left and several minutes later returned with the order.

"You only seventeen, but I guess you're old enough to know what it mean to be a military man."

"What's that?"

"Sometimes it mean killin' other men." Morgan took a bite from the hamburger and swallowed it down with beer. "And sometimes," added the waiter, "it mean dyin'."

The Detroit sky was dark and full of heat lightning when Morgan stepped down onto the depot's platform. He felt woozy from the four beers he had drunk, the last one a free one from the waiter, who had said, "It's my treat, boy. You keep your money because you might need it in this hootchy-koo town."

Seventeen and woozy drunk, and alone in Detroit on a hot August night, Morgan felt great. The train had carried him miles from home and dropped him off in a strange city. Left behind, and in his excitement almost forgotten, were his parents. Momentum now carried him. Had he wanted to, he could not have gone back. Ahead of him waited the induction center at Fort Wayne and basic training at San Antonio, Texas.

He lit a cigaret. Killing and dying. That is what the black waiter had told him. "If that's what it takes, that's what it takes," he said, picking up his overnight bag and walking toward a line of taxis.

— 3 —

The taxi deposited him at the Fort Wayne recruitment center. Morgan entered the administration building. A clerk signed him in, issued him sheets and a blanket, and directed him to a squad bay where about three dozen men were already sleeping. He made his bed, then went out into the dim hallway and deposited twenty cents into a Coke machine. He sipped at the cold drink and began thinking.

This Vietnam thing. This Vietnam what? Issue? Conflict? He knew that Vietnam had been a major issue in the 1964 presidential campaign. Morgan had been a junior in high school then, and on television he had watched President Johnson solemnly promise to keep America out of Vietnam's internal affairs, while Johnson's opponent, Senator Barry Goldwater, had declared it his intention to go into Vietnam and get it over with.

Morgan swallowed more Coke and lit a cigaret. Is Vietnam a conflict? he wondered. He knew that Korea had been called a conflict and that it had ended in a draw, with a truce line drawn at the thirty-eighth parallel between the Republic of South Korea and communist North Korea.

Something clicked in his head: the republic of South Vietnam and communist North Vietnam; a truce line separating them at—what?—the seventeenth parallel? After the French had been defeated at a place called Dien Bien something, back in the fifties?

Then maybe Vietnam is a conflict, Morgan thought. It is too small to be a war. There is only the South Vietnamese army, and some American advisors, and now the marines. Less than three months ago he had seen on television a group of marines landing at Danang. There had been a band and pretty Vietnamese girls who had placed a lei around the neck of each marine as he waded ashore. The marines had not stormed ashore like they did in the movies, so it could not be much of a war, Morgan thought.

"To hell with it," he muttered. "I'm too tired to think." He extinguished his cigaret in a sand-filled ashtray, swallowed the last few drops of Coke, then padded barefoot to his bunk and climbed in. He could barely make out the sound of a radio nearby playing the tune "Detroit City."

— 4 —

At 5:00 A.M. a PFC entered the squad bay and flicked on the overhead lights. "Rise and shine, rainbows. Ya got fifteen minutes to shower, shave, and shit. Ya got it? Fall out."

Morgan wiped sleep from his eyes, peered down at the bunk underneath his, and saw that it was empty. The night before it had been occupied by a black youth, and Morgan had heard him saying, "Them Vietcongs ain't never done nothing to me. The only place I'm going is back home." Morgan guessed that the youth had done exactly that. After attending to their toilets, the group of young men ambled in a disorganized procession to the chow hall.

Breakfast consisted of a bowl of oatmeal with a cold piece of toast thrown on top of it. "You wanna look at it instead of eating it, then move the fuck outta the line, lardass," the cook snarled at a chubby kid. Orange juice and coffee completed the meal.

The first light of dawn was filtering through the windows when the group returned to the squad bay. A corporal was waiting for them.

"O.K., listen up. We're going to do this by the numbers. Form a single line and follow me." He started off down the corridor. Mildly confused and apprehensive, the recruits followed him, at times shuffling their feet as their line bottlenecked at turns in the corridor, at other times quickstepping as their line stretched out. The corporal halted abruptly. Men at the back of the line lurched into the men in front of them, causing mild complaints and laughter.

"Shut up and listen up. This is station one. The personnel here will tell you what to do. You don't do anything but keep your mouths shut and do what you're told to do. Does everybody understand?" The ensuing silence was broken only by the sound of coughing.

"After you're through here, you follow the red arrow that's painted on the wall. You'll come to station two. You do what the personnel there tell you to do, then you proceed to station three, and so on until you're done."

"When will that be, sir?" someone asked.

"When you're done, dipshit," answered the corporal. "You're done when you're done."

The recruits were given triplicate forms to fill out. The sergeant in charge of station one spied two whispering recruits. "I didn't give you permission to talk," he growled.

"I was just asking how to spell September," one of the youths explained. "For where it says to put your birthday."

"September is spelled n-i-n-e, and it ain't your birthday, asshole, it's your date of birth." After finishing with station one, the group followed the arrow to station two, where they filled out more papers. The rest of the stations entailed more of the same, plus a physical examination.

The doctors who examined the recruits were civilians who had been contracted by the Department of Defense. Most of them looked as if their years of medicine had been so devoted to healing the sick that they had neglected their own health. These physicians peered into the recruits' eyes, ears, and noses. Stomachs were palpated. The sole duty of one doctor, who chewed on a dead cigar, was to peer up the anuses of the recruits as they spread their cheeks.

Station eleven was psychiatry. The doctor sat behind a desk, his shirt-sleeves rolled up. Morgan sat down across from him.

"Have you ever been in trouble with the law?"

"No."

"Trouble in school?"

"No."

"What are your hobbies?"

"Waterskiing, baseball, reading."

"Have you ever had a girl friend?"

"Yes."

"Any homosexual tendencies?"

"No."

"Last question. Name three U.S. presidents."

"Kennedy, Johnson, and Chester Arthur."

The psychiatrist looked up. "Have you ever been a smartass?"

"All my life, I guess."

"Good. You'll need a sense of humor in the army."

"The air force," corrected Morgan.

"Air force. Right. Good luck. Next."

After the long day spent processing, the recruits were allowed to leave and go out into the city for the night.

Morgan rode a bus to Briggs Stadium and watched the Tigers lose as he sat in the general admission section. Afterwards he took another bus downtown and ate a chili dog at a greasy spoon. He flushed it down with a Coke, the ice in it melting rapidly in the night's muggy heat. He had started back to Fort Wayne when a sidewalk hawker, a disheveled man with wine stains on his shirt, grabbed his arm and insisted he buy a ticket to a burlesque show. Morgan did not need all that much persuading; he bought the ticket, went into the theater, and sat near the back. He felt conspicuous when his eyes adjusted to the darkness and he realized that he was the only clean-cut person among a peppering of old men.

On a stage a rubber-faced comedian, wearing a straw boater and a seersucker coat, told stale jokes. The sparse audience responded with feeble groans and slightly more energetic calls of "Bring on the broads."

And on they came, one at a time, bewigged, bejeweled, begloved, each stripper's face caked with make-up which failed to hide the deep lines of failure. Their eyes, heavily mascaraed, stared unseeingly over the heads of the audience. Glossy lipstick smiles were frozen on each stripper's face. Each girl took five minutes of time to perfunctorily strip down to pasties and G-string as they danced and bumped and ground in haphazard time to phonograph records. As each stripper departed the stage after her allotted time, a bored, unshaven man sitting behind a set of drums at the edge of the stage did a series of uninspired rimshots.

The audience became more vocal as a well-endowed young blonde came to center stage and began her act.

"Shake yer tits, baby," a voice down front demanded.

"Oh, mama, let me dive in," hooted a voice in mock frustration.

"C'mon, honey," challenged a voice as the stripper teased her fingers over the front of her G-string, "show me that true-blue, blonde pussy."

Morgan knew it was time to leave when an obviously drunken voice slurred out, "Mama, let me lick your sweet asshole."

— 5 —

Awakened at 5:00 A.M. by the loudspeaker, the youths were ushered into a small room. A staff sergeant entered and walked onto a small stage that was flanked by the American and the Department of the Air Force flags.

"Repeat after me," he said. "I, and say your name here . . ." Morgan and sixty-four others repeated the oath of enlistment. Done, the sergeant, a jocular fellow with Eddie Cantor eyes, wrapped himself in the Ameri-

can flag and said, "Congratulations, men, you now
have the chance to die for your country."

The air force recruits were bussed to Metropolitan
Airport, where they killed several hours by playing pool
and watching television and memorizing their service
numbers. That night they boarded a chartered plane and
left Detroit behind them. After a brief stop in Indian-
apolis to pick up more recruits, they continued through
the night, some of them sleeping, some of them playing
cards.

The plane landed at Houston in the early morning.
The men filed off, walked across the already hot tar-
mac, and boarded another plane. After flying over the
Astrodome, the plane turned to the southwest, flew over
the sere Texas flatlands, and brought them down at San
Antonio, Texas, home of Lackland Air Force Base.

— 6 —

For Morgan, basic training was a grind. There
was so much to learn, so many things to be done. Their
first lesson in discipline had been no more than fifteen
minutes after the bus had driven them from the airport
to their old, two-story barracks on the sprawling military complex. Their drill instructor, a whip-thin staff
sergeant named Cody, had bellowed for the youths to
hit the floor and give him fifty push-ups. The startled

and bewildered recruits complied as best they could, and
after Sergeant Cody had left them studying the Uniform
Code of Military Justice, one boy from Kalamazoo
broke the apprehensive silence and said what they were
all thinking—"We're in for a world of shit."

And then it was six weeks of up at 0500 and lights out
at 2200, the days filled with calisthenics, marching, formations, obstacle courses, the firing range, and learning
military courtesies, with Sergeant Cody pushing them
all the way, sometimes begging them to tighten up and
become a homogeneous unit, but most of the time bully-
ing them to. Barking at their heels all day, Sergeant
Cody ushered his recruits through the first week of mass
confusion to the sixth week of cohesiveness of ninety
young men, and transformed the callow civilians into a
dedicated, disciplined group of airmen.

There had been two incidents during the basic training of Morgan's group that had marred it. The first was
the attempted suicide of a quiet blond youth who, on
the third day of training, sawed through his wrist with a
razor blade and ran around the barracks screeching like
a disinterred wraith until other recruits wrested him to
the floor. Sergeant Cody had slapped the youth several
times and then had driven him to the base hospital.

By common silent agreement the young man was
never again mentioned.

The second incident involved death. As the unit was
marching in the 105-degree heat, a tall, lanky boy
named Paladino collapsed. He was hurried off to the
hospital, and that night Sergeant Cody had come back
to the barracks to announce that Paladino had suffered
heat stroke and had died. In a subdued tone Sergeant
Cody had imparted the idea that the rest of the basic
training he dedicated to the memory of Paladino, and at
the end of the sixth week Morgan's unit had graduated
as the squadron's honor flight.

Morgan received orders to report to Sheppard Air
Force Base near Wichita Falls, Texas, to begin technical
school, and after five and a half additional months of

training in the transportation field returned home for a month's leave before reporting to Travis Air Force Base, California, for a flight to Guam, which would become his duty station for the next eighteen months.

— 7 —

Morgan sat in the bustling air terminal at Travis Air Force Base and watched the people around him. Going out one door was a group of soldiers bound for Japan, and coming in another was a group of soldiers arriving from Hawaii.

"Your attention, please. Flight one-o-seven to the Republic of South Vietnam is now boarding." A ragged cheer went up from the crowd, and 162 soldiers, sailors, and airmen stood and formed a line in front of one of the doors.

Several hours later Morgan boarded a Boeing 707, which flew him and 161 others to Guam via Hawaii. It was now April 1966 and Morgan, barely eighteen, with one stripe on his arm, was overseas.

— 8 —

February 1967. Guam; 2240 hours. Morgan sat facing the communications console in the Air Traffic Control Center. A piece of red plastic embedded in the console lit up and, simultaneously, the earphones to his headset buzzed. He leaned forward and flipped a black toggle switch; the earphones filled his head with the bored voice of an airman at the Airlift Command Post. "The medevac is down."

"Roger the medevac," confirmed Morgan. He then flipped the switch that connected him with Medevac Assistance, Air Freight, and Fleet Service. As he waited for them to answer he looked out through the double doors and saw the landing lights of the C-141 Starlifter run past out on the runway, and heard the thunder of its four jet engines. Morgan saw a blue half-ton truck with a flashing electric bulb arrow in its bed waiting at the far end of the runway, ready to guide the Starlifter to its parking stand.

On the far side of the runway, guarded by Strategic Air Command police, a fleet of camouflaged, shark-tailed B-52s waited silently in the darkness for their crews.

The medevac was guided into its parking stand at 2255, and blocked. Morgan was relieved of duty at 2300 and went out through the double doors and down to the medevac. He stood near the medevac and watched the swirl of activity. Ground support crews hustled about, their movements economical and efficient. Hutch, a tall kid from Connecticut, was busy pumping out the mede-vac's toilets and checking the gauges on the side of the large, yellow honey wagon.

Morgan smiled at Mr. Cruz as he brushed past, his powerful, mahogany arms laden with box lunches. A Filipino, he had served as a valet to an American officer

in Manila and had staggered along with the officer on
the Bataan death march. The officer had died in intern-
ment, but Mr. Cruz had endured, and when he had been
liberated by MacArthur's soldiers, he had pointed out
the officer's unmarked grave in the jungle. Amidst the
confusion of liberation, Mr. Cruz had been evacuated
to Guam and had been there ever since. His thick hair
had now turned steely gray, and he bore a crescent-
shaped scar etched around his right eye that extended to
mid-temple, which caused him to appear continually
sad. Even after all these years, he was still serving Americans on their journeys of pain.

Irritated by the flashing red light mounted on a medevac ambulance, Morgan moved away, climbed the steps
of the plane, and disappeared inside. To his left and up
a short set of stairs, the crew sat on the flight deck, the
pilot and copilot drinking coffee while the navigator
was hunched over a table which was hidden under a
complexity of charts. Morgan turned to his right, then
pressed against the bulkhead as an air force nurse made
her way through the narrow passageway. As she passed
him, his nostrils picked up her scent: perfume, soap,
and weariness. She climbed up into the flight deck, and
he watched her buttocks working under blue slacks. He
walked past the latrines until he stood looking into the
cavernous belly of the plane.

The bulkheads were lined with litters, and each litter
held a wounded or sick GI. Because the interior of the
plane was cold, each patient had been issued a heavy
woolen blanket. IV bottles hung above most of the litter
cases. Plastic tubes snaked down from transparent
bottles and fed sustaining fluids into the wounded
young men. Other tubes appeared from under the
blankets and emptied urine into plastic bags. Several
nurses and corpsmen moved among the litters, monitor-
ing their afflicted charges.

The floor area between the bulkheads was filled with
neat rows of seats. Strapped into them, the ambulatory

patients talked quietly among themselves in groups of two and three. Some chewed on sandwiches, compliments of Mr. Cruz. These patients wore the blue robes issued them at Cam Ranh Bay.

Although wounded or diseased, these men shared a bond that casualties of all wars had shared: they had fought, been hit and, most importantly, had survived. Behind the pain and exhaustion that their eyes reflected, there was a glimmer, a knowledge that they had triumphed and survived to tell about it. There was also something else present among these men, an electriclike vibration: They were going home.

In the tail section, isolated from the rest, two casualties slumped in their seats. Their arms and legs were tied to the seats with restraining straps. One of them was sleeping, his face angelic. The other soldier was awake. He sat ramrod straight in his seat, occasionally testing the leather cuffs which held him. His eyes glared savagely from his ravaged face. His lips moved constantly as he inaudibly repeated some insane litany. His eyes stabbed out toward Morgan. Morgan met the crazed stare. The man hawked up phlegm and spat it at Morgan.

"What the fuck are you staring at, asshole?" screamed the deranged soldier, then added prophetically, "You're next, you know."

A B-52 lumbered down the runway, its eight engines thundering; gradually gaining speed and reaching rotation, the Strato-fortress lifted gracefully into the star-filled sky.

Nine other B-52s followed. Banking westward while climbing to an altitude of twenty-six thousand feet, the flight flew in formation toward the Red River Delta region of North Vietnam, over which each B-52 would disgorge its lethal bomb load of thirty tons. Over the Philippines a flight of KC-135 tankers would refuel the B-52s in midair. The twenty-five-hundred-mile round trip would take twelve hours to complete.

A Russian trawler stood twenty-five miles off the end
of the runway at Guam, riding the gentle swells of the
Pacific. Communications antennae on its bridge bristled
like the whiskers of an indolent cat. Below decks Soviet
intelligence personnel sat hunched over pale green radar
scopes. An encoded message was beamed from the
trawler to a communications center on Hainan Island,
which then transmitted the message to Hanoi. Sam
missile sites were alerted. Civilians sought shelter. North
Vietnam waited patiently for the impending arrival of
the skyborne rolling thunder.

— 9 —

July 1967. Guam.

"Airman Second Class Preston reporting as requested, sir."

Colonel Breen, the squadron commander, returned
Morgan's salute and told the airman to sit down. "I
wanted to tell you that your request for a consecutive
overseas tour has been approved. You'll be leaving for
Vietnam on One October. You'll be going to an air
cargo unit at Vung Tau."

"Where's that, sir?"

"It's southeast of Saigon, on the coast. It's an R 'n' R
site, so I hope you enjoy your tour."

"Thank you, sir. Is that all?"

"Almost. I just wanted to personally congratulate you. You're the first man from my squadron who has volunteered for Vietnam, and that makes me proud."

"Thank you, sir."

"One other thing, Airman Preston. Why did you volunteer for Vietnam after spending eighteen months here?"

"Well, sir, I figured that if I rotated to the States after this tour, I'd only be in the States a couple of months before they cut orders for me to go to Vietnam. I just thought I'd beat them to the punch."

"Still and all I find your volunteering commendable."

"Thank you, sir."

"You're dismissed, young man." Morgan saluted and left.

— 10 —

The night before he left Guam for Vietnam, Morgan's friends threw a party for him. They drank until dawn and gave him a present—a slalom water ski.

"Have fun with it at Vung Tau," said Ayres.

"Boy, did you ever luck out on an assignment," said Singleton. "Everyone else is fighting through rice paddies, and you're going to an R 'n' R base."

"Be careful," they all said in one way or another.

— 11 —

October 1967. The Boeing 707 jet landed on the
tarmac at Tan Son Nhut and taxied to a stop in front of
the terminal. The 162 men on board filed out of the
plane and into the terminal, which was in a state of
controlled chaos. One hundred and sixty-two soldiers
waited to go on R 'n' R to Hawaii. Two loudspeakers
were blaring simultaneously, one in English, one in
Vietnamese. An Air Vietnam flight was boarding, destined for Phnom Penh and Vientiane. Vietnamese children fidgeted in their mothers' arms. MPs and Quan
Canh, the Vietnamese police, stood idly by. Vendors
selling warm Cokes moved through the crowd.

The inbound men passed through customs and traded
their dollars for MPCs, or military scrip. Trucks were
waiting outside to ferry the men to their respective destinations.

"You can walk to your unit," one of the MPs told
Morgan, giving him directions. "It isn't very far."

Morgan walked outside into the ninety-degree night,
carrying his duffel bag and water ski. The first thing he
saw was a huge billboard advertising toothpaste in Vietnamese. He walked past the brightly lit air freight area
operated by the Ninth Aerial Port Squadron and found
the transient barracks.

"The orderly room don't open until morning, and all
our bunks are full," said the man on duty. "You'll have
to sleep in one of the chairs on the porch. What's with
the water ski?"

"I'm going to Vung Tau."

"Easiest duty over here."

'So I've been told."

Morgan sat in a chair on the porch, sweating profusely. The humidity was oppressive; his lungs felt full
of moisture. A flight of four Phantoms tore into the sky
with a flash of afterburners and headed north. A C-130

transport landed, its four turboprop engines roaring. An Air America helicopter lifted and disappeared toward Saigon.

Morgan lit a cigaret. From somewhere distant came the sound of muffled explosions. Mortars, he guessed. A green flare arced into the darkness, followed by a red one. The faint stuttering of a machine gun immediately followed. A jeep full of MPs drove slowly by. From inside the barracks came the radio sound of a Beatles song. Morgan slept fitfully.

In the morning he ate at the chow hall, then went to the Ninth Aerial Port Squadron orderly room.

"What's with the water ski?" asked the personnel sergeant.

"Orders for Vung Tau," said Morgan, handing over his personnel records.

"Uh, we're redlining all incoming people. Sorry 'bout that, but we're forming a new mobility group, and we need seventy men. You're number fifty-eight. Wanna sell your water ski?"

"How much?"

"Ten bucks, MPC."

"Sold. What's a mobility group?"

"Seventy of you will be permanently assigned to fly with cargo and troops to wherever they're going," explained the sergeant. "You'll unload cargo and load the birds with whatever's going out. Sometimes you might stay in one spot only a couple of hours, and sometimes a couple of weeks. You'll get to see a lot of Vietnam."

"That doesn't sound too bad."

The sergeant laughed drily. "The last mobility unit we had had fifty men in it. About half of them are dead or missing."

"You're sure you can't just send me to Vung Tau?"

"Orders are orders."

"I guess," sighed Morgan.

"Good luck. And keep your head down."

Morgan was assigned to a two-story barracks housing

eighty men and, while awaiting the formation of the
mobility unit, was put to work filling sandbags for the
squadron commander's personal bunker. He quickly
became friends with Horner, a tall kid from Nebraska
whose nickname was Easy, and Dandreau, a gangly,
pimple-faced youth from Ohio. The three of them
worked every day for two weeks filling sandbags under
the supervision of A1C Conrad, who had been incountry for eleven months and was killing time until he left
for the States. While in Vietnam, Conrad had cornered
the market on selling submarine sandwiches and Cokes
to the eight hundred men in the squadron, and cigarets
and other PX merchandise to the Vietnamese.

"You guys wanna sublet my apartment downtown?"
Conrad asked. "It's got two bunks and an overhead
fan. The view ain't much, but the latrine's inside. The
gook family that lives below wants only thirty dollars a
month. It'll get you outta them crowded barracks."
Dandreau declined, saving his money for a car when he
returned to the States. Easy and Morgan rented the
apartment, which was on Trung Ming Giang Street,
about halfway between Tan Son Nhut and downtown
Saigon. After a boring day of filling sandbags, Morgan,
Dandreau, and Conrad were drinking beer in the Tan
Son Nhut Airmen's Club when a swarthy, mustached
figure in camouflage fatigues sat down at their table.

"Flim-Flam Man," greeted Conrad, "where you
been this time?"

"Con Son Island," said Flim-Flam Man, ordering a
beer. "I heard they had tiger cages out there. I figured
they must have a zoo, so I got hold of a couple of tigers
and . . ."

"How'd you get the tigers?" interrupted Morgan.

Flim-Flam Man fixed him with piercing blue eyes.
"Very carefully, that's how. Anyway, I sailed out there
and found out that what they have in these tiger cages
are political prisoners, criminals, and a few VC. The
camp commander wouldn't let me unload my tigers, but

he did give me a nickel tour. These tiger cages are set in the floors of old buildings and covered with metal grates. They're too small for a man to stand up in or even to stretch out. Some guards pulled this one poor bastard out for interrogation. His legs were so wasted that he couldn't even stand up. He crawled like a crippled crab.'' Flim-Flam Man paused and downed his beer.

"My boat crew was getting antsy, and my tigers were pacing and growling in their cages. The captain told me that he knew of a minister over by Bac Lieu who might be interested in my tigers, so we got back on board and set sail for his island.''

"A minister?'' said Conrad.

"The Reverend Nam. He's not your typical Presbyterian-type preacher, but he's something. His followers call him the Palm Tree Prophet.'' Flim-Flam Man lit a cigaret and continued.

"We tied up at a dock in the Mekong River. It was made out of plywood and cut into the shapes of North and South Vietnam. The Reverend Nam met us and invited us to his temple. He really smelled ripe, and he must have seen me wrinkling my nose because he apologized for not taking a bath in seventeen years.''

"Seventeen years!'' exclaimed Dandreau.

"He said it had something to do with his religion.''

"Dude definitely ain't a Baptist,'' said Conrad.

"He invited us to spend the night. He fed us a good dinner, then he showed me this cat that he had taught to let mice suckle its teats. He said this proved that North and South Vietnam could learn to coexist peacefully. He called it a living allegory.''

"Shee-it,'' Conrad said scornfully.

"It got to be pretty late, so he showed me where to sack out. He even gave me a girl for the night.''

"Was she good?'' asked Dandreau.

Flim-Flam Man grinned. "It's always good. Even when it's bad.''

"You spent the night on the island?" prompted Morgan.

"Yeah. I woke up about four in the morning and heard this weird sound coming from outside. I got up and went out and found the Reverend perched up in a palm tree, singing to himself like a bird."

"Vietnamese voodoo," said Conrad, rolling his eyes.

"I didn't want to disturb him, so I whispered, 'What are you doing, Rev?' He said he was praying to Buddha and Jesus, and asked if there was anything I'd like him to pray for. I told him offhand I couldn't think of a damned thing, but if he could get a backup band together, I'd be his agent." Flim-Flam Man drained his second beer.

"What about the tigers?" asked Morgan.

Flim-Flam Man wiped foam from his lips. "Oh, he loved them. He traded me a gold statue of Buddha for them. The last I saw they were chained to each side of his temple doors. It sort of reminded me of the Chicago library. How long you been incountry, Morgan?"

"Two weeks. I'm waiting for my first mobility mission. I've spent most of my time filling sandbags."

"Been to Saigon yet?"

"Not downtown. I rented an apartment on Trung Ming Giang."

Flim-Flam Man stood up. "Meet me here at eight o'clock tonight. I'll take you on a tour of the city. How about you, Dandreau? You want to go, too?"

"Sure."

Flim-Flam Man left. "What's his story?" Morgan asked Conrad.

"I don't know. He comes and goes. You see him, and then you don't."

"What branch of service is he in?" asked Dandreau.

Conrad puzzled. "To tell you the truth, I don't even know if he's in the service. All I know is that he's one interesting son of a bitch."

"Roger that," said Morgan.

— 12 —

The three men met at eight o'clock and walked to
the front gate, where they piled into a taxi and headed
downtown, passing the illuminated and ghostly-looking
Presidential Palace, which was surrounded by gun-tot-
ing ARVN Rangers. Flim-Flam Man directed the cab
driver down a narrow unlighted street, not far from the
United States Embassy. They stopped in front of a large
building. Several hundred pairs of shoes and sandals lay
in front of the entrance, which was covered with a
blanket.

"This is a Buddhist temple," said Flim-Flam Man.
"Take off your boots here."

They stepped inside. The temple echoed with the
sound of a brass gong. About fifty bonzes, clad in saffron robes, knelt in front of a candle-lit altar, from
which a large statue of Buddha gazed sightlessly. Flim-
Flam Man led Morgan and Dandreau behind the monks
and up a short flight of stairs. Reaching the closed door
at the top, Flim-Flam Man knocked on it once. It
opened. A Vietnamese man squinted at the trio, bowed
to Flim-Flam Man, and stood aside.

A cloud of cigaret smoke roiled toward the ceiling,
from which naked light bulbs cast a harsh glare on the
regulation-size boxing ring that dominated the room.
Two hundred Vietnamese men, sitting on wooden
benches, surrounded the ring. Flim-Flam Man led his
companions down to the front row. No sooner had they
sat down than a silence filled the room.

Two legless Vietnamese emerged from a side room
and moved down the aisle by walking on their bare
hands, their torsos swaying gently. Reaching the ring,
the maimed men were lifted up by their seconds until
they were able to grasp the lowest rope and squirm
under it, their fish-out-of-water motions vaguely ob-

scene. They perched their scrawny butts on wooden stools that had had their legs considerably shortened. The tattered hems of both men's trunks, scuffed on the canvas mats in the boxing arenas at Qui Nhon, Nha Trang, Phan Thiet, and a score of other towns, were tinged a permanent gray. The two boxers stared dispassionately at each other.

The older of the two fighters wore purple trunks with yellow stripes. His nose, broken in a half-dozen fights, had had its cartilage surgically removed; it lay flat against his face, which was a mask of scar tissue. His mouth gaped open, allowing him to breathe. His obsidian-black eyes were expressionless.

The younger boxer wore white trunks with red stripes and sported fresh facial wounds, including a tear at the left corner of his lip which was held together by a series of black sutures. His hair was spiked high on his head, giving him an electrified look.

Dandreau closed his gaping mouth long enough to ask, "Where the hell did they get the Everlast trunks?"

"From me," answered Flim-Flam Man. "I own the concession for athletic equipment in Southeast Asia." Dandreau and Morgan stared at him.

"I have a friend in Special Services who's authorized to order any equipment he needs—for our troops, of course, but the Vietnamese need it, too. They're an incredibly sports-minded people."

"So you're sort of the sports director for Vietnam," said Morgan.

Flim-Flam Man smiled. "Sort of. Soccer is big over here. I've sold more than three hundred soccer balls to the Ninth ARVN Division. Regulation Voits. About a month ago I sent enough baseball equipment to the ROK Whitehorse Division to outfit half a dozen teams. The Koreans are great emulators of anything American.

"Of course," he chortled, "the ROK commander sent the gloves and protective cups back with a note explaining that his men didn't need the gloves because their hands are hardened from practicing the martial arts, and they didn't need the cups because they can draw their testicles up into their groins, just like Sumo wrestlers. I'm temporarily overstocked on both items, but I heard they love the baseball shoes. I wouldn't doubt it if they wear them into the bush and slide into the VC, spike high.''

The ringing of a bell interrupted Flim-Flam Man's discourse. A scholarly looking, bespectacled Vietnamese climbed into the ring and stood at its center, dabbing perspiration from his forehead with a monogrammed handkerchief. His white shirt was stained down the back and under the arms with sweat. Hematite cufflinks flashed as he raised his arms for silence and addressed the crowd, his reed-thin voice whining above the spectator noise.

Flim-Flam Man leaned toward Morgan and said, ''This is an interservice match, so we should see some good fighting. See the man in the purple trunks with the tattoo on his chest? It says 'Sat Cong,' which means 'Kill communists.' It's only worn by Vietnamese Navy Special Forces. If he'd been caught by the VC, they'd have carved the tattoo out of him with a dull knife before killing him. He's lucky that he only lost his legs.''

''That's bad enough in itself,'' said Morgan.

Flim-Flam Man shrugged. ''He's alive, and that's not bad when you consider the alternative.''

He motioned toward the other boxer. ''He was an officer in a Ranger battalion. He trained in the States at Benning and Bragg, then came back here and lost his legs in Laos. He's a bleeder but game. It should be a good match.''

Dandreau asked, ''How do they fight? I mean, it's obvious they can't slug it out toe to toe.''

''Chin to chin, actually,'' said Flim-Flam Man. ''They don't need footwork for what they do. Traditional Vietnamese boxing is a combination of western boxing and the Thai or French savate style of kicking, but these two

will just hit each other until one of them falls and can't
get up." He pulled a cigar from his pocket and lit it.

"No referee?" asked Morgan.

"No referee."

The announcer, finished, left the ring. The crowd
buzzed in anticipation. Last-minute wagers were made.

"Is this fight sponsored by Gillette Blue Blades?"
Dandreau asked.

"No," replied Flim-Flam Man patiently. "It's sponsored by the Southeast Asian Boxing Commission."

"Which consists of you, no doubt," said Morgan.

Flim-Flam Man exhaled a fragrant cloud of smoke.
"No doubt," he said, smiling like the Cheshire cat.

"How many rounds to this fight?" Dandreau wanted
to know.

"Only one, but it's a long one. I should have explained earlier that each man has been anesthetized.
Their fists and faces are shot full of novocaine. They
won't feel any pain, just the impact."

Morgan was incredulous. "If they can't feel pain and
there isn't a referee, then how can the fight be stopped
before they really hurt each other?"

Flim-Flam Man puffed easily on his cigar and smiled
benignly. "That's the point. It can't be."

The bell rang. Both boxers advanced on their hands
to the center of the ring. The animalistic roaring of the
crowd drowned out sounds of flesh hitting flesh. . . .

— 13 —

"You guys seen enough for the night, or do you want a drink?" Flim-Flam Man asked as they left the Buddhist temple.

"I think I need a drink," said Morgan.

"Me, too," chorused Dandreau.

"Good. I'll take you to my favorite hangout when I'm in Saigon. We can walk it from here." They walked in silence for several minutes, turned a corner, and were on Tu Do Street.

Tu Do Street was riotous with people and traffic. The sound of horns was everywhere. Cyclos whisked by, carrying American soldiers to various destinations. Honda motorcycles bearing entire Vietnamese families competed with blue-and-yellow Renault taxis, which were driven kamikaze-style. An American Motors jeep, painted candy-apple red, crept through the traffic. Its mudguards were embossed with the Playboy logo of a white rabbit wearing a black bow tie. The driver, a lieutenant commander in the Vietnamese navy, drank from a bottle of Chivas Regal and leered with gold teeth at his passenger, an American girl wearing a Red Cross uniform.

Dope dealers and pimps shared the sidewalks with black market vendors who squatted behind mounds of jungle boots, shoe polish, camouflage fatigues, Zippo lighters, American cigarets, and paintings of nudes done on velvet. Beggars of all ages pleaded everywhere. Hostesses beckoned from the doorways of bars. The Hollywood Bar sat next to the New York Bar, which sat next to the Coconut Grove.

Flim-Flam Man, Morgan, and Dandreau crossed the street, running the gauntlet of traffic.

"Here it is," announced Flim-Flam Man. The neon sign flashed Cherry Tree Bar. He ushered Morgan and

Dandreau inside. An emaciated crone, her lips stained black from years of chewing analgesic betel nuts, perched on a stool near the door and fed coins into a Wurlitzer jukebox, her bony fingers randomly selecting tunes. Rock and Roll music filled the long and narrow room. Dandreau began snapping his fingers.

"Don't start singing," warned Morgan. No more than four steps into the bar the three Americans were surrounded by a band of miniskirted hostesses, each one chattering in a rapid patois of Vietnamese, French, and English. "Troi oi! You beaucoup numbah one GI. Buy you me tea?"

Nodding politely and speaking to them in their native tongue, Flim-Flam Man led the way through the crush of hostesses. To their right was an elevated dance floor, behind which a gold-veined mirror reflected the dancing images of four girls in velour bikinis. A strobe light affixed to the end of a slowly turning fan shot shafts of light into the mirror; the refracted effect seemed to make the walls of the bar undulate. Miniature blinking Christmas tree lights added their twinkling colors to the Felliniesque atmosphere.

About twenty GIs sat at the teakwood bar drinking either San Miguel, a Filipino import, or Ba Muoi Ba, the locally brewed, formaldehyde-fortified Biere 33. Other GIs sat at tables, accompanied by hostesses who sipped Saigon tea, a colored-water drink, for which the GIs paid one dollar and fifty cents per glass.

One hostess, her siliconed breasts grotesque on her diminutive body, was flirting unselfconsciously with the soldiers at the bar.

"Vietnam's version of Carol Doda," noted Flim-Flam Man. "She had some doctor from Hong King fix her up." The siliconed hostess stopped in front of a warrant officer, flicked out her tongue, licked his ear, chin, and neck, then pulled down one cup of her under-wired bra, revealing an erect, inch-long nipple. With long-nailed fingers she beckoned the warrant officer to touch her; when he did, she instantly went into a parox-ysm of feigned passion, grinding her belly against his knees while her fingers opened and closed surrepti-tiously around his genitals. After ten seconds her pre-orgasmic smile vanished, replaced by a quizzical look as her hand left the warrant officer's lap and raised, palm up, to the level of his eyes, awaiting, expecting, de-manding a tip. The red-faced man gave her some money. She kissed him chastely on the cheek and moved on to the next man.

"Toledo doesn't have anything like this," said Dan-dreau.

Flim-Flam Man looked at him coolly. "Every place has a place like this." Dandreau ambled off to sit in front of the dancers.

"I'm supposed to meet someone here," Flim-Flam Man said to Morgan. "Crazy Gina. She runs the place for Mamasan."

"You sure seem to know your way around."

Flim-Flam Man shrugged and lit another cigar. "I've been over here a long time."

"How long?"

"A long time."

"Flim-Flam Man! Wha's happen?" Flim-Flam Man introduced Morgan to Crazy Gina. Her hair was combed down in bangs over her forehead. Her eyes were the color of slate and just as hard. She smiled con-stantly, a technique learned when she had been an Air Vietnam stewardess. A black bra showed through her three-buttons-undone orange blouse, which was tied in a knot under her straining breasts. The upthrust swelling of breast flesh was covered by a sheen of per-spiration and trembled slightly when she laughed. A butterfly-embossed buckle held together the belt which encircled her tiny waist. Her lushly flaring ass was clearly outlined in skintight jeans.

"We hab business to discuss," she said.

"Let's take a walk, Gina. Excuse us, Morgan." Morgan sat alone for a while and finished his beer. He got up and went to the bar to get another one, and was stunned by the beauty of the young barmaid. Her hair was pulled back in a ponytail. She had high, delicate cheekbones, testimony to a dash of French blood in her veins. A livid burn scar on the right side of her face marred her natural beauty. She was no older than seventeen.

"GI?" she asked Morgan.

"Beer, please." He watched her closely.

"Wha' kind?"

"I don't care," he mumbled. She left and returned with a San Miguel. He paid her and asked her name.

She averted her eyes when she said, "Tam," then turned away to take another customer's order. Morgan returned to his table.

Flim-Flam Man reappeared and sat down.

"Can I ask you what that was all about?" said Morgan.

"Sure. Gina's my business partner. We were discussing a trip I'm taking shortly to the Golden Triangle."

"Where's that?"

"It's where Burma, Laos, and Thailand come together. They grow the best opium in the world up there, and I'm going to get some."

"Are you bullshitting me?"

"Not a bit."

"Then why are you telling me this? I mean, what if I told somebody?"

"Who would you tell that would believe you? I don't even exist. Besides," he said evenly, "if I thought you'd tell anybody, I'd kill you."

"Just like that?"

Flim-Flam Man sighed. "It's a cold world, Morgan. I thought you learned that at the boxing match."

"What are you going to do with the opium?" asked Morgan.

"Bring it down to Ban Houei Sai on pack horses.

That's where Tom Dooley had one of his clinics. There are people who still say he spent all that time in the hills working for the CIA. Anyway, from Ban Houei Sai we'll fly it to Luang Prabang and sell it to the Chinese for gold. I'll fly the gold to Bangkok, trade it for American dollars, bring the greenbacks back to Saigon, and trade them for more gold in Cholon."

"Sounds complicated," said Morgan.

"Not really."

"What if you're traced?"

Flim-Flam Man smiled. "I already told you, I don't even exist."

"Well, you're right about one thing."

"What's that?"

"No one would believe me if I told them."

Flim-Flam Man wiped sweat from his forehead. "I'm right about something else, too."

"What's that?"

"If you told anybody, I'd kill you."

Morgan smiled weakly. "What happens to the opium after you sell it at Luang Prabang?"

"The Chinese contract an Air Vietnam flight to take it to Vientiane where it's made into heroin. From there it goes to Bangkok, Phnom Penh, and Saigon. Most of the Saigon shipment gets sent to the States."

"How?" asked Morgan, finishing his beer and lighting a cigaret.

"In the caskets they ship our people home in. There's a connection in the morgue at Travis Air Base."

"That's fucking sick!" protested Morgan.

Flim-Flam Man shrugged again. "It's a fucking sick world. Where there's a demand, there will always be a supply."

Dandreau, flush-faced and perspiring copiously, rejoined Flim-Flam Man and Morgan. He raised his bottle to his lips, half missing them; a stream of beer ran down his chin. "My God!" he sputtered. "See that blonde chick dancing? The one that ain't a gook? She danced right in front of me, looked me right in the eye and pulled her G-string down, and said, 'I'm from Argentina.' "

"What did you say to her?" Morgan asked.

"What the hell could I say? I told her that some of my best friends are from Argentina. She's a real blonde, too. What a muff!"

Flim-Flam Man yawned. "She's Swedish-German, actually."

"Well, she told me she's from Argentina," huffed Dandreau.

"She is."

"A Swedish-German from Argentina," said Morgan. "How does that work?"

"Her father was an SS interrogator during World War Two. Just before Berlin fell, he escaped to Argentina and married a Swedish girl who worked at the embassy in Buenos Aires. She died in childbirth. The girl you see dancing is their daughter."

"Why's she over here?" Dandreau wanted to know.

"Let me explain all of it. After his wife died, the German hired a Uruguayan couple to raise her. He was too busy running guns to Ecuador, Chile, and a few other countries to be much of a father. He got tired of gun-running, went to France, and joined the Foreign Legion. He served in Morocco for a while, then was shipped to North Vietnam during the Indochina War. He was in charge of interrogation in Hanoi, then got sent to Dien Bien Phu to interrogate Viet Minh prisoners."

"What's Dien Bien Phu?" Morgan asked.

"It was a French garrison near the Laotian border. Anyway, the prisoners told him that General Giap's troops were setting up heavy artillery in the mountains around Dien Bien Phu—actually carrying dismantled howitzers up the sides of the mountains, one piece at a time, then reassembling them. The French commander didn't believe the German, either because he didn't think Giap's troops could carry the artillery, or else because he didn't like the German. Probably a little bit of both."

Flim-Flam Man paused to drink from his beer. "Anyway, the German said he'd stick around and see for himself. About a month later the Viet Minh artillery opened up. Everyone was surprised except the German and his prisoners. A short time later the garrison surrendered and, as the story goes, while the French were being lined up to be marched away to POW camps, the German walked up to the French commander and said, 'I told you so.' "

Dandreau stared blankly at a beer stain on the table, trying to decide whether to hum "Venus" or "Blue Velvet."

"This was all back in fifty-four," continued Flim-Flam Man. "The German was repatriated and sent back to France, then to Algeria, where he interrogated FLN rebels. Then he switched sides for a while, and finally wound up back here, where he took a position with one of the rubber plantations. Michelin, I think. He worked for them until 1965, and then disappeared."

"Disappeared where?" asked Morgan.

"Let me finish. His daughter arrived here later that year, using the last of the money he sent her to buy a one-way ticket to Saigon. She went to the plantation to find her father, and they told her that he had disappeared."

"Disappeared where?" Morgan asked again.

"She dances to make money so she can go back to Argentina. She could make a lot more by hooking, but she won't do it. Probably her Catholic upbringing."

"But where did her father disappear to?"

"He had a lot of enemies. Jews, Viet Minh, Moroccans, Algerians, French. Some say the CIA had a contract on him. Some say Mossad, the Israeli intelligence, was after him. Take your pick."

Dandreau, drunkenly oblivious to the conversation,

was now muttering fragments of the song "Winchester Cathedral."

Morgan said to Flim-Flam Man, "Do you know the girl behind the bar?"

Flim-Flam Man turned and looked. "Sure. That's Tam. She's worked here maybe six months."

"I'd sure like to take her home with me tonight."

"Why don't you ask Mamasan?"

"Gina?"

"No. Gina only manages this place. Mamasan owns it. She's behind those beads," he said, gesturing toward a beaded curtain at the rear of the bar. "Just go in and ask her," he prompted.

"I think I will," said Morgan, getting up.

Morgan parted the bead curtains and entered the room. A portable television sat in a corner, its horizontal hold rolling. The Armed Forces Television channel was playing an episode of "Combat"; ersatz battle sounds filled the room as Vic Morrow mowed down a line of advancing enemy soldiers.

"Yes?" a woman's voice asked from the darkness.

"Chau ong, Ba?" asked Morgan.

"Do not address me in Vietnamese, American. It demeans us both. Your grasp of the language is less than rudimentary. Besides, I am Tau. Chinese."

Morgan shuffled his feet in embarrassment. "Sorry," he said. His eyes adjusted to the darkness. He saw an obese woman sitting cross-legged on a wooden pallet, her pudgy arms folded across the expanse of her stomach. Her hair was tied in a bun, and her eyes reflected a mixture of curiosity and cynicism.

She lit a Gitane cigaret and inhaled deeply. Exhaling, she said, "You inquire as to how I am. Of late my hostesses show me a grievous disrespect, an ill-tempered spirit plagues my bones, and my television is failing. Made in Japan, phaw!"

"Maybe I can fix it."

"You are inclined mechanically, American?"

Morgan walked to the television, found the horizontal control, and adjusted it. The picture stopped rolling. He turned down the sound and said, "Ma'am, I need your services."

The fat madam began laughing, the sound ending in the rasp of a heavy smoker. Coughing behind her hand, she said, "American . . . I have neither . . . offered . . . nor been asked . . . for . . . my . . . services . . . in a length of . . . time . . . I care not . . . to remember."

Morgan blushed. "That's not exactly what I meant. I'm interested in one of your girls."

The madam smiled scornfully. "Of course you are, American. Why else would you grace my establishment with your presence?"

"Not one of your hostesses," he said.

"Oh?" she said, arching a plucked and heavily penciled eyebrow.

"No. It's the barmaid. The girl who tends the bar."

"Tam?"

"Yes. I want to take her home with me."

The madam arched both eyebrows. "To America?"

"I have an apartment on Trung Ming Giang."

The madam smiled wryly. "A particularly neglected neighborhood. Not to cast aspersions on Americans, but all of Saigon has fallen into a state of sad disrepair since the French departed. The French . . ." she repeated wistfully, closing her eyes as she revived some distant memory. She opened her eyes and said, "She is scarred in the face, American. Perhaps one of my hostesses would be more tasteful to the palate of your desire."

"I want her," reiterated Morgan.

"But she is disfigured," she said more strongly.

"I think she's beautiful," countered Morgan.

The madam sighed. Her voice took on a businesslike tone. "Fifty dollars for Tam, American."

Morgan looked at her incredulously. The madam smiled. "A fair price, I think, considering your ill-concealed eagerness." Morgan reached into his pocket for his wallet, counted out the money, and handed it to her. She recounted it and placed it in a cigar box.

"Thank you," she said.

"Thank you," said Morgan, turning to leave.

"A last thought," she said. Morgan stopped and turned around. "Tam's deformity is a result of napalm," she said in a flat voice. "She will go with you tonight and do your bidding. She will please you well. But in the morning she will still hate Americans, American."

Morgan went back to his table to wait for Tam to finish work. Flim-Flam Man had disappeared. Dandreau was sitting with a hostess whose fingers were busy in his lap.

"I'm a he man," he said to her, "and you're a she man, see? And a he man always goes with a she man." The hostess, understanding little, nodded her head in agreement. "And," he continued, fighting to focus his eyes, "if a he man can't get a she man, he . . ."

"He wha' . . . ?"

"He . . . I don't really know what he does."

"You buy me 'nother drink?"

Dandrea grinned lopsidedly. "A drink for the wench with the fire in her eyes."

"No buy for wen'. Buy for me," protested the hostess.

"Make it a double," he yelled.

— 14 —

Tam finished work at midnight and walked over to Morgan's table. "Mamasan say I go with you," she said. There was no emotion in her voice.

"Yes. I don't live very far from here." Morgan nudged a semi-dozing Dandreau. The three of them left the bar. Morgan hailed two taxicabs, one to take Dandreau back to Tan Son Nhut, the other for Tam and himself.

They had driven no more than several blocks when, while waiting for a light to change, a Quan Canh, or Vietnamese policeman, approached them, armed with an M-16 rifle. He struck his head through the cab window and said something in an inquisitory voice to Tam. Tam turned to Morgan. "Give him one thousand piasters an' he go 'way." Morgan paid the bribe without saying anything. They continued on.

A speeding Lambretta motor scooter flashed from a side street on a collision course with the taxi. The cab driver turned the wheel sharply and hit the brakes. Tam's head smashed against the window as the cab sideswiped the scooter, sending its driver sprawling.

Morgan got out and helped Tam out of the cab. He guided her over to the curb where she sat down unsteadily, holding her head. The cab driver stood next to the downed Lambretta, swearing at its driver, a youth in his midteens who sat on the pavement, cradling his right arm. Morgan walked over and examined the arm; blood oozed from a nasty-looking cut. He took a handkerchief from the dazed youth's pocket and tied it neatly around the wound. He helped the young man to his feet, and the two of them uprighted the motor scooter. He then went back to the curb and retrieved Tam, helping her back into the cab. They proceeded to the apartment on Trung Ming Giang.

Easy awoke as they entered. Morgan led Tam to a

chair and helped her sit down. He went into the bathroom and returned with a cold compress, which he pressed against the bump on her head.

"What happened?" asked Easy.

"Just a little accident," explained Morgan.

"You want me to get out of here and sleep in the barracks?"

"No. Just go back to sleep."

"O.K. Have fun," he said, turning his back. "Oh, I almost forgot. I've been assigned to Ops. I'll be in charge of picking who goes on what mobility missions."

"What a skate job," said Morgan, shaking his head.

"Yeah, but what if I pick someone to go on a mission, and he gets blown away?"

"I guess that's bound to happen. All the missions won't be easy ones."

"You want me to schedule you for the milk runs, Morg?"

"Nope. Just throw my name in the hat with the others."

"Whatever's fair," said Easy, laughing. "You're flying on your first one this morning, at o-seven-thirty."

"Your timing leaves something to be desired, Easy."

"Sorry 'bout that," he said, closing his eyes.

Tam looked at Morgan with questioning black eyes. "Why you help him?" she asked, referring to the boy on the motor scooter.

"He was hurt," he said, applying a fresh compress.

"But he Vietnamee, not American."

Morgan shrugged. "He was still hurt."

"We make love now?" she asked.

"Listen, we don't have to do anything. You've got a pretty bad bump, and I've got to get some sleep before my mission."

"But you pay for me." She walked over to the bed and took off her clothes. Her body was slender and firm. She lay down on the bed and waited, her arms behind her head. Morgan stripped and turned out the light. Instead of making love they talked.

"Where are you from?" he asked, smoking a cigaret in the darkness.

"Quang Ngai Province. Village name Song My. Song My titi place."

"Real small, huh?"

"Very small."

"Ah, how old are you, Tam?"

"I sixteen."

"Only sixteen?"

"Da. Sixteen."

"You're very young to be working in a bar so far from home."

Tam understood most of his words. "I have big family to help. Beaucoup brothers and sisters." She caught him staring at her scarred face. "You look my hurt. I tell you. American planes come, drop many bomb. Some bomb bring fire. Fire hurt me."

Morgan squirmed uncomfortably. "It must have been an accident."

"GI? What mean 'accident'?"

"A mistake. The bombs must have been dropped by mistake."

"Da. Mistake. Americans here make big mistake. Bring many hurt. Bring many death. Bring too many tears."

Morgan kissed her on the cheeks. "Tam?"

"GI?"

"I hope I see you again."

When Morgan awoke at six, Tam was gone. He dressed and rode in a cyclo to Tan Son Nhut, eager to experience his first mobility mission.

— 15 —

Morgan's first mobility mission started with a flight to Ham Tan, a coastal city eighty miles east of Saigon. The C-130 he and five other mobility members flew in lumbered through monsoon squalls and landed at the airstrip, which consisted of pierced steel planking. They offloaded several pallets of C-rations and took on board several dozen Vietnamese civilians and a disabled jeep, which they chained to the floor of the huge transport plane. Morgan sat next to a Vietnamese woman who alternately suckled a dysenteric baby and vomited into an air-sickness bag all the way to Tan Son Nhut, where the mobility members offloaded the civilians and the jeep, and loaded five pallets laden with bags of United States Aid cement which were destined for a Civic Action Program at Vinh Long, a Mekong River town. Offloading the cement, they pushed two howitzers on board and transported them to My Tho, then returned empty to Tan Son Nhut. Later that night Morgan helped load the troops and equipment of one of the Big Red One's battalion and returned, tired and wet, to the Harem, his Saigon apartment. He was surprised to find Tam waiting for him on the sidewalk.

"My night off," she said, smiling shyly.

"How's your head?"

"Head O.K. How you?"

"Tired."

"I stay with you tonight."

Morgan smiled at her. "All right," he said.

Once in the room they undressed quickly. Her skin under his hands was slightly rough, as if it had been gone over lightly with fine sandpaper. They made love in the quietness of the room, the only sound that of the slowly revolving fan.

Easy came in from work. Heading for the shower, he

said, "You've got a mobility in the morning. Be at Ops
at o-five-thirty."

Sleepy-eyed, Morgan kissed Tam good-bye and
caught a cyclo to the airbase, where he checked out an
M-16 from the weapons room. He ate breakfast quickly
and walked over to the Ops room, where five other mobility members and a briefing sergeant already were con-
gregated.

"You're going to a place called Loc Ninh. It's a district town a few miles from the Cambodian border,"
said the sergeant. "You'll be taking supplies to the
Special Forces camp there and spending a couple of
days with them. They've been hit three or four nights in
a row by a large North Vietnamese force, so watch your
ass."

The six mobility members climbed aboard a C-130
which had already been loaded with pallets containing
C-rations and other necessities. The transport plane
trundled from its parking stand and moved to the end of
the runway, awaiting takeoff. Paris Control gave the
go-ahead; the C-130 lifted off into the dawn and headed
north. Morgan looked at the ground from out of one of
the windows.

A farmer below walked behind two lumbering oxen,
cultivating a rice field. Smoke from a dozen fires spiraled thinly into the sky from the west. Four sampans
tied together floated down a narrow river. A column of
tanks headed toward Quan Loi. Two helicopter gun-
ships hovered low over the ground like huge dragon-
flies. A flight of six Vietnamese AlE Skyraiders passed
above, headed for An Loc. Clusters of huts stood in
jungle clearings. Rubber plantations were laid out in
neat symmetrical rows; the orange-tiled roofs of the
plantation villas stood out in stark relief. Fire-support
bases had been carved out of the jungle.

Cemeteries dotted the ground everywhere with their
above-ground tombs. Huge areas of jungle had been
decimated by Agent Orange, a defoliant that had been
sprayed from C-123s working under the code name of

Operation Ranch Hand. Naked trees lifted their bare
limbs to the sky as if in supplication.

But Morgan was mostly impressed with the amount
of bombs that had been dropped on the countryside.
The lush green below was interspersed with sere, bomb-
pocked areas. Small craters and large, filled with
brackish water, scarred the earth. Some areas were completely spared, while others looked like a landscape of
the moon.

The land gently rose into a forested, hilly plateau. Beyond it, in sleepy Cambodia, was hidden the headquarters of the Communist High Command, or COSVN.

The C-130 descended over a rubber plantation and
landed at Loc Ninh. Morgan and the others offloaded
the pallets, then warily exited the plane.

A Green Beret captain walked up to them. "You're
staying the night?"

"Yes, sir. We've got more supplies coming in tomorrow."

"Why don't you come inside the compound and get
something cold to drink?" He pointed toward the rubber trees. "Everything's quiet out there. For now."

The captain led them through three rings of concertina wire. The spaces between the rings were filled with
trip flares and low tangles of barbed wire. The camp
itself had been made in the shape of an elongated dia-
mond and was constructed largely out of logs and
earthen walls. The command bunker was made of three-
foot-thick concrete and was completely buried. A gaso-
line-powered generator supplied the bunker with air
conditioning.

The captain pulled seven beers from a refrigerator
and distributed them. Sipping at his, he briefed the men.
"If Charlie hits us tonight, and we have no reason to
believe he won't, he'll be coming from the rubber trees
directly across the runway. We've got an artillery piece
positioned at the south end of the runway, and that
should deter him some. When the shit hits the fan, I
want all of you to remain here in the main bunker. If we

need you, we'll come get you. No sense running around in the dark if you don't have to. Charlie'll hit sometime between o-two hundred and o-four hundred, so get some rack time early. Any questions?"

"Yes, sir," said Stanton. "How safe are we here?"

The captain laughed. "Just as safe as the rest of us, airman. No more, no less."

— 16 —

Darkness fell quickly at Loc Ninh. The Special Forces camp's eighty-two-millimeter mortar began lofting illumination flares into the night. Suspended from nylon parachutes, the flares swung gently above the airstrip, starkly lighting it and casting long shadows into the rows of rubber trees. At 2300 the illumination rounds were alternated with H and I rounds meant to harass and interdict enemy movement. The whumping sounds of the mortar shells exploding seemed amplified by the darkness.

Green Berets and Montagnard mercenaries manned the camp's perimeter, crouched down in firing positions behind the earthen breastworks. Claymore mines strung out in the concertina wire were activated, ready to be command-detonated. M-60 machine guns held full belts of ammunition.

At 0215 twenty shadows detached themselves from the rubber trees and ran, screaming and firing their automatic weapons, onto the runway. The 105 howitzer fired a beehive round, thousands of steel fléchettes punctured the NVA soldiers, who fell moaning and writhing to the ground. M-60s in the camp opened up, spraying the fallen bodies with hundreds of rounds.

At 0225 fifty NVA assaulted from out of the treeline. The camp's machine guns opened up on the band of advancing soldiers, knocking fifteen of them immediately to the ground. The howitzer fired again; still more NVA fell. The remaining North Vietnamese reached the concertina wire, threw several grenades which fell short of their marks, then retreated into the treeline, dragging some of their comrades' fallen bodies with them.

From the rubber trees a light machine gun opened up. An angry red stream of tracers sprayed into the camp, slightly wounding one Montagnard, who was immediately dragged into the command bunker and treated by the Green Beret medic. Individual shots rang out from the treeline, answered by shots from within the camp. The rate of gunfire intensified, slackened, intensified again, then died down to only a few occasional rounds.

The main assault started at 0305. Two hundred North Vietnamese charged out from behind the rubber trees, firing from the hip as they came. The howitzer fired round after round, bowling over soldiers like tenpins. One hundred and twenty NVA reached the concertina wire. The lead soldiers flung crude bamboo ladders over the razor-sharp wire and were hit in the process by the camp's machine guns. The night air filled with the screams of the wounded and dying, and the acrid smell of gunpowder and blood.

Dawn was heralded by the lonely sound of one jungle bird singing. The run rose hot and burned off the purple morning haze. Dozens of shapeless black forms littered the runway and the concertina wire, like ragdolls thrown haphazardly by a willful child.

Morgan, Stanton, and Desnoyers crossed the littered runway, carefully avoiding boobytraps, and entered the first rows of the rubber trees. Stanton, the smallest and most agile of the three, shimmied up a slender tree, smearing himself in the process with white sap which oozed from numerous bullet holes and shrapnel gouges.

"Even the trees blend in Vietnam," muttered Desnoyers.

Stanton used his knife to cut the tangled shrouds from several flare-bearing parachutes; the white silk floated gently to the ground. Desnoyers stooped to pick up one of the small chutes and quickly released it when he realized that it wasn't snagged on a root, but rather on the exposed leg of an NVA soldier who had been ignominiously dumped headfirst into a hastily dug grave by his retreating comrades. A Ho Chi Minh sandal, partially melted, stuck to the charred remains of the foot. Gagging, Desnoyers abandoned the parachute.

Thirty meters to the left, a shout of discovery went up from a foraging helicopter crew. One of them was kneeling on the ground, working on something in front of him. He stood and held up his trophy. Impaled on a stick was an NVA head. The facial skin had been burned off, the eye sockets were empty, and the mouth was fused in a wide-open, jaw-breaking grimace, suggesting that the soldier had been shouting in pain or anger when the jellied gasoline had incinerated him. His skull was partially hidden under a burned bush hat, from under which sprouted an ash whiteness of once-thick black hair. The toothlessness of the burned skull owed less to the lack of oral hygiene than to the American holding the skull; a large pair of pliers dangled from his utility belt, and hanging from his neck was a small leather pouch almost full of teeth: amulets taken from the vanquished.

An NVA sniper, hiding behind a rubber tree, aimed at a second lieutenant and squeezed the trigger. One side of the lieutenant's face disappeared in a welter of blood and bone. His mouth opened in a wide crimson grimace.

Broken teeth fell from his mouth as his shattered jaw gaped. The sniper's second bullet tore through his heart, silencing him forever.

Immediately, a line of soldiers assaulted the treeline, firing M-16s on automatic. An M-79 grenade buzzed into the undergrowth and exploded. Someone threw a white phosphorus grenade; several rubber trees began burning at their bases. An observation helicopter hovered overhead, its rotors drowning out the sounds of battle below.

Three men plunged into the treeline and cautiously approached the sniper's position. They found the man sitting on his haunches, mortally punctured by several bullets. Blood dripped from his useless fingers, which were spasmodically trying to pull the trigger, onto his SKS rifle, which was pointed at the ground.

One of the Americans placed his rifle barrel to the eyeball of the wounded NVA and pulled the trigger. The back of the sniper's head blew out, spraying the foliage behind him with gore.

Morgan walked over to the smashed pallet of C-rations that had been air-dropped during the second day of the battle and had drifted into the first row of rubber trees on the far side of the runway. Stepping over several torn bodies, he unsheathed his bayonet to cut through the wires encasing the boxes of rations. He severed the wire and tore the cardboard open. Rummaging around inside, he came up with a can of peaches. He sheathed his bayonet and opened the can with a P-38 that dangled from his neck.

As he sipped the sweet juice, he looked at the far end of the runway where a yellow bulldozer had just finished carving a huge pit in the red earth. The dozer's operator, begrimed and shirtless, sat languidly at the controls of his stilled machine and smoked a cigaret.

Near the center of the runway a cargo net had been laid out. A work party was busy tossing VC bodies onto it. The dead, stacked three high, had been counted, photographed, and looted by intelligence specialists whose job it was to piece together all the information contained in documents and personal diaries, and to determine the fitness of the enemy by examining the bodies for signs of malnutrition and disease.

Morgan watched as a Chinook helicopter clattered into sight above the trees and descended to four feet above the cargo net and its load of death. The rotors created a towering, debris-filled cloud of red earth which blew over a radius of several hundred feet with a skin-tingling force.

Two men, bent over at the waist and wearing protective goggles, scurried beneath the Chinook's belly and wrestled the net's cables over the protruding hook on the helicopter's underside. This accomplished, the two men scuttled away from the turbulence, one of them turning around long enough to give a thumbs-up to the white-helmeted figure piloting the Chinook.

The pilot's practiced fingers moved nimbly over the bank of instruments in front of him, and the helicopter responded by rising, imperceptibly at first. The cables tautened. The pilot increased power until the engine whined in protest. The Chinook leveled off at thirty feet, gracefully executed an arcing turn, and hovered over the open pit.

Inside the chopper the gloved hand of the crew chief pulled back sharply on the hook retraction knob. One cable slid free. The side of the net opened downward, and the lifeless bodies fell in a tangled mass of flailing arms and legs which were silhouetted against the cloudless sky, as if the dead were belatedly protesting their ignominious disposal.

The din of the Chinook's threshing rotors hid the thumping sound the bodies made as they collectively hit the bottom of the open grave. The chopper wheeled and darted toward another body-filled net while a group of soldiers carrying bulky paper bags, their faces covered with surgical masks, descended into the grave and covered the first group of bodies with a thick layer of quicklime.

The ferrying, dumping, and liming process took two hours. Then the bulldozer moved in and pushed the raw, red dirt into the grave with unhurried precision. It then ground back and forth over the spot, tamping the earth level beneath its steel treads, leaving its imprint on the grave: an American imprimatur, irrevocably signed and sealed. No marker was erected to identify this as the final destination of four hundred Asian revolutionaries. In all, more than six hundred and fifty NVA had perished during the four-day battle and retreat.

The unaccounted-for dead, well hidden in the depths of the rubber plantation and alongside the paths leading to Cambodian sanctuary, would be dealt with by the natural forces of the jungle. Tropical heat and monsoon rain, myriad insects and foraging animals would all collaborate with time to reduce and transform flesh and blood and bones into the most basic of elements, which would then become an integral part of the jungle.

The souls of the dead, however, having been violently separated from their bodies, were destined to restlessly roam the countryside for eternity, as prescribed by Asian religion. These disembodied spirits would join the ghostly ranks in a limbolike dimension already crowded with infinite numbers of Vietnamese, Chinese, Japanese, French, and a steadily growing representation of Americans.

Already the ghosts of Dien Bien Phu stood on the sides of heavily misted mountains, waiting to greet the newly deceased arrivals.

Amid the rubber trees an American battalion was making contact with the NVA rearguard, chipping away at the demoralized enemy. Bird Dog planes circled lazily overhead as their pilot-spotters searched out stragglers. The coordinates were radioed back to the artillery battery at the airstrip; thin spirals of smoke rising from the trees marked the shells' points of impact. Huey gunships crisscrossed the area, dipping their noses toward the ground as they pumped thousands of bullets into the trees and disgorged rockets from their pods.

Another Chinook helicopter landed at Loc Ninh.
Forty NVA bodies were placed on a cargo net. The
Chinook carried this load over the plantation and
dumped the bodies on the route the main element of
NVA were using to reach sanctuary in Cambodia. This
particular maneuver was ordered by a Special Forces
Psyops team, which knew that the bodies would spook
their retreating comrades.

The running battles continued for thirty-two hours,
until recondo teams reported all surviving NVA units
had entered Cambodia. The American units pulled back
into defensive perimeters and hacked out landing zones
for the helicopters which would ferry them back to the
airhead at Loc Ninh

— 17 —

Morgan spent the next two weeks flying non-
eventful milk runs to various airfields. Howitzers were
flown to the Twenty-fifth Infantry Division at Cu Chi.
Troops were ferried to Chi Lang in the Mekong Delta,
Dau Tieng, and Quan Loi. Food and ammunition were
delivered to a Special Forces camp near Bu Dop. Bodies
were loaded on board for their trip to the morgue at Tan
Son Nhut from Tay Ninh, Lai Khe, Long Xuyen, and
Xuan Loc. A full-grown elephant, used by the Montagnards as a beast of burden, was anesthetized, tied to two
pallets, and flown from near Bu Dop to a Montagnard

settlement at Bo Duc. ARVN soldiers were flown to
Song Be, Ben Cat, and Can Tho. The plane returned
to Tan Son Nhut from Can Tho with a load of blind-
folded, surly looking VC prisoners. One airman, Ser-
vantes, was wounded in the buttocks by metal fragments when a bullet punctured the skin of a C-130 as it
descended on the airfield at Tan Chau. Three more
mobility members, Cords, Wallace, and Masur, were
lost when a C-123 Provider, loaded with five thousand
pounds of ammunition, blew up on takeoff from Tan
Son Nhut.

"You're flying to Dak To," Easy told Morgan one
night just before Thanksgiving. "The NVA blew the
ammo dump, and there's quite a few GIs stranded on
the side of Hill Eight Seventy-Five. You'll be carrying
ammo and food and medical supplies."

Morgan looked down from the C-130 as it descended
on the airfield at Dak To. A wide black hole in the earth
showed where the ammo dump had been located. A
lieutenant from the 173rd Airborne Division greeted
them upon landing.

"We can really use this stuff," he said as the supplies
were offloaded. "Your outgoing payload will be fifty-
six body bags."

A trio of American fighter planes swept over the top
of Hill 875 in the distance; a mushrooming cloud of
napalm ripped the air as the men at the airstrip heard
the concussion from two seven-hundred-fifty-pound
bombs.

"What's going on?" asked Morgan.

"Shit really hit the fan," said the lieutenant. "Our
planes accidentally dropped bombs on the battalion
command post up there. We got dead and beaucoup
wounded that we can't get off the mountain." The body
bags loaded onboard, the C-130's engines began turning.

"Good luck to you, Lieutenant," said Morgan,
climbing aboard.

"Thanks. If we take the top of the mountain by

Thanksgiving, we're going to feed the troops hot turkey dinners. Hell, even if they don't take it by Thanksgiving, they're still going to get hot turkey."

The C-130's back ramp closed. The plane taxied onto the dirt airstrip, gained speed, and lifted into the sky, carrying its grisly cargo back to Tan Son Nhut.

— 18 —

Morgan took a cyclo to the Cherry Tree Bar. Tam was behind the bar, wiping up some spilled beer.

"Hi, Tam," he said. "I missed you."

"Morgan. I too miss you. Truly." A group of soldiers came into the bar and were immediately surrounded by the chattering bar girls. The jukebox was turned on; Otis Redding started singing "Sitting on the Dock of the Bay."

Morgan leaned close to Tam. "Did you enjoy the other night with me? At my apartment?"

Tam shyly lowered her eyes. "Yes. I enjoy. Very much."

"I've got a proposition for you."

"A wha'?"

"A proposition. A plan."

"Oh. Wha' plan?"

"I'd like you to live with me."

"Live with you?"

"Yes. I'd like you to move into the apartment."

"Why?"

"Because I want to be near you as much as possible. Because I miss you when I'm out on missions."

"But I mus' work."

"You can still work. All I'm asking is that you live with me when you get out of work. What do you say?"

"Give me time to think," she said. "I mus' ask Mamasan."

Morgan had several beers while Tam went into the back room. Returning, she said, "Mamasan want talk you."

Morgan parted the beaded curtain and entered Mamasan's domain.

"You would have Tam live with you?"

"Yes."

"Why?"

Morgan shrugged his shoulders. "Because I want her to."

"Because you want. All Americans want. All Americans think of nothing except themselves."

"I want to make her happy."

"You want to make a Vietnamese girl happy. How admirable."

Morgan stood silent. Mamasan lit another cigaret. "And what of Tam? You would live with her while you are in Vietnam, but what happens when you leave? Maybe you would leave her with a child?"

"I'd never do that. I promise."

Mamasan made a sound of disgust. "Americans and their promises. I've heard Americans promise many things, and the promises have been lies. Americans pervert the truth."

"I don't lie," Morgan said firmly.

"Understand me, American. I do not like you. It is not to be taken personally; I don't like any American. But if it is Tam's wish to live with you, then I cannot forbid her."

"Thank you."

"Don't thank me, American, make me one of your promises, since you proclaim yourself to be truthful. Treat Tam gently so that when you leave she will have fond memories of you, not sad ones."

— 19 —

Carrying a small suitcase containing all of her belongings, Tam followed Morgan into the apartment.

"You can hang your clothes next to mine," he said. Tam began unpacking.

Easy came in.

"We have a new roommate," said Morgan.

Easy smiled at Tam. "O.K. by me," he said.

Morgan spent the first three weeks of November on mobility missions, sixteen in all. He would arrive back at the Harem tired and be asleep when Tam came in after work. More often than not, they would make love until early in the morning. Easy slept through it all.

On Christmas Eve, Morgan, Easy, and Dandreau began the party early. Dandreau turned the radio on. Rock and roll music filled the room. The three men drank steadily while listening to the music, which made them homesick.

There was a knock at the door. Easy opened it, and Flim-Flam Man entered with an entourage of three girls, two of them Oriental, one of them Caucasian.

"A roundeye," Dandreau yelled. "An honest-to-God roundeye!"

They all gathered around Flim-Flam Man. "Glad you're back," said Easy. "Who've you got with you?"

"These two are Siamese twins, Mai and Tai. I picked them up in Bangkok. And this is Millie. She's from Liverpool. I met her at Penang."

"Hi, Millie," said Dandreau, grinning.

"Hullo, luv." She smiled back, revealing a gap between her front teeth. She was dressed in a purple miniskirt, sandals, and a see-through blouse.

"Liverpool, eh?" said Dandreau. "Did you ever get to see the Beatles?"

"Oh, sure. Me and my chums used to go to the Cavern every Saturday night. We was regulars. We even knew them when they were called the Quarrymen."

Morgan got beers for Flim-Flam Man and his three female friends, and the party continued.

Two hours later everyone was drunk. Millie began doing an impromptu strip to the music. Naked, she stood in the center of the room. With a whoop Dandreau caught her up and laid her down on Easy's bed. He fumbled out of his clothing and lay down on top of her.

Millie opened her eyes. "Thirty dollars, ducky," she slurred. "This ain't free love, you know."

A half hour passed. Flim-Flam Man, dreamy-eyed, sat in a corner of the room fondling the breasts of his Siamese twins while they held his beer and opium pipe. Millie, clothed again, was drunkenly but quietly conversing with Easy. Dandreau, passed out, lay naked on the floor. Morgan waited for Tam to arrive.

"Is too many people here. We go to special place tonight," said Tam, taking Morgan's hand and leading him downstairs to the street where she hailed a taxi that took them to the outskirts of the city.

"Is it safe here?" Morgan asked, watching the taxi's receding taillights.

"Is it safe anywhere in Vietnam now?" parried Tam.

They went into the lobby of a small hotel. Tam paid the desk clerk, and he gave her a key. They went up the short flight of stairs and into the room.

Tam took Morgan's clothes off and undressed herself. Leading him by the hand she went into the bathroom and turned the shower on. The warm water felt good on their skin as Tam soaped them both down. They rinsed and dried off with terry cloth towels. She silently led Morgan back into the main room and turned out the light.

From her purse she extracted a small ball of opium and a pipe. After preparing it she held it to Morgan's lips. He inhaled deeply.

— 20 —

The mellifluous chanting of the shaven-headed monks reverberated with the temple's smoke-stained brick walls, then seeped through crevices in the crumbling mortar of the ancient structure. Wafting across moonlit paddies, the mantra entered Morgan's and Tam's room. Diminished by the distance of its journey, only a muted sound reached their ears.

Naked, Morgan sat in a rattan chair at the foot of the bed. Narcotic fingers of opium coursed through his veins, holding him gently. His eyes were fixed hypnotically on the vision in front of him.

Tam lay face down on the bed, the flickering lights from several candles creating moving shadows that wove exotic patterns across her bronzed body. She drew up her knees slowly until they nestled under her breasts. Her slim buttocks jutted into the air. Her sparse pubic hair encircled but failed to conceal her slightly engorged labia.

She spread her legs apart and began undulating her hips from left to right, moving in time to music which only she heard. Her right hand appeared between her legs. She extended a tapered index finger, drew it downward across her anus, then pushed it into the groove of her vaginal lips, until it disappeared inside her.

Morgan's eyes filled with this sexual display. The optical image of Tam entered his brain, suffusing it with a golden heat.

Tam's finger reappeared, glistening with her own wetness. She massaged her clitoris until, distended, it descended from its protective cleft. Her expert ministrations caused the small button of flesh to become even more engorged.

Morgan felt something rhythmical born within him, something akin to but separate from his heartbeat. Single-purposed in its goal of overwhelming him, the beat became stronger until he heard thunder from somewhere inside himself.

By now Tam's entire body was reflecting the effect of her masturbatory touch. Her hips sawed forward and backward in imitation of intercourse. Her head arched toward the ceiling, supported by her graceful neck, which now revealed a faint network of bulging veins. Her small mouth was open; a silent O pushed from her lips as her tongue played over dual rows of ivory-white teeth.

Tam shuddered as she urged herself toward completion. Her thumb rubbed against her clitoris while her finger, joined by two others, was busy whipsawing in and out of her vagina. Moist sucking sounds could be heard, punctuated by her tortured breathing as she rode her hand up a vast, internal wave, reached its crest, and stayed there, suspended between the narrow margin separating ecstasy and pain. She screamed as her orgasm overwhelmed all of her senses.

After several minutes of rest Tam got off the bed and knelt at Morgan's feet. She opened a bottle of baby oil and poured a large amount in her hands. She began rubbing the warm oil into Morgan's scrotum and along the length of his erection. Under the soft light his belly glistened. His hips began moving involuntarily, thrusting against her sliding hands.

"Is good?" she asked. Morgan was beyond answering.

"Is good," she concurred. She held his penis lightly in her hands while he came. Then, reverently, she took him between her parted lips.

— 21 —

Britt, Chase, and Morgan sat down at the table in the Airmen's Club. Dandreau, lost in the music the Filipino band played, remained standing, dancing in place.

"Hey, you ofay Chubby Checker, sit down," ordered Chase, his dark eyes laughing.

"Do-wah, do-wah, o mama, do-wah!" sang Dandreau, tapping his fingers against the table top as he took his seat.

A Vietnamese waitress, clad in a miniskirt, fishnet stockings, and high heels, took their order, smiled perfunctorily, and left. The Filipino band was loud but failed to drown out the noise of three hundred airmen who sat in front of the stage, drinking and talking among themselves.

"These rear-echelon cookies are something else," noted Britt as he surveyed the roomful of tailored-fatigued, well-groomed airmen.

Chase and Morgan looked around but said nothing. Dandreau still tapped his long bony fingers, keeping rhythm with the Filipino drummer, flecks of spittle flying out of his mouth as he sang along. His eyes were glazed.

"Don't you be getting none of them 'leptic fits around me," Chase warned Dandreau. "If you bite your tongue, I'll let ya bleed to deaf."

As the waitress returned with their order, Dandreau seemed to notice where he was for the first time. He focused on the waitress and screamed at her, "You're groovy."

"Wha' you say?" she yelled over the din of the club.

"You're groovy! Groovy, groovy, groovy!" Chase, Morgan, and Britt laughed. Airmen seated at nearby tables turned to watch Dandreau's antics.

"You grooby, too," she shot back, consternation written all over her face. "Numbah one grooby." Dandreau, smiling lecherously, reached out to grab her. She backed away. "Now give you me four dolla' for drins."

"I can dig it, I can dig it, I can dig it!" Dandreau sang as he paid her.

"Hey, there's the Commander!" Morgan hooted, referring to another of the Seventh-team members, Sisco, a small man who was much taken by the fact that he was of Nordic descent. Sisco's wavy blond hair was combed straight back, his eyebrows and lids were white; he

almost seemed to be an albino. Off duty he affected a
black turtleneck which, to the others, gave him the appearance of a U-boat commander; hence, his nickname.

"Hey, Commander!" Morgan yelled, waving his arm
to get Sisco's attention. He spotted Morgan, got up,
carried his chair over to them, and sat down.

Chase looked up at Sisco, smiling. "Where's your
U-boat, Commander?"

"Out in the motor pool," he replied, unruffled by the
teasing.

"Dive! Dive!" wailed Dandreau, greeting Sisco.

"Dandreau, you doin' whites again?" Sisco asked.

"Uh, uh, uh, uh!" exclaimed Dandreau, tossing his
head back, his eyes rolling up into their sockets.

"You're doin' whites, you asshole," Sisco concluded.
The five of them drank steadily. They and three hundred others cheered madly as an Australian stripper
teased her way down to a lacy black bra and matching
panties.

"More!" cried the crowd as she walked off the stage.

"More music, more music!" Dandreau demanded
plaintively. Britt glanced up.

The Three Musketeers—Jacques, Fisher, and Zeke—
suddenly materialized. They each carried an appropri-
ated chair and sat down at the already full table. There
were now eight members of the mobility force gathered
together.

"Goddamn, a party!" exclaimed Morgan, already
feeling light on two beers.

"More damn crackers," grumbled Chase, his voice
mock-serious.

"We no hab crackers," apologized the Vietnamese
waitress, overhearing the jest as she took the Three
Musketeers' orders.

"Not eating crackers, babysan," corrected Chase.
"These here Three Musketeer crackers."

The Three Musketeers laughed.

She looked at Chase uncomprehendingly, then
shrugged. Dandreau, who had been watching the wait-

ress, now snaked out an arm and pinched her on the butt.

"You dinky-dau GI," she screamed as she jumped away from his groping hand.

"Sit on my face, you truck-driving mama!" invited Dandreau.

"We not serb that here," she shrilled at him, not understanding his words, but the blush which tinged her face implied understanding of his lecherous intent.

Jacques ordered a draft. He wore a drooping Fu Manchu mustache, which he was invariably fussing with, using Pinaud wax to shape it perfectly.

"Seven-seven for me, please," said Fisher, a dark-featured, polite man from Billings, Montana.

"Tuborg!" demanded Zeke, the last of the trio, his fierce blue eyes fixed on the waitress's face. Ever since he had been incountry he had asked for Tuborg beer. The club had never carried it.

"I 'member you from before," she told him. "An' we still no hab Tubor' for you. Nebah happen."

"Hell of a note when a man can't get a decent beer," grumbled Zeke.

"Hell of a note when a man can't get a decent lay," added Jacques, as he toyed with his mustache.

Fisher was watching Dandreau who, forgetting the waitress, was now crying softly. Tears trailed down his cheeks as the band played "Runaround Sue." Sue was his girlfriend's name.

"Well, then, I'll just have to settle for San Miguel," Zeke sighed disgustedly. "Bring me six of 'em and an empty pitcher."

She left, threading her way through the crush of tables, and returned with the order. Without ceremony Zeke poured the beer from the six San Miguel bottles into the pitcher, hefted it with both hands, and guzzled, lines of beer streaming out from the corners of his mouth.

"Disgusting," muttered Sisco.

"But quenching, Commander," added Fisher.

"Drown it out, drown it out!" Dandreau sang, improvising his songs as he became more stoned on the combination of downers and beer.

"Where. you guys been?" Morgan yelled into Jacques' ear over the rumbling noise of three hundred drunken soldiers.

"Up at Khe Sanh," said Jacques, referring to the old French garrison in I Corps, located near the Laotian border.

"What you take in?"

Jacques took a swallow of his drink. "Beaucoup shit for the marines. Ammo, med supplies, rats, and a hell of a lot of body bags."

"Some shit brewing up there, Jackie?" Morgan asked as he lit another cigaret.

"There's a division of NVA regulars running around up there in the hills. Two divisions, maybe."

"Who we got on the ground up there?" Morgan yelled.

"The Bird," Jacques began, referring to a man whose thick eyeglasses gave him an owlish expression. "The Bird, Singleton, Voight," he continued. "Voight's got dysentery or something. He's shitting all over the place. We just dropped him off at the dispensary." Jacques turned away from Morgan and clapped a hand on Britt's shoulder. "Mr. Britt, you got orders from Easy."

Britt grimaced and scratched at his bald spot. "Where to?" he asked resignedly.

"Khe Sanh."

"When?" Britt wanted to know.

Jacques smiled, mock sympathy twisting his features. "Soon's you finish your drink. Bird leaves in an hour."

"Did Easy write me up for this one?" Britt asked, reaching for his bush hat with one hand, finishing his drink with the other.

Jacques shrugged. "He had to—it's your turn in the barrel."

Britt stood up, swaying slightly from the effect of

the drinking. "What's it like up there at—what?—Khe Sanh?" he asked.

Jacques coughed into the palm of his hand, then said, his eyes thoughtful, "It's O.K. now, but you're likely to have unfriendly company at any time."

"Far out!" bitched Britt, then laughed. "You fuckheads are my friends, and I don't even like any of you. What do I want to go up there for where there aren't any friendlies at all?"

"The marines are friendly," offered Chase.

"The marines are animals," Britt threw back.

"They love you, too," laughed Morgan.

Britt smiled his lupine smile, his teeth showing even and white.

"Adios, Britt," yelled the rest of them, with the exception of Dandreau who sang, "Lover don't leave me for no mean marine."

Sisco adjusted his turtleneck and told the others he had to get back to his U-boat.

"Don't forget to use your turn signal when you leave the motor pool," Chase admonished him.

Sisco laughed and then left.

The Three Musketeers, sneaking out a couple of beers which they intended to take over to the dysenteric Voight at the infirmary, were the next to leave.

"If he's going to shit," explained Jacques, wrinkling his nose, "he might as well shit San Migs."

Chase, Morgan, and Dandreau stayed on, drinking.

Morgan and Chase talked, their heads huddled together over the middle of the table to block out the noise.

Morgan, curious, asked Chase what it was like to be a black man from a Chicago ghetto.

"No different than being a Polack from a Chicago ghetto," Chase laughingly answered, "e'cept we able to hide out better in the dark."

They both laughed, ignoring Dandreau who seemed to be mesmerized by the music. He sat with both hands propping up his head, his eyes almost completely shut.

Their waitress returned with still another round of drinks. Morgan and Chase broke off their conversation and sat back as she put their drinks in front of them. Rather than go around the table to give Dandreau his drink, she leaned across it. Chase and Morgan both chanced glances at her cleavage as her blouse fell slightly away from her slender body.

Seemingly oblivious and subdued, Dandreau came to life, scream-singing, "Do it, do it, do it!" He reached across the table, with a motion so rapid it was difficult to follow, and squeezed one of the waitress's breasts in each hand.

She screamed.

"Honk, honk, honk, taxi coming through!" he bellowed, yanking the terrified Vietnamese girl over the table.

She screeched, her buttocks hit him in the chest, and her legs, seeking balance, involuntarily wrapped around Dandreau's neck. Her sudden weight upset Dandreau's center of gravity and the chair. They toppled over backwards onto the floor. Chase and Morgan stood up to watch, as did a dozen soldiers seated nearby.

Dandreau lay on his back, holding the waitress against him. She kept screaming as he nipped at her leg.

Morgan, Chase, and the others cheered wildly, which encouraged the drunken, grappling Dandreau.

A foot lashed out, narrowly missing Dandreau's head. "Let her go, motherfucker!" boomed the fat, black sergeant-at-arms whose face was livid with anger. "I said, let her go!"

Dandreau, his mouth full of nylon, mumbled, "Mime mying moo, mutt my mouts muck!"

Morgan knelt down to help Dandreau.

Chase attempted to calm the enraged NCO. "Hey, Sarge, we'll take care—"

"Don't 'Sarge' me!" raged the fat man. "I'm a ser-GEANT to you, airman!" He spat the last word in disgust.

"You a nigger to me," Chase told the man, a murderous rage in his eyes. "An if you don't get yo' motha-fuckin' mouf off me, I'll make you a dickless nigger." He stood in a crouch, ready to carry out his threat.

The sergeant started to say something, hesitated, then his own voice going low in his throat said, "Nigger, you an' your friends get outta my club. Now."

"We're going, Ser-GEANT," Morgan said, as he helped Dandreau to his feet.

"Going, going, gone," Dandreau sang as Chase and Morgan helped him out of the club.

Weaving drunkenly, the three of them stumbled back toward the barracks. In front of the Seventh Air Force Headquarters, Dandreau suddenly became frantic.

"Take off your hats, take off your hats!" he ex-horted them. Morgan and Chase humored him.

"Attention!" Dandreau yelled as he threw up his right hand in a salute and began singing "The Star-Spangled Banner" to the flag on top of the head-quarters building. Chase and Morgan stood rigid and saluted. They would have continued to play out this drunken scenario had it not been for the looming presence of an air policeman who, hearing them, came over to investigate.

Hooking Dandreau's arms at the elbows, they dragged him away as fast as they could, then dumped him into a ditch near the barracks.

"Let the fucker sleep it off here," said Chase as Mor-gan and he started walking toward the barracks.

Another song issued from the darkness of the ditch behind them. They stopped, listened, and laughed. Dandreau, in the darkness, was singing "Goodnight, Irene."

Two days after Christmas, Morgan and Dandreau received orders for a mission to Song Be.

— 22 —

January 1968. Sitting with his back against the yellow forklift, Morgan drank from his canteen and passed it to Dandreau. Grimacing, the airman waved it away. "I pass. In all the time I've been here I still can't get used to the taste of purification tablets. They make the water taste like piss."

"In all the time you've been over here you haven't caught dysentery, either," Morgan chided. "Besides, this has Kool-Aid in it. Grape. Try some."

"Jesus," groused Dandreau, "the only thing that tastes worse than purification tablets *is* Kool-Aid." Shrugging, Morgan capped the canteen and set it aside. He lit a cigaret and squinted pensively through its smoke at the mountain which towered above the airstrip.

Reading Morgan's mind, Dandreau said, "You think Charlie One Shot will make an appearance today?"

"Why should today be any different from the other times?"

"Oh, I don't know. It's just that he . . ." Dandreau let his thought trail off, then with some agitation said, "It's crazy! One mortar round per plane? Every two weeks?" He pointed his chin at the jungle-covered mountain and made a sound of disgust. "That gook son of a bitch has the ultimate skate job, don't he?"

Still staring at the mountain, Morgan said, "Be thankful he hasn't hit anything."

Dandreau laughed cynically. "So far, so good, so what? Law of averages says he's got to connect sooner or later." Morgan did not respond. "Maybe," continued Dandreau, "it means they don't have much left to throw at us. Maybe Charlie is runnin' outta gas. Maybe there is light at the end of Westmoreland's tunnel."

It was Morgan's turn to laugh. "Dandreau, Charlie is

going to be fighting this war long after we've gone home.''

"Maybe we've won all their hearts and minds," persisted Dandreau.

"He's probably going to win, too," Morgan said quietly.

"Bullshit!"

The droning sound of turboprop engines interrupted their conversation. Morgan glanced at his watch. "Right on time," he said, standing up and brushing laterite dust from his clothing.

Dandreau got up and climbed onto the forklift. "How many days you got left, Morg?"

"Two hundred and seventy-two."

"Is that counting your wakeup? You have to count your wakeup, you know." Both men watched the C-130 descend from the cloudless sky.

Tonelessly, Morgan said, "There isn't a wakeup, Dandreau. This whole war is just a dream, and it goes on forever."

Dandreau threw back his head and laughed. "Ninety-three more days of this 'dream,' and I'm gone. And that's counting my wakeup."

The C-130 transport plane, its belly filled with supplies for the isolated artillery compound near the Cambodian border, skimmed over the threshold of the dirt runway and landed.

On the side of the mountain, well hidden from the airstrip below, Fighter Second Class Mu squatted next to his mortar, his skinny buttocks inches from the ground. Wrinkling his nose to dislodge a pesky fly, he panned his binoculars away from the forklift and focused on the cargo plane. The roaring sound of its engines carried up to his firing position as he watched the plane roll down the runway, slow, then turn and lumber toward the loading area.

Morgan walked to the edge of the loading area, raised his arms over his head, and guided the plane toward him. The pilot and copilot were visible through the

flight deck's windshield as the C-130 closed on the
beckoning sergeant. He clenched his fists and crossed
his arms at the wrists; the C-130 braked to a halt, its
Snoopylike nose bobbing gently.

Fighter Second Class Mu picked up a shell and held it
above the mortar, which was a World War Two relic
that had been captured from the French by the Viet
Minh at Dien Bien Phu in 1954 and had been transported to South Vietnam via the Ho Chi Minh Trail,
carried on the backs of impressed Montagnard tribesmen.

The C-130's back ramp slowly opened, revealing the
cavernous interior of the plane. Chained to the floor
was a jeep.

Fighter Second Class Mu dropped the shell into the
mortar tube and covered his ears.

Just as Morgan reached in to work the chain release,
the single mortar round dropped in and exploded forty
meters away, sending a jagged shard of shrapnel
through the ramp's hydraulic system. The ramp immediately fell onto his left foot and crushed it into the
ground.

Morgan's nervous system was wracked with the sensation that his whole being was on fire as a grenade of
pain exploded in his brain. That part of his brain that
dealt with logic frantically sought to establish a cogent
reason for this fiery sensation and ravaged by the pain,
failed to do so. Totally defenseless against the excruciat-
ing sensation, unable to escape the pain, Morgan threw
back his head and screamed, his eyes staring at the sun
without seeing it.

When the mortar round had exploded, the C-130's
loadmaster had taken cover at one side of the ramp-
chained jeep. He had seen the ramp fall away, had
watched Morgan jerk and stiffen, and had seen Morgan's head snap back on his neck, tendons bulging as his
mouth opened wide. However, the noise from the inboard propellers had drowned out Morgan's screaming.
Ignoring his own safety, the loadmaster crawled to

the end of the ramp and looked questioningly into Morgan's unseeing eyes, then peered down to where Morgan's foot disappeared beneath the ramp. Comprehending, he stood and jumped to the ground and ran over to the bunker where other mobility members had taken refuge.

By this time Morgan was screaming, "Get it off me! Get it off me!" His words were lost beneath the overriding sound of the propellers.

The loadmaster emerged from the bunker, followed by several other airmen. Dandreau jumped in the seat of the forklift. Two men appeared on either side of Morgan and supported him while the loadmaster directed the forklift driver. Maneuvering the vehicle to one side of the ramp, Dandreau lowered the forks until they rested on the ground, then slid them under the ramp and pulled back on the lift lever. The ramp raised it far enough for the two men to pull Morgan away. He wrestled free from the mens' grips on him. In denial of the reality, Morgan told himself his foot was only sprained. He tried to walk, his first step transmitting a pain which brought nausea; he fell, writhing and moaning, to the ground. The two airmen reached down, hooked Morgan under his armpits, and dragged him to a jeep parked near the bunker. Without ceremony they threw him into a jeep and, sandwiching him between their bodies, drove down the road toward the artillery compound.

Needing to somehow deal with the intolerable pain, Morgan began beating his fists against the jeep's windshield, on which his high school class ring did a proficient job: a portion of glass the size and shape of his balled fist crumbled into a spiderweb pattern; his gouged knuckles became slick with blood. He continued the assault, working a fast, tattooing succession of blows to the shattered glass while the airman to his right tried to restrain him. The jeep's driver, a grizzled master sergeant, yelled, "Sonny, if you don't stop, I'm gonna set your ass out right here an' you can crawl the rest of the way."

"I can't stop. I can't," Morgan moaned between pain-clenched teeth.

By the time the jeep deposited him in front of the medical bunker, there were three more shattered areas imprinted in the windshield.

Two corpsmen half-dragged and half-carried Morgan down into the semidarkness of the medical bunker. His first thought was that it was cool down there, much cooler than under the sun at the airfield. The black face of the senior corpsman appeared in front of him. "Where you hit?" he asked matter-of-factly.

Morgan forgot about the coolness of the bunker. "My foot doesn't work anymore."

"Let's get the boot off," the corpsman said, his voice staying at a conversational level as he unlaced the boot and pulled.

"Ah, God, no!" screamed Morgan. "Not like that."

"I gotta get the boot off somehow."

"Give me a knife," ordered Morgan. The corpsman turned away momentarily, than handed Morgan a scalpel. Morgan took it and began sawing at his boot. He gripped the remnants of the boot with both hands and, with an indrawn breath, pulled it off.

Blood from the injury saturated his once-white sock. Morgan peeled it off gingerly and looked at his foot. From the ankle down, the entire foot was a swollen, red-and-purple, bruised mess. A rivet mark, testimony to the weight of the ramp as it had crushed his foot, was impressed in the flesh over the knuckle of Morgan's big toe, which was mashed to half of its original thickness. A portion of yellowish white bone protruded from its tip. Morgan tried to wriggle his toes; the pain made him gasp.

"You got something for the pain?" he asked the corpsman.

The medic sliced open Morgan's fatigue pants with a razor blade and with a fluid motion plunged a syrette into the exposed flesh. Morgan's heart pounded and skipped several beats as the morphine suffused him. He was filled with a sense of euphoria. The pain subsided.

"That's some good stuff," he said appreciatively to the corpsman whose face seemed to Morgan to have melted until it resembled a rubbery Halloween mask. "Yes, sir, that's some good stuff."

— 23 —

Morgan was driven past the crippled C-130 and taken directly onto the runway where he and the jeep driver smoked and talked while waiting for the medevac dustoff. Stuporous and smiling, he heard the chopper thirty seconds before it came into view from behind the mountain. Its rotors made a monotonous sound which, as it neared them, changed in pitch until the airfield reverberated with the din.

Morgan popped smoke and threw the canister away from the jeep; a thick scarlet plume spiraled into the sky. The pilot flew his chopper directly toward the spot, coming in low over the picket line of ARVN bunkers which acted as the first defense against a ground attack on the artillery compound. As the dustoff crossed this line at no more than twenty feet high, the ARVN soldiers who were running themselves and playing elaborate pebble games jumped up and hurried to pull their freshly washed fatigues off the commo wire that served as a clothesline, then scurried into their bunkers. A flock of scrawny chickens, which were carried live on the soldiers' backs while in the field to serve as fresh meat, squawked and ran in erratic circles. One ARVN soldier, clad in a diaperlike roll of cotton, stood defiantly on the sandbagged roof of his bunker and shook his fist at the medevac. He unleashed a torrent of Vietnamese curses as the chopper thundered overhead, its red-painted crosses brilliant against the dull camouflage markings on it sides. Beside himself with the futility of his epithets, the ARVN soldier stood in the blast of rotor wash, raised his middle finger on his right hand, and thrust it at the receding medevac's tail. Red and white chicken feathers, caught up in the down draft of the rotors, whirled into the air, then settled slowly, like autumn leaves, on the dusty red laterite.

The medevac hovered briefly near the smoke canister, then set down gently on the runway, engulfing Morgan and the jeep driver in a maelstrom of laterite dust, pebbles, and pieces of C-ration cardboard. Morgan and the driver were both wearing goggles to protect their eyes; bandanas covering their noses and lower faces gave them the look of Tuaregs caught in a sandstorm. Morgan covered his goggles with both hands and grooved on the noise made by the medevac. Rotor-generated wind tore at his clothing. He loved the sensation and imagined himself to be in the Sahara desert.

"Don't need no o-a-sis," he sang to himself, still high on the morphine, as he climbed unassisted into the medevac. He sat on the floor behind the pilot, adjusted a safety belt, and gave a thumbs-up. The engine whined louder as the chopper shuddered and bounced; the helicopter tilted its nose toward the ground, lifted, and swept off across the airfield.

On the side of the mountain, Fighter Second Class Mu squatted in a bush and watched the helicopter lift away from Song Be, a prideful smile crossing his weathered face.

Morgan, with a goofy smile on his face, leaned out the doorless side as far as he could, craning his neck.

The copilot turned in his seat and saw him, and hooked up a spare headset that he gave to Morgan.

"What are you looking for, chief?" asked the copilot, his voice disembodied in the earphones.

"Where's Morgan?" Morgan asked. In his morphine-clouded mind he was looking for himself down on the receding airfield.

The pilot flew his craft at treetop level over the canopied jungle. Enthralled, despite the morphine in his bloodstream Morgan was hyper-aware of each tree they passed over. He saw a pillar of black smoke trailing up from the jungle to the west. In this state of mind he was once again reminded that before the Indochinese War, when the Emperor Bao Dai had hunted tigers in the royal hunting preserve at Dalat—the beautiful mountain city which now housed Vietnam's sole atomic reactor—Vietnam must have been one of the most beautiful countries in the world.

The medevac flew over an area which had been defoliated by Operation Ranch Hand. This Air Commando project had sent formations of C-123s over the land, spraying toxic chemicals in order to deny the Viet Cong their jungled sanctuaries. In addition, the chemicals contaminated the crops and water tablets, affecting both people and livestock.

The villagers were forced to abandon their land. They gathered their children and the elderly, and their few possessions, emerged from the dying forest, and walked the oxcart trails south, where they were met by other farmers-cum-refugees. They left behind their ruined soil, nervous and wheezing livestock, and the whitewashed, well-tended tombs of their ancestors. The ranks of the VC swelled with these villagers, their soft black eyes revealing nothing of the revenge they nurtured in their hearts.

The area Morgan looked down upon contained thousands of defoliated trees, their bare blackened branches reaching toward the sky as if in appeal. Further on, the chopper crossed a B-52 strike zone. Geometric patterns of bomb craters dotted the jungle, the craters glinting blackly as the sun reflected off the brackish water which half-filled them.

After a half-hour flight, the helicopter landed at Quan Loi, where Morgan was carried off and placed in a nearby Quonset hut. A dead soldier was also carried in and laid down on the floor. A medic checked Morgan's foot and told him that another medevac would soon drop in and take him the rest of the way, to Long Binh. Drowsy from the morphine, Morgan nodded slightly to the medic, who then left, closing the door to the hut behind him.

Morgan stared at the tin ceiling and fumbled in his pockets for his cigarets, only to discover that he hadn't any matches.

"Hey," he said to himself at this revelation, "I don't have any matches." He got up on his elbows and looked at the closed door. "Hey," he yelled, "I don't have any matches." No one answered. He tried to get to his feet but, overcome with a wave of dizziness, eased back on the cot. The roof and walls of the hut rattled as debris blew against it, heralding the arrival of a helicopter on the pad outside. He waited impatiently, his glazed eyes fixed on the door. It did not open. He heard the helicopter lift off.

He needed a cigaret badly. He slowly scanned the semi-darkened interior of the hut and spotted the body lying in the corner. He cleared his throat.

"Hey," he said in a church-soft voice, "you got a light?" He sat up and rolled his feet over the side of the cot, tentatively testing the weight potential of his crushed foot. He decided against walking and got down on all fours. He crawled over to the dead soldier, who was lying face down in the dirt. He grabbed the body by the shoulder and hip and flipped it over. The soldier's face had stiffened in death; his blue eyes stared ceilingward at nothing. His lips were compressed in a tight line of wryness, as if in comprehension of the cruel joke life had played on him at such a young age. The lapels of the dead soldier's shirt were embroidered with the insignia of a second lieutenant. Morgan quickly patted down the man's pockets but didn't find any matches.

"Then how about the time?" Morgan asked. "You got the time? Shit, you got all the time in the world." He leaned over the man and read the Rolex on his wrist: Almost three hours had passed since Morgan's foot had been crushed.

He rolled the body back into its face-down position. Staring at the back of the dead lieutenant's head, he tried to think of something to say, something appropriate to the circumstance. His mind could not work past clichés. He decided to leave whatever words there were to the minister who would deliver the stateside eulogy.

"Thanks for the time, sir," he muttered before he crawled back to the cot and fell into a drugged sleep.

— 24 —

Practiced hands pulled him from the medevac and laid him down on the aluminum gurney. As he was wheeled toward triage, Morgan waved back at the medevac crew, which was already engrossed in takeoff procedures. Morgan looked up and through a hazy mist saw a large plywood sign over the cement sidewalk that led into the cluster of hospital buildings. His mind painstakingly put the letters on the sign together:

WELCOME
to the
93rd Evacuation
Hospital
Ready Now

His mind wandered, and he wondered how men who were blinded would know where they were. Maybe, he thought, one of the medics told them. But, his mind argued, what if the men were not only blind but deafened? Maybe, he thought, they have someone here like that woman who taught Helen Keller to communicate with her hands. But, his mind continued to argue, what if the men are blind, deaf, and have had both hands blown away?

Fuck this, thought Morgan. If the men are that fucked up, they won't care where they are. Exhausted, he tried to stop thinking and said, "Me, too."

"You, too, what?" asked the medic at the head of the gurney.

"I'm ready. Now."

"Good for you," drawled the medic, grinning widely. "We've been waiting for you."

Morgan was wheeled through the triage doors. A doctor, nurse, and orderly surrounded him. The doctor read the casualty tag.

"Left foot," he said. The orderly began taking an oral history from Morgan, writing the answers down on a chart. The nurse, a freckled blond with tired eyes, used a pair of surgical scissors to cut along the seam of Morgan's fatigues, slowly exposing his leg. Reaching midship, she realized he was not wearing any undershorts.

Smiling, she said, "My mama told me that when a man undresses, a lady leaves the room." Morgan felt his face redden. She gave the scissors to the orderly and walked over to another litter where she fussed with the IV drip that fed glucose into the arm of an unconscious soldier.

After his pants had been cut away, Morgan was covered with a green surgical sheet. The doctor examined the foot, briskly but gently probing at the damaged tissue, bending the ankle backward and forward. Morgan watched, curious yet detached. The doctor flashed a perfunctory smile. "Well, Sarge, I don't know how much of it we can save, but we're gonna try for the whole thing, just as soon as Jackson cleans it up. We'll throw some sutures in it and see what Mother Nature does."

"Thanks," said Morgan. The doctor left.

Jackson, a corpulent youth from Arizona, anesthetized the wound. He inserted a syringe in four different spots around the damaged area and then several more injections directly into the wound. He offered Morgan a piece of gum, and they both chewed while waiting for the novocaine to take effect.

The triage doors burst open suddenly. A gurney was rushed into the room, pushed by three orderlies. The writhing soldier lying on it had no visible wounds, but his face was ashen and contorted with pain. His ragged breathing made a hoarse wheezing sound.

The same doctor that had worked on Morgan leaned down and yelled into the soldier's ear, "What's wrong with you, trooper?"

The soldier opened his mouth to speak. A frothy pink bubble formed on his lips, then burst.

"MPs brought him in," explained one of the orderlies. "They ran him over with a jeep."

The doctor grunted. "Hell of a thing to be in a war and get run over by a car." His hands and eyes moved expertly over the injured soldier's body. "This guy's chest is crushed," he pronounced. "Oxygen," he ordered. "And get a chest man in here."

Morgan watched this scene intently, fascinated by the casualness of the medical personnel. Each of them moved knowledgeably around the triage room in coordinated, purposeful patterns.

"You feel this?" asked Jackson, snapping Morgan

out of his reverie. Morgan watched Jackson probing at the edges of the wound.

"I can feel pressure from your fingers but no pain."

"Good. We'll start now." Jackson picked up a bottle of Betadine and poured a large quantity of the antiseptic directly on the wound. Next, he used what looked like an ordinary toothbrush and began scrubbing the wound, starting on the outer edges and gradually working his way into the rawness of it.

Morgan sat upright and watched Jackson working. He was intrigued by the fact that although it was himself being worked on, he felt as if he were watching someone else. Must be the morphine, he thought, mentally shrugging his shoulders.

Jackson stopped scrubbing. "Ah, I gotta clean the bone now, so you might not want to watch this part."

"It's my foot."

"Suit yourself." The orderly inserted his index finger under the bone that protruded from Morgan's big toe and began scrubbing it roughly. Since Morgan felt no pain, he simply watched.

A loud voice said, "Casualties coming in. Five from the Cav."

"Fuck!" muttered Jackson. "More overtime again." He prepared an antitetanus injection, which he injected into Morgan's hip. "Well," he said, "you ain't gonna die, but you ain't gonna walk all that well for a while." He tossed the disposable syringe at a wastebasket eight feet away. It landed on top of a stack of bloody bandages. "Two points," he exclaimed, walking away.

Morgan eased down on the gurney and closed his eyes. He smiled when he remembered what the medic at Song Be had told him: Bone damage didn't readily heal in this climate; Morgan was probably destined for an outcountry hospital. Maybe in Japan, hoped Morgan, nodding off.

He was jolted awake as the gurney was slammed against the wall. "We got beaucoup hurt coming in," explained Jackson. "Those sutures will have to wait."

Morgan nodded and noted that the triage was rapidly filling with doctors, nurses, and more orderlies. Through the wall he could hear whapping sounds as casualty-carrying choppers made their way to the Ninety-Third. The sounds of rotors slapping air became louder, closer.

"They're down," someone said.

The personnel in triage became silent as everyone waited for the casualties to be wheeled in. Morgan sat up on the gurney, his back against the wall. He wished he were someplace else, but since he wasn't, he decided to watch everything that was about to happen.

The parade of hurt began. The triage doors flew open as the first gurney smashed through them. The body of an eighteen-year-old from Texas was hurried into the room. One side of the soldier's face was covered with a blood-soaked pressure bandage; the other side was caked with drying blood. His dirty blond hair was matted with it. A doctor bent over the still form, looked intently into the soldier's eyes, and sighed.

"This one's DOA. Put him in the freezer."

The next litter held a twenty-six-year-old from Colorado whose left leg had been traumatically severed. He had been hit by the same booby trap that had killed his Texan friend.

"Good tourniquet job," noted the doctor as a nurse monitored the soldier's blood pressure. "The blast probably cauterized the artery. He's a lucky son of a bitch. Prep him. He's going straight to OR. Petrie, you do him."

"Roger that," acknowledged a doctor who was working on a nineteen-year-old from Oregon who, as a result of shrapnel, was missing a kneecap and oozing blood from numerous wounds which dotted the entire length of his body. The soldier was softly blubbering.

"Stabilize the shock, type and cross-match him, then get going on the knee," Dr. Petrie told an assistant. "He's going to need at least two units of whole."

A twenty-two-year-old from Wisconsin walked unassisted into the room. He was untouched except for a needlelike piece of Plexiglass that protruded from his right eye. A doctor put his arm around him and ushered him to a chair.

"Get pictures of this," he ordered, "and keep the tape on the eyelid. And," he added, addressing the soldier, "don't you dare blink." The soldier nodded silently, his hands clasped in his lap.

A twenty-year-old from Alabama was pushed in on the last gurney. The stump of his left arm was neatly bandaged. His good hand was buried between his legs and seemed to be working at something.

A doctor approached him. "What you got there, trooper?"

The young soldier looked up, his eyes imploring. "I need help, sir."

"Sure," soothed the doctor. "That's what I'm here for."

The soldier smiled wanly and raised an object from between his legs, offering it to the doctor. "Can you help me get my wedding ring off this?" he asked apologetically. "My wife would kill me if I came home without it." The doctor accepted the amputated hand. Necrotic fingers curled tightly into its palm. Encircling the third finger was a plain gold band flecked with minute spots of blood.

"Get rid of this," ordered the doctor, tossing the hand to a passing orderly. "And make sure this gentleman's ring is returned to him."

— 25 —

With a towel tied around his midsection, and using crutches, Morgan worked his way down the green-tiled hallway and stopped at the morgue's door. He pushed the button that was inlaid in the wall and heard a buzzing sound from within. The door opened. A pale, effeminate-looking man stood in the opening. "Yes?" he said, arching his left eyebrow.

"Medic said I could get some clothes from you."

"Well I suppose you can," he said testily. "Come on in and close the door behind you."

The artificial chill of the room prickled Morgan's skin. A body lay on a stainless steel table, naked except for a pair of jungle boots, one of which pointed at the ceiling while the other pointed at the floor. Morgan's nose wrinkled at the coppery smell of blood.

"Follow me," said the attendant, flouncing off into an alcove whose floor was covered with GI clothing. Out of a small window at the rear of the clothing room Morgan saw three naked bodies hanging upside down from what looked like a miniature goalpost. A soldier garbed in a rubber jumpsuit, gloves, and boots was using a hose with a high-power nozzle to clean the bodies. Water dripped off them and formed pink-tinged puddles beneath the dead soldiers' heads.

"Well, are you going to try on some clothes or are we just looking today?" the attendant said, impatiently tapping his foot.

"Sorry," said Morgan. "I was just looking at that . . . It's like something out of a butcher shop."

"Hmmm," replied the attendant. "Will you please hurry?"

Morgan laid his crutches against the wall, reached down, and picked up a shirt which he held gingerly between thumb and forefinger.

"Too big," he said, letting the garment fall back into the pile.

"Fussy, aren't we?" said the attendant, looking pointedly at his watch. The next shirt Morgan selected was the proper size, but it had been torn from lapel to bottom pocket. Small pieces of flesh adhered to a long trail of dried blood. Morgan discarded it.

"Your name's not Beau Brummel by any chance?"

"Who's he?" asked Morgan.

The attendant ran nervous fingers through his hair. "He was a very fastidious person."

"Is he dead?"

"Oh, never mind!"

The shirt Morgan finally selected bore the cloverleaf patch of the Fourth Infantry Division. The embroidered name tag read Waite. Morgan found his own pants lying on top of the pile. "A couple of safety pins will fix these up. Do you have any?"

"Sure." The attendant led the way over to a desk. "Are you sure you don't want a matching cummerbund?"

Morgan looked down at his bandaged foot and smiled. "Nah. I think my prom days are over."

Morgan fixed the pants with the safety pins. The attendant held the morgue door open wide as Morgan hobbled through it.

"Don't do anything I wouldn't do," said the attendant coyly.

"I'm sure there's very little that you don't do," said Morgan, winking broadly.

"How precious!" simpered the attendant, slamming shut the door.

Morgan left the hospital complex. The crutches chafed his underarms and sweat stung them. He worked his way to the side of the Bien Hoa-Saigon highway and waited, massaging a cramp in his left thigh. A military police jeep drove by, the driver and M-60 gunner both glancing at him curiously.

A column of armored personnel carriers clanked by in

the opposite direction. Attached to each vehicle's antenna was a South Vietnamese flag: three horizontal blood-red stripes on a field of saffron, the latter symbolizing the fertility of Vietnam's soil, the former symbolizing happiness.

To Morgan the ARVN APC commanders, small-statured to begin with and further diminished by the American helmets and flak jackets that they were wearing, looked like unhappy schoolboys heading toward an unpleasant situation.

An ancient bus lumbered toward him, jammed with farm families returning from market. Several heads craned out of each window. Wooden cages containing chickens and ducks were lashed to the bus's roof. An unseen piglet squealed its fright. As the bus drew abreast of Morgan, he saw fire-breathing dragons painted on its side. He looked up into the faces of the passengers. They stared back at him stonily. Something wet and viscous hit his cheek. Watching the receding bus, Morgan wiped the spittle away with the back of his hand.

An army deuce-and-a-half thundered toward him. Morgan stuck out his thumb. The large truck downshifted and lumbered over to the side of the road, covering Morgan with dust. The driver, sporting an enormous red mustache and wearing a piece of camouflage silk tied around his head, opened the passenger door.

"Where ya headed, man?" he yelled.

"To hell," said Morgan, handing his crutches to the man.

The driver tugged thoughtfully at the corner of his mustache. "Well, I'm only going as far as Saigon."

"Close enough," muttered Morgan, easing his way into the cab.

— 26 —

Morgan checked himself into Third Field Hospital in Saigon, where he was put on a ward with twenty other patients. In a corner bed a Viet Cong lay dying, covered with massive burns.

Easy and Tam came to visit him, both of their faces showing concern.

"What's the doctor say, Morg?"

"Not much up to now. He's afraid I'll get gangrene, but he's not sure."

"Gangrene? Wha' mean gangrene?" Tam wanted to know.

"Just a bad infection," Morgan reassured her.

Morgan met a man from his own state, who was recuperating from a shoulder wound.

"Where do you live?" Morgan asked.

"Traverse City."

"Isn't that where they have the cherry festival each year?"

"That's the place."

"Must be pretty country."

"Roger that," said the other man, whose name was Bruckner. The two of them became tight friends, and Morgan looked on the older Bruckner as an elder brother.

One night the two of them watched a movie, *To Sir with Love*, in the hospital's courtyard, along with about fifty other patients. Morgan's foot had hurt so badly that after the movie Bruckner carried him back to the ward in his arms.

That night the burned VC died.

"About time," muttered a warrant officer whose helicopter had been shot out from under him. "I was getting tired of hearing that motherfucker moaning all the time. I don't know why they put a VC in with us in the first place."

Morgan's foot was progressively turning blacker; his toes were covered with a dry, crusty layer of skin. The pain was terrific.

Tam visited him almost daily, and Easy came after work, bringing Morgan his mail and filling him in on what was going on.

"We had a bad accident at the base last night. A C-123 was getting ready for takeoff, and a Phantom came barreling in and hit it. He was supposed to land at Bien Hoa, but I guess he ran out of gas. Everyone in the C-one twenty-three made it out O.K., but the Phantom pilot went right through one of the one twenty-three props, and it took his head off. His plane exploded and burned, and we were all out there in the rain looking for his head. What a night!"

Dandreau came down from Song Be and visited him, and Morgan thanked him for lifting the C-130's ramp off his foot.

"Shucks," said Dandreau, blushing. "Think nothing of it."

Morgan and his new friend, Bruckner, spent most of their days sitting in the hospital snack bar, listening to tunes on the jukebox. Since the movie, Morgan's favorite song was "To Sir with Love." They met another soldier who didn't have a nose.

"I was riding in a jeep with a one-o-six recoilless rifle mounted in it," explained the noseless man. "We hit a mine and the jeep rolled over, and the one-o-six crushed my nose to shit. The doctors are going to make me another one out of plastic. I guess I'll never have to worry anymore about having the sniffles."

At the end of January, two days before Tet, the lunar New Year, Morgan's doctor decided to send him to Japan.

"They'll have to operate on you. I don't know how much of your foot you might lose. Maybe all of it and maybe none. We just can't do anything more for you here."

The farewell between Morgan and Bruckner was emotional. The two men had grown close during their stay in the hospital.

"I'll be going back to my unit in a few days," said Bruckner.

"Well, be careful," Morgan admonished his friend. "I'll look you up when I get back from Japan. If I get back from Japan."

"Try to get a pass while you're there. I hear the Japanese women fuck your brains out."

"I'll do that," promised Morgan. It was time to board the bus for the ride to the medevac at Tan Son Nhut. The two men hugged each other spontaneously, and when they released each other, both had tears glittering in their eyes.

Morgan was carried aboard the C-141 medevac on a litter. After the plane was filled with casualties, it took off and, several hours later, landed in Japan.

— 27 —

February 1968. "Would ya just look at that snow," marveled one of the casualties as the bus carried them to the air force hospital at Tachikawa.

"Is that Mount Fuji?" asked another soldier. "Man, I shoulda brought my skis."

Morgan was processed at the hospital and admitted to an orthopedic ward. That night a surgeon came into his room and, using sharp surgical implements, peeled away the dead skin on Morgan's foot.

"I'm sorry to cause you any pain," said Dr. Bonnin. "I'll have the nurse give you something for it as soon as I've finished."

The next day Morgan was transferred to the main ward, which held twenty beds, all of them full with the human debris of the war.

The bed next to Morgan contained a man named Gerber whose jaws were wired together.

"I was lying in a tent at Lai Khe when this guy came in and shot me. I mean, he pointed a pistol at me and shot me through the chin. He told the military police that he was playing Russian roulette. I hope they give the sorry son of a bitch life at Leavenworth."

The bed on the other side of Morgan contained a man who had a fractured pelvis.

Morgan had to soak his foot in peroxide a half dozen times a day, then apply a strip of coarse gauze. After the peroxide had dried, he had to rip the gauze off.

"I know it's painful," soothed the nurse, Lieutenant Alexander, "but it keeps the wound fresh and free of germs and dead tissue."

Morgan met Wolfe, a youth who had severely broken his arm in a fall from the wing of a Phantom F4C.

"When you get that foot fixed," Wolfe told him, "we'll go downtown together and get some nooky."

"O.K.," said Morgan. "Except I don't know when they're going to operate on me."

"Sooner or later," said Wolfe. "They won't forget you."

That night they received word that the North Vietnamese and Viet Cong had invaded almost every town in Vietnam during the celebration of Tet.

"Did you see the *Stars and Stripes* yet?" asked Wolfe. "It says that the VC even tried to take over our embassy in Saigon. Man, they must be crawling all over the place."

Morgan spent the next week soaking his foot with

peroxide and writing letters home and to Easy. He asked
Easy to say hello to Tam for him, and for her not to
worry, that he would be back eventually.

A new man arrived on the ward. His name was
Tobey, and he was missing his left eye, left hand, and
his left leg from the knee down. He was unconscious
and moaning.

"He's a marine, and he stepped on a land mine,"
Lieutenant Alexander explained to the rest of the patients. "Try to keep the noise down so that he can get
some rest."

That night Tobey was taken from the ward and
operated on. The next night he was also taken out and
operated on.

"What the hell is going on with him?" Morgan asked
the lieutenant.

"The artery in his leg keeps breaking, so they have to
keep amputating more of it," she explained. "I don't
really think he's going to make it."

On his tenth day in Japan, Morgan was operated on.
Lieutenant Alexander gave him a preoperative injection and wished him good luck. Sedated, Morgan was
wheeled into the operating room.

"Good morning," said Dr. Bonnin. "We'll have you
done and out of here in no time." An IV was attached
to the back of Morgan's hand. "We're going to put
some Pentothal in you to make you sleep now," explained Dr. Bonnin. "I want you to start counting backward from one hundred."

"One hundred, ninety-nine, ninety-eight, ninety-
seven, ninety-six, nine . . . ty . . . five . . . nine . . . ty . . .
four . . . nine . . . ty . . . thr . . ."

Morgan woke up in the recovery room. "Jesus
Christ, that hurts!" he exclaimed. A nurse shushed him.
"Be quiet. And no swearing," she ordered.

Morgan looked down and saw that his foot was encased in a freshly plastered cast. A small circle of blood
stained it. He was wheeled back to the main ward and
assisted into his bed.

"How ya feelin'?" asked Wolfe. "You feel like going downtown for a quickie?"

"Not today," said Morgan, laughing weakly. "Give me a couple of days and I'll be O.K."

Dr. Bonnin visited Morgan. "All we had to do was take off about half your big toe and peel away a lot of other dead skin. You'll need a little physical therapy, but you'll walk O.K. We'll be sending you back to your unit in about four weeks."

Morgan thanked the doctor.

Tobey was wheeled off for another operation. "He doesn't have much left to his leg to fuck around with," said Wolfe. "I hope he either makes it or dies soon. This waitin' is getting to be a bitch."

A week later Tobey opened his eyes for the first time and asked for a root beer float. Lieutenant Alexander was ecstatic. "He's going to be O.K.," she said.

"He's quite a way from bein' O.K.," Wolfe told her. "Especially with all the parts he's missing."

"I was speaking relatively," said the nurse. "He's going to live, and that's what counts here. He'll be rehabilitated back in the States."

Morgan met Marr, a brooding individual who said little. Marr's right leg was encased in a knee-high cast. "It's just a bone chip," he said.

Morgan had been up and around for almost a week when Lieutenant Alexander asked him if he wanted a weekend pass.

"Hell, yes. Wolfe and I have business downtown."

"I'm not even going to ask what kind of business it is," she said, laughing.

"Mind if I tag along?" asked Marr gruffly.

— 28 —

Doug's Place was like any other bar near Tachi-kawa that served Americans. A long wooden bar with a mirror behind it dominated the room. One wall was sectioned off into private booths, while the area between the booths and bar was filled with tables and chairs. A jukebox sat against the rear wall, next to the door that led to the bathroom. When Morgan and Marr entered, it was empty except for an army major and a marine second lieutenant sitting together at the bar.

Morgan and Marr took a table near the door. A pleasant-looking woman waited on them; they both ordered Kirin beer. The woman smiled and bowed, and turned to leave.

"Excuse me," said Marr. "Who's Doug?"

"Doug? That Doug," she replied, pointing to a poster-sized picture hanging on the mirror behind the bar. The man in the picture was a Caucasian in his mid-twenties with dark, thick hair. A mustache grew from his upper lip. Aviator sunglasses hid his eyes, but the compressed line of the man's lips, the sharp nose, and the aware tilt of the head told the story: tough, impassive, someone not to be fucked with.

"Who is he?" Marr wanted to know.

"I tell you already," said the woman. "That Doug."

"No. I mean, what does he do? Does he own this place?"

"Doug not own Doug's Place. Doug dead," she said in a barely audible voice. "Doug hurt in war, come here to 'merican hospital." She closed her eyes and blushed. "Doug, I, rovers for rong time. He tell me he hit man from New Yor' before war and now secret hit man for Uncle Sam."

"Hit man, hell," said Marr. "Why's Uncle Sam need secret hit men when he's got a whole goddamn army full of them?"

"Doug say he work for big bird," the hostess said, shrugging.

"Big bird?" Marr shouted. "A hit man who works for birds?" Marr turned to Morgan. "I think this whole story is for the birds."

"I cannot say," said the hostess. "Doug only tell me he work for big bird that die in fire, then rive again."

"The Phoenix?" asked Morgan.

"Hai. You know this . . . Feeneek?"

"I've heard about a program called the Phoenix. It's based in Nha Trang."

"Hai. Doug say Nha Trang."

Marr laughed. "The army has people in Nha Trang who work with birds. Now we're not only winning their hearts and minds, but their birds, too. Why not? It makes as much sense as anything else."

"I think it has something to do with Special Forces and CIA people weeding out the VC political leaders in the villages," said Morgan. "Some guy told me they sneak into the villages disguised as ARVN and assassinate VC suspects. Weeding out the infra-something. The infrastructure. I also heard that they take the VC out in the ocean, tie them up with chains, and throw them overboard."

"Yeah?" sneered Marr. "Who's their leader, Captain Al Capone or maybe Major Bugs Moran?"

Morgan shrugged. "Like I said, it's just something I heard." The hostess listened to the exchange intently, nodding at the words she understood, frowning at the ones she didn't.

"Soldier come for me," she said. "He say Doug dead. He make me sign paper. He say Doug make me bennifishy. Soon I get money from 'merica."

"Bennifishy?" said Morgan. "Beneficiary? Doug made you beneficiary of his GI insurance?"

"Hai."

"Ten thousand dollars American," hissed Marr. "What's that in yen?" His eyes rolled toward the ceiling as he figured the conversion. "That Doug left her

something like three and a half million yen." He whistled. "Son of a bitch. And she probably bought this bar
with it."

"That would explain why it's called Doug's Place,"
said Morgan.

The hostess left and returned with their beers.

"To Doug," toasted Marr.

"To Doug," repeated Morgan. The army major sitting at the bar turned, raised his glass, and joined the
toast.

The marine second lieutenant scowled. "Yeah, yeah,
you cub scouts."

The major smiled tolerantly. "Relax, Lieutenant,
they're just having fun."

Morgan stood up and limped toward the bathroom.
Weaving between tables, he imagined himself to be a
halfback engaged in broken-field running.

"Touchdown," he roared, slamming the restroom
door open with a forearm which would hurt in the
morning.

He stood at the urinal pissing, his forehead pressed
against the coolness of the tiled wall. A few drops of
urine dribbled onto his toes where they protruded from
the cast. Even through the anesthetic effect of the beer,
his foot ached dully. He moved to the sink and splashed
cold water on his face. Patting his face dry with paper
towels, he looked at himself in the mirror and frowned
at his image. More beer, he thought.

Coming out of the restroom, Morgan saw her sitting
alone at one of the booths, drinking tea. Her hair,
combed up and held in place by several pearl-tipped
pins, was jet black. Loose tendrils of it curled down
in front of her ears and along her delicately carved
cheekbones. Her eyebrows were thin crescents, and her
almond-shaped eyes had in their center pupils as black
as the darkness in a cave. Her nose, flattened slightly at
the sides, fit her face perfectly. Her slender body was
covered by a yellow blouse and a beige knee-length

skirt. Morgan limped past her and sat back down at his table.

Wolfe barged through the door holding a pink teddy bear in the crook of his elbow cast. "Hey! Hey! I finally found you fuckers," he panted. "Man, I been to damn near every bar in this town looking for you. Where the hell you been?" Flushed and smiling, he sat down.

"Right here," gruffed Marr. "Who's that with you, Winnie the Pooh?"

"His name is Pinky."

"Win him at a Pachinko parlor?"

"He's a gift. From a lady friend."

"How was she?"

"How was she?" Wolfe hooted. "Ask me how the hell was I?"

"O.K. How were you?"

"How was I?" He looked surreptitiously around the room before answering, then said, "I was so good she gave me Pinky as a prize."

"Prize for being the fastest?" needled Marr.

"No. Prize for being the best. She gave me Pinky because I fucked her with my cast." He gave out a rebel yell.

The marine second lieutenant turned on his stool and yelled, "Quiet down, asshole."

"Fuck ya, lifer," Wolfe shot back. "Wanna smell my cast?"

"It's physically impossible to fuck someone with that cast, Wolfe," said Marr.

Wolfe grinned. "I'll tell you how I did it if you buy me a drink." Marr motioned at the hostess.

"And one for Pinky, too," Wolfe said adamantly.

"I'll buy your drink, you crazy asshole, but I ain't buying one for your fucking Pinky," growled Marr.

"Then I won't tell you how I did it."

The hostess approached. "Two beers," groused Marr.

Morgan mustered his courage, got up, and sat down

next to the girl. His face was flushed, and he couldn't think of anything to say.

"Name you?" she asked, smiling. Her teeth were impossibly white.

"Name me . . ." he began. Then, not wanting to talk pidgin, he corrected himself and said, "My name is Morgan."

She giggled. "More-gun funny name. My name is Yuki."

"I guess so. I don't know. I don't know anything right now except that I'm drunk and you're pretty, and I apologize." His face reddened more. "I mean, I apologize for being drunk, not for you being pretty."

She giggled again. "You good-lookin', More-gun. Why you don't smarrow?"

"Smarrow?" he said, perplexed.

"Smarrow." She smiled at him. "You know?"

"Oh. Smile. Smile! I don't know why I don't smile."

She looked at him steadily, compassion in her eyes. He suddenly felt like crying. "I guess I haven't smiled in a long time."

"Are you happy?"

"No."

"Then I make you happy."

"What?"

She smiled again, this time shyly. "Then I make you happy," she repeated, slowly enunciating each word. She placed a hand over his. He looked down and was mesmerized by the hollow on the inside of her wrist.

"For one night, More-gun, I make you happy."

She laid money on the table. "We can go now," she said. They stood. Morgan helped her on with her coat, and arm in arm they headed for the door.

A drunken Marr looked up as they neared him. "Hey, Morgan . . ." he began in a raspy voice.

"Marr, don't say anything except good night," Morgan said.

Marr shrugged. "What the hell. Good night, Morgan."

" 'Night, Morgan," said Wolfe. "Pinky says good night, too."

The marine second lieutenant at the bar muttered, "That dumb fuck flyboy is gonna get the clap."

The army major smiled tolerantly. "Lieutenant, that young man is going to get what he needs tonight, while you and I are only going to grow older and fight the rest of this war."

"And win it, too," said the lieutenant belligerently.

"Then fight the war after this one," continued the major.

"Goddamn straight," growled the lieutenant, trying to focus his eyes. "What war after this one?"

"Lieutenant, there's always a next one," the major confided.

The marine lieutenant pondered this for a while.

"Skoal," said the major, raising his glass. "Now, Lieutenant, if you'll help me with my crutches, I'll help you with yours, and we'll depart this fine establishment."

— 29 —

Morgan and Yuki walked through the maze of narrow streets. It was drizzly and cold, and Morgan tried not to limp too noticeably.

"It gives you much pain?" she asked, pressing close to him.

"A little," he admitted, more sober now in the night air. For fifteen minutes they walked silently, then she stopped in front of a small wooden house.

"I live here," she said with a touch of pride. Morgan pulled at the wooden door handle. When it failed to open he pulled more forcefully; the entire front wall of the flimsy house jiggled. Smothering a laugh behind her hands, Yuki said, "In Japan, doors sride." Morgan pushed laterally on the knob; the door slid open effortlessly. He stood aside, allowing Yuki to enter first. She flicked on a light, then bent and took off her shoes just inside the threshold.

Morgan stood behind her and surveyed the room. In the combination living and bedroom, a futon lay on the floor against the far wall with several blankets folded neatly at the head of it. In a corner of the room an old Victrola sat on a wicker chair with a stack of record albums next to it. To his immediate left an alcove no bigger than a closet served as a kitchen. Several pots and pans hung from nails hammered into the wall. Water leaked slowly from a single faucet. A shelf held a few cups and bowls. A battered teakettle sat on a hot plate.

Morgan took off his boot and sat it next to her shoes. She bent down and wiped off the bottom of his cast with a piece of cloth.

"Please sit," she said, gesturing at the futon. "I make tea. Excuse me, please."

Morgan sat on the futon and rubbed the raw skin at the top of his cast. He could hear Yuki busy in the kitchen. She entered and kelt down in front of him. Unbuttoning his shirt, she said, "I take your clothes. Dry them." He tried to assist her. "No," she softly chided him, pushing his hands away. "You rest."

He relaxed, luxuriating in her closeness as she peeled the wet garment from him. With her index finger she touched the medal around his neck.

"You Cat-o-lick?" she asked.

"Sometimes."

"When sometimes?"

"When I need to be," he said.

"When you scared in war?"

"Yes," he said, then asked, "Are you a Buddhist, Yuki?"

"Oh, no. Confucian."

"What's that?"

"No important. I live now. Someday I die. Then I live again."

"Oh. Reincarnation."

"No. Confucian."

Removing her fingers from the medal, Yuki traced a line down the middle of Morgan's chest, stopping at his navel.

"Japanese men not have many hairs," she said.

"I don't either," he said, smiling.

"You smarrow, More-gun. First time you smarrow."

"You make me smile, Yuki," he said. "Thank you."

Her fingers left his belly and lightly pinched one of his nipples. Morgan's back arched with the touch. His erection was immediate.

"I make you smarrow even bigger soon," she promised. Her hands went to his belt buckle and deftly undid it. Morgan raised his hips as she pulled one trouser leg off, then carefully worked the other trouser leg over the cast. As in Vietnam, Morgan didn't wear any underwear. Naked except for the medal around his neck and the cast on his leg, he sat on the futon, his erection jutting from between his legs.

Yuki eyed it judiciously. "Japanese men not so very big," she said.

Morgan blushed.

Yuki affectionately caressed the tip of his penis. "Smooth," she said. "Like vervet."

The teakettle whistled shrilly. Yuki took her hand away from him, stood up, and walked into the kitchen. She returned with two cups of tea.

"Drink, please," she said. "It warm you nicely."

Morgan took the proffered cup and sipped the fragrant steaming brew.

Sipping her tea, Yuki walked over to the stack of record albums and selected one. She put it on the Victrola and lowered the needle into place. In a few moments Elvis Presley's voice filled the small room, singing "Love Me Tender."

Wordlessly she walked across the room and entered a darkened doorway which Morgan hadn't noticed before. A light clicked on. Yuki stood with her back to him. She took off her blouse, revealing the straps of her plain cotton bra. The knobs of her spine stood out in subtle relief while her shoulder blades were lost in shadow. She fumbled with the hook and eye of her bra, then leaned forward and shrugged her shoulders in a universally feminine way. Her left breast in profile was pear-shaped, its nipple a dark brown. She unzipped her skirt and let it fall around her feet. Stepping out of it gracefully, she bent down and scooped it up. Clad only in panties, she looked over one shoulder at Morgan, smiled shyly, and closed the door.

Through the closed door Morgan could hear the sound of running water. He sipped the tea and absently massaged his aching leg. He was also aware of the ache which had started in his testicles and edged upward into his groin. He heard the bathroom light click off.

The door opened, and Yuki walked into the room, dressed in a silken kimono the color of jade. She knelt at the dressing table and undid the pins holding her hair. Loosened, it cascaded down her back, the ends touching the floor. She picked up a brush and began running it through her hair with long, measured strokes. A smile played at the corner of her lips.

Morgan set his teacup down, reached out and took the brush away from her, and pulled her to him. Yuki fitted herself in his arms, carefully avoiding putting any weight on his cast.

They kissed—slowly and gently at first, each tentatively tasting the other. Yuki parted her lips. Morgan touched them with his tongue, and they parted more, allowing him into her mouth.

Yuki separated from the embrace long enough to get up and turn off the light, then returned to Morgan.

"You relax," she said, pushing him back on the futon. Taking off her kimono, she climbed astride him, reached down between his legs, grasped the midsection of his penis, and guided it slowly into her. Morgan was surprised that she was already slick enough that his entry caused no pain to either of them. The walls of her vagina held him tightly.

He could barely see her face in the darkness, but he heard the smile in her voice as she murmured something in Japanese. She made love to him unhurriedly, moving her pelvis fluidly. She sighed each time she sank down around his penis, taking all of it, then pulling back until only its tip penetrated her. She drew him into her center and began a series of milking movements. Morgan grasped her hips and held her motionless as he trembled toward orgasm. As his ejaculate filled her, he whispered her name.

Rising from him, she said, "You tired. You sleep now." She cupped a hand under her crotch and went into the bathroom. Drowsy, Morgan heard the Victrola: "click . . . click . . . click . . ." I should get up and turn it off, he thought just before he fell asleep.

Sometime later he woke up. Yuki lay next to him, her buttocks nestled against his belly, her body radiating warmth. His left arm was draped across her neck; he could feel her pulse beat against his forearm and her warm breath against the palm of his hand. He parted the spill of hair covering her neck and kissed its nape.

Yuki stirred, took his hand in both of hers, and pressed it to her lips. Outside, rain beat lightly on the roof. They slept.

Morgan dreamt that he was warm and safe and with a woman, and when he awakened shortly before dawn,

the realization that the dream and real circumstances co-
incided made him happy. Yuki still slept snugly against
him. He rose up on an elbow and peeked at her face. A
strand of hair had worked its way into her mouth, and
she chewed on it softly. Morgan lay back down, careful
not to disturb her.

His groin tingled pleasantly; his penis swelled and
pressed against her buttocks. She opened her legs
slightly. Her tiny hand grasped his penis and rubbed its
head against her vaginal lips in a slow and circular motion. She opened like a flower, and Morgan eased into
her. She sighed and pushed her buttocks against him.
Morgan reached around and fondled her breasts and
erect nipples, feeling their pebbly texture.

So joined together, they fell asleep again.

Yuki awakened him around 9:00 A.M. by gently stroking the side of his face. Clear-eyed and without a hangover, he smiled his thanks as she handed him a cup of
freshly brewed tea.

"More-gun, you must go soon," she told him, the
words simultaneously gentle and firm.

Morgan sighed. "I know, but I don't want to."

"More-gun, I promise to make you happy for one
night," she said. "Did I for you do this?"

Morgan stood and kissed her on the forehead. "Yes,
for me you did. You made me very happy."

She suddenly laughed, the sound crystalline and
fragile in the silence of her home. "I even make you—"

"Smarrow," said Morgan, completing the sentence
for her, smiling as he said it. Then his face turned serious.

"Yuki?"

"Yes, More-gun?"

"Thank you," he said, and bowed. She smiled and
returned the simple gesture.

"More-gun?" she said.

"Yes?"

"You wercome."

After he had cleaned up and dressed, Morgan took

out his wallet and offered Yuki all the money he had: about four-thousand yen, or eleven dollars. She accepted it reluctantly. As he finished his third cup of tea, Yuki left her home for a few moments, then returned.

"Taxi waiting for you, More-gun. You must go now."

"But I—"

"I pay, More-gun," she explained. He handed her the empty cup, and stood facing her. Yuki's face wore a smile, but her eyes showed a certain sadness.

"Good-bye, More-gun. Take care yerserf."

He kissed her then, a soft and brief touching of his lips to hers, then left without a word.

The taxi driver drove him back to the hospital. He opened the passenger door for Morgan.

"For you," said the driver, holding out a small white envelope. Puzzled, Morgan accepted it, opened it up, and removed the contents: a photo of Yuki and the yen he had given her. He put the photo back into the envelope and tucked it into his pocket.

"Big tip for you," he said to the cab driver, handing him the yen. The cab driver smiled, showing half a dozen gold crowns.

"Thank you, itchi bon chee hai," he said.

"You're welcome," said Morgan. He turned and limped toward his hospital ward, smiling all the way.

— 30 —

.

The movie, *The Good, the Bad, and the Ugly*, was playing on the hospital's psychiatric ward. Morgan walked in and took a chair. After the movie he spoke with three of the psychiatric casualties who seemed anxious to talk.

"We all grew up on John Wayne movies, Iwo Jima, and all that shit," said a tall man named Karras. "A clean wound in the chest and tell Laura I love her. Bullshit! They never showed a sucking chest wound. You never heard a sucking chest on a sound track. Never showed brains in Technicolor. Audie Murphy and catsup. Shit!"

The second man, Woodruff, said, "It was just a routine sweep through some scrub brush, and we walked into a mine field. Motherfucker was unmarked. At least the lieutenant's map didn't show it. Tullar lost a leg. Ferguson got his belly laid open, and Ramirez the Greek got instantly dissected.

"We called in a dustoff, then worked our way back toward base camp. We came to this creek full of mud and scummy shit, and filled our canteens. There was these two water buffs and a slope kid who was washing them down. One of our guys, Leon, was really hot about the mine field. He and Ramirez the Greek were max tight, dig it, and so Leon goes and opens up on the water buffs." He emitted a high-pitched laugh and continued. "Like, he used a couple of clips on those buffs before they went down. You wouldn't believe how much lead those motherfuckers took before they gave it up. Bellowing like their nuts had been cut off while Leon stitched them with bullets. Blood and guts and shit everywhere." He laughed again.

"Patton would have loved it," said Karras.

"What about the kid?" asked Morgan.

"Ah, shit, he was easy. Leon only needed one bullet to waste him. He didn't put up a fight at all. But them buffs, now that was something to see."

The third psychiatric casualty jabbed Morgan in the forehead and said, "I had a buddy who got it right here. He's dead. AWOL from life, you know?"

Morgan remained silent.

"I jumped behind the fifty cal and saved the POL dump. Them sapper cocksuckers was everywhere. But they got the ammo dump, you know? They blew the sky red. Hey, whatever turns the little cocksuckers on, right?"

"Right on," said Morgan.

"But me and that fifty cal saved the POL dump. No gook got up after I was done sprayin' the area."

"Right," said Morgan.

"I was raised Catholic, O.K.?"

"O.K. So was I."

"I don't think I can go to Communion again." He wiped his eyes with his thumbs. "Can I?"

"I think you can if you want to."

"It'd be nice."

"Yes, it would," said Morgan.

"Can you do me a favor?"

"What's that?"

"Please call a priest."

At the end of six weeks Morgan was released from the hospital. He said good-bye to his friends and went down to the air terminal to catch a flight to Saigon.

— 31 —

After a refueling stop at Taiwan, the plane continued on to Vietnam. As the jet touched down at Tan Son Nhut and the engines were reversed, Morgan looked out the porthole window and saw the burned remains of a C-47 lying next to the runway. Further on he spotted the charred hulk of a C-123; both planes had been mortared by the Viet Cong during Tet.

The jet taxied up to the terminal and stopped. The passengers began filing off. After six weeks in Japan, Morgan was unaccustomed to the Vietnamese heat and humidity; the underarms and back of his uniform darkened with perspiration as he crossed the tarmac to the terminal.

The terminal building had been reinforced since Tet. Rolls of barbed wire were strung in front of it, and several sandbagged machine-gun positions, manned by ARVN, had been hastily erected.

Inside the terminal everything was confusion as milling throngs of Vietnamese mixed with Americans. Loudspeakers blared in Vietnamese and English. To one side duffel bags were being opened and inspected by customs personnel.

An Air Vietnam DC-6, its tail emblazoned with a green dragon, pulled up to the terminal and disgorged its human cargo into the already full terminal. The pretty Vietnamese stewardesses, all dressed in matching, colorful ao dais, moved gracefully through the crowd.

Morgan smoked a cigaret while he waited for the customs man to finish searching his duffel bag, then shouldered it and walked through the exit. He signed into the orderly room, perfunctorily answering questions about his foot and only smiling slightly when the office personnel made sexual remarks about what a great time he must have had in Japan.

Sergeant Blandeau, who was passing the war by taking papers out of the In basket and placing them in the Out basket, had just returned from a thirty-day R 'n' R to Greece, his reward for extending his tour of duty.

"So how was Greece?" Morgan asked him.

Blandeau didn't answer. Instead, he pulled open a desk drawer and held up a plastic vial which was filled with short black hairs.

"You shoulda seen her, Morgan," he said, a lupine smile on his face. "You would have got your rocks off just watching her sashay her ass through them old pillars at the 'cropolis."

"Pussy hairs?" asked Morgan.

"Hell, no. They're from around her asshole. You know what them Greek women are like. They ain't like gook women. They got hair all over 'em, under their arms, on their arms, even on their legs. They got mustaches so thick they tickle you."

Morgan felt tired. His foot began to ache. He said good-bye and went into the chow hall for a cup of coffee. Easy was sitting at a table, and the two friends exchanged greetings.

"Anything exciting happen while I was gone?" asked Morgan.

"Just Tet."

"I really missed something, eh?"

"Hell, we even had action right here in the chow hall. We were sitting here at about o-three hundred one morning, and this VC runs right through the screen on the front door. There were three skycops following him with M-16s. We all hit the floor, and the VC ran out the back door with the skycops right behind him. We heard a lot of shooting. It sounded like the Fourth of July."

Morgan shook his head in wonderment.

"I haven't told you the best part. The cook was standing in the kitchen, taking all of this in, and when it was all over he walked to the back door and hollered. 'And stay out!' "

"Keystone cops," laughed Morgan.

"Roger that."

"How's Tam?"

"I don't know," said Easy, stirring his coffee. "She left about three weeks ago. Said she was going back home for a while. Said she missed her family. She told me to tell you that she'll be back soon."

"Good enough."

"Are you patched up enough to let me assign you to mobility missions?"

"No. I'm supposed to go to physical therapy at Third Field. That should take about a month."

"Just let me know when you're ready to go again."

"Will do."

Morgan caught a ride to the Harem, took a shower, and sacked out.

— 32 —

Morgan reported to Third Field Hospital early the next morning. The physical therapist instructed him on a series of exercises designed to strengthen his foot, then went on to work with a little Vietnamese girl who was being fitted with an artificial leg.

A radio was playing in the room. President Johnson was giving a speech in which he said that he would not seek a second term in office.

"How can he quit on us?" wondered the physical therapist. "How can he just quit when we're stuck over here? It doesn't make any sense."

"You're catching on," said Morgan, finishing his exercises. He left the therapy room and walked over to the hospital's snack bar.

He ordered a Coke, then walked over to the jukebox. He slotted a quarter and punched up a song by Lulu. Next, he sat down at an empty table in the half-filled snack shack and began skimming through the latest edition of the *Stars and Stripes*, idly wondering if the North Vietnamese government published a similar paper for their soldiers. Probably called it the *Hammer and Sickle*, he mused.

•   •   •

On the sixth page of the paper, the casualty report filled a column and a half: neat ink-printed rows of the latest American deaths. Morgan usually skipped over this section without a glance—disembodied names told him nothing about the dead or the circumstances of their deaths. Besides, if he wanted to know about casualties, all he had to do was look around him at the ambulatory wounded who sat at other tables in the snack shack, or else go down to the morgue which was only a short distance away. This time, however, the casualty list somehow beckoned him; he felt compelled to read it. Morgan sighed and began from the top:

Stimac C. Cpl. USMC Bayonee, New Jersey
Chase S. A. SP4 USA Missoula, Montana
Pershing R. D. 2Lt. RA Key West, Florida

Any relation to Blackjack? Morgan wondered. He's a West Point lieutenant somewhere over here.

Turnbow R. SP4 USA New York, New York
Turnbow D. SP4 USA New York, New York

Brothers? Morgan wondered. Twins? A typographical error? He continued.

Prindle H. T. MSGT. RA Fort Ord, California

Morgan grimaced. A lifer to the max, that one.

Santiago J.A.L.D. PVT. USA San Juan, Puerto Rico
Presnell P.J. CW03 RA Alexandria, Virginia

Chopper pilot, Morgan concluded.

Bruckner D. K.

The letters lay small and dead on the page. Morgan
felt his face flush. Bruckner . . .
The eight letters of his friend's name were pulled into
Morgan's eyes, drawn through his optic nerves, and
decoded by his brain, then thrust down with a searing
finality into his heart. He was burned to the quick by the
knowledge of what had happened to his friend, who was
a member of the Twenty-fifth Infantry Division.
Oh, Bruckner . . . was the only thought that came to
him. Morgan slumped forward in the chair. As his eyes
continued absorbing other words, some internal part of
himself began shutting down. Words rolled across the
periphery of his consciousness in a slow and melting
fashion, sounding in his mind the way a record does
when the plug is pulled in mid-song, then ending, finally, in silence.
His eyes went back to the name.
Bruckner . . .
Other words on the page moved in an undulating motion. From . . . missing . . . dead . . . hostile action.
Bruckner . . .
Dead . . .
Missing first . . .
Ah, God . . .
The *Stars and Stripes* lay open and forgotten as
Morgan, numb, pushed the chair away from the table
and stood on rubbery legs. He braced his knees momen-
tarily, then forced himself to walk.
After first bumping hard into some object in the
snack bar, Morgan stumbled out into the hospital plaza
where Bruckner and he had, less than two months

before, watched the movie *To Sir with Love*. When the movie was over, Bruckner had carried Morgan in his arms up the two flights of stairs that led to their ward. They had sat up well after lights out and had spoken to each other in hushed voices about their hopes and dreams when they got back to the real world.

Morgan was seeing only dimly as he walked stiffly toward the hospital exit. Everything he saw seemed monochromatic, and none of what he saw made any sense to him. He never heard the brief conversation between two wounded soldiers who sat at the table that he had lurched against during his near-blind exit from the snack shack.

"What the fuck's wrong with that dude?" the first man asked.

The second wounded man never stopped licking at the ice cream cone he held. "Probably stoned," he absently answered, reveling in each taste of the cold, sweet refreshment.

— 33 —

"You guys Wolfhounds?" Morgan asked the trio of dirt begrimed, tired soldiers. He had been walking down a side street in Saigon, avoiding the bustle of Tu Do, when he had spotted the Tropical Lightning patch of the Twenty-fifth Infantry Division on the three men's clothing.

The three soldiers stopped and studied Morgan.

"Yeah," one of them warily confirmed. He was a blond corporal with a raspy voice. "What cha need?"

"You know a guy in the two-twelve, name of Bruckner?"

"Bruckner . . . Bruckner . . ." repeated the corporal. "Lemme think."

A tall, skinny SP4 interrupted. "He's a big dude? Carried an M-sixty?"

"That's him."

"Yeah. Sure, we knew him," continued the SP4. "He's the one that got wasted at Hoc Mon. What ya want to know about him?"

"How he died," said Morgan, his voice flat.

The SP4, remembering Bruckner vividly now, said, "He was running a patrol through some village, and Charlie spiderholed him. Just popped outta that hole and put two or three AK rounds through his chest."

"Which?"

"Which what?"

"Two bullets or three?"

The third soldier in the trio laughed. Morgan looked at him—a bespectacled black man whose sleeves bore the three inverted chevrons of a sergeant. The black man met Morgan's stare, his arms going out in front of him, palms up, begging for understanding.

"Hey, my man, it don't really matter, ya know? After the first round, it don't matter how many more there be."

All three soldiers laughed at this, but when they saw that Morgan did not laugh, they stopped.

"Hey, man, you a friend of his?" asked the corporal.

"Yes."

"Umm," the corporal hummed judiciously. "Well, hell, we don't mean nothing by laughing. It's just that when you're dead, your dead. That's all, you know? Fini."

"I need to know the details—start to finish," demanded Morgan.

"Well, fuck me," said the SP4, "the man's a masochist! Tate," he said to the black sergeant, "give him the whole nine yards."

The sergeant stared at Morgan for a long moment, then spat in the dirt.

"Like Perkins told you, your buddy got spiderholed out by Hoc Mon. Two or three rounds in the chest. Rest of the squad got blown away, too. Seven or eight dudes all together. Good dudes," he added emphatically.

"Then what?" pressed Morgan.

The sergeant's eyes were lost in thought as he continued.

"Later that day we reconned in force and picked up the bodies. Charlie took their weapons and most of their clothes and stuff, and didied before we got there. We just went in smokin' and pulled our guys outta there."

The black man paused. Morgan waited.

"So anyway we got 'em back to our laager site and laid 'em out behind the tracks," he recounted, referring to the armored personnel carriers that provided security at the campsite.

"We got hit bad a couple of hours before sunup, and when the tracks moved on-line one of them . . ." He stopped.

"One of them what?" demanded Morgan.

"Ah, fuck!" the sergeant exploded, incredulous at Morgan's determination. "You wanna know that bad? O.K." He sighed. "One of those tracks ran over your buddy and a couple other stiffs. You happy now, or you want more?" The man was glaring at Morgan.

"I want all of it," Morgan told him, returning the look.

The sergeant shook his head morosely, not understanding Morgan's macabre curiosity, then rapidly spat out the rest of the story.

"Your buddy was crushed flatter than shit, and Doc could only tell who he was from a letter he dug out of his pocket.'' The sergeant's voice took on an apologetic tone. ''After that, man, I don't know. They loaded him and the other stiffs on a dustoff and took 'em away.'' He shrugged his shoulders. ''And that's all I know.''

The sergeant and Morgan continued staring at each other. The other two men—the SP4 and the corporal —looked down at their torn and dirty boots, their hands jammed in pockets, embarrassed by the intimate details of death.

''So you don't know where they took him?''

''No, I don't, man. Sorry.''

Morgan thanked the trio and left, looking for an out-of-the-way place where he could get quietly drunk. He wanted to drink enough to remember everything he could about Bruckner, and then he wanted to get drunk enough to blot out every last memory of him.

But as he walked through the doorway of some nameless bar, Morgan knew that no matter how much he drank or how often, he would never be able to forget.

— 34 —

Relatives and friends gathered at the funeral home, muddying the foyer with slush from the last snowfall of 1968.

A minister who had never known Bruckner delivered the eulogy. He spoke of the vagaries of premature death and about the mysteries of life, mysteries to which God alone had answers. The minister also expressed his own deep-felt conviction that Bruckner had died the most gallant and ennobling death an American man possibly could: on the field of battle in the service of his country, fighting to ensure that the people of South Vietnam who desperately wanted to live in a democratic nation would be able to do so.

The minister had never served in the military, but he was hawkish on the war, as were the majority of the mourners who listened intently to his every word. They sat on hard folding chairs, their reddened, sniffling noses hidden in handkerchiefs: the four stoic brothers; Bruckner's stone-faced father, Bruckner's mother, slumped against her husband's bony shoulder, her eyes misting; Bruckner's widow, who simply stared at the flag-draped casket.

They listened to the minister and believed his words, believed that Bruckner indeed had died in the cause of furthering democracy. They all had to believe, for to do otherwise—to come to the realization that one they had raised and loved had been killed in a senseless war— would have shattered their faith in the rightness of the war, would have caused them to question the actions of their own government. And these simple and humble people just could not do that. Rather, they chose to believe that Bruckner had died heroically, and for a just cause.

The hearse-led procession of cars, moving slowly under the gray Michigan sky, snaked its way through the streets of Traverse City. This cortege halted at the entrance to the hilltop cemetery. Six solemn pallbearers —classmates of Bruckner's—pulled the casket from the back of the hearse. They grasped the cold brass handles tightly, then stared up to the burial site.

The ragged line of mourners followed.

Amid gnarled, bare-limbed trees, the mourners as- sumed respectful attitudes of attention as two members of the VFW honor guard, chafed by the cold, fumbled

with and finally folded the flag that had covered
Bruckner's casket. One of them, a World War II vet-
eran, approached Bruckner's widow and offered the
flag to her.

She accepted it, her eyes never leaving the casket.

The seven man honor guard fired three salvoes with
their old M-1 rifles. The gunfire was briefly carried on,
then silenced by, a vicious wind that whipped in off
Lake Michigan.

A young soldier wet his lips and raised a bugle to his
mouth. The sounds of "Taps" carried sadly across the
cemetery.

Shortly after the last bars echoed into silence, the
minister had a few last words to say. The mourners, cut
to the bone by the weather, impatiently shuffled their
feet in the dirty remnants of snow.

In one last, loving gesture, Bruckner's widow walked
to his casket. She placed a single red carnation on its lid.
The wind toyed with the flower for a moment, then
swept it up and deposited it in the freshly turned grave.

With faces aged beyond their years by the harshness
of their lives and now by the harshness of Bruckner's
death, the mourners walked, huddled and hunched
against the cold, back to the cars.

On the back side of the hill, two men emerged from
the warmth of the cemetery's toolshed and walked toward Bruckner's burial site. Both men carried shovels,
and one of them bore a slender white cardboard box. Inside the box, furled around its pinewood staff, was a
miniature replica of the flag of the United States of
America.

Shortly, the Bruckner house filled with a large gathering of relatives and friends. Aunts and cousins bustled
about the kitchen preparing casseroles and pouring stiff
shots of whiskey for the men.

Everyone ate, drank, and laughed too much.

The teenaged cousins grew bored with the gathering
and piled into one car, leaving to find a place and a way

of their own to pay their last respects to Bruckner.

The younger children played quietly at the feet of their parents, aware of some new and strange current of emotion at this specific gathering, but too young to grasp its significance. After a while the young boys wondered why their fathers were regarding them with such long and thoughtful stares, and became restless.

One by one the friends and relatives paid homage to Bruckner's parents, brothers, and widow—a brief murmuring of sympathetic words, a touching of lips to cheeks. The men firmly took Mr. Bruckner's hand, each man trying to massage into the old man's flesh their own messages of empathy, compassion, and sorrow. They, too, had sons.

By dusk the gathering was over. Bruckner's brothers left en masse, after first kissing and hugging their parents and sister-in-law.

There were no more words to be spoken. The three of them stood in the middle of the living room and embraced. Then Bruckner's widow left for her own home.

Mr. and Mrs. Bruckner sat in the living room as the night deepened. Mrs. Bruckner read silently from a well-thumbed Bible, stopping every so often to take off her bifocals and wipe them with Kleenex. Bruckner's father sat in his armchair and stared at a photograph that sat atop an end table.

The photo was of Bruckner at sixteen. He was standing tall and proud, holding a rifle, next to a deer he had killed. The dead animal was dangling from the branches of a pine tree, head down. Its eyes open and glassy—lifeless. But Bruckner's eyes, as shown in the photo, were clear and smiling, alive with the first burst of youth, the intimations of manhood already showing on his face.

Bruckner's father stared at the photograph. Every once in a while the old man cleared his throat.

At 9:00 P.M. Bruckner's father arose from his chair and turned on the radio. He and his wife listened to the news and, after the local weather report, prepared for bed. They performed the same presleep rituals that they had throughout their thirty-seven-year marriage.

They walked through the suddenly too big, too empty living room and up the stairs to their bedroom: Bruckner's father and mother together, alone.

Seven blocks away, Bruckner's widow walked into her bedroom, alone.

In the safety of their room Mrs. Bruckner prayed, petitioning God to take good care of her son.

Mr. Bruckner tried to hold back his tears but, under cover of darkness, surrendered to the pain of the loss of his youngest son. The old man's throat spasmed with hopelessness; his tears began rolling freely down his ruddy cheeks. He tasted his own salt and grief; his chest heaved as he openly expressed his pain. He instinctively reached out toward his wife, as she had to her God. His trembling fingers were met halfway in their search by his wife's careworn hands. They huddled together in their bed of thirty-seven years and held each other tightly, the tears on their seamed faces mingling.

Seven blocks away, Bruckner's widow sobbed as she embraced the pillow which had once cradled her husband's head.

— 35 —

Three weeks into his physical therapy Morgan received a letter from one of his friends who explained that he was now in Vietnam, was a medic, and was based out of Dau Tieng. He told Morgan that he would enjoy seeing him if he got a chance.

Morgan climbed aboard the Dau Tieng-bound C-130 and sat down. The flight took only about twenty minutes. Disembarking at the rubber plantation, he sought out directions to his friend's unit.

"Damn, it's good to see you," said Doc Wrench. "No shit. A face from home."

The two men ambled over to a makeshift enlisted men's club and drank warm beer while they exchanged tales. After about half an hour they heard what sounded like thunder.

"Incoming!" someone yelled, and everyone hit the ground.

Two 122-millimeter rockets crashed into the motor pool and exploded. Several trucks began burning.

"Aren't we going to help put out the fire?" asked Morgan.

"I'm not a truck jockey, I'm a medic. They'll handle it themselves."

Night fell and the two men continued drinking behind one of the barracks.

"Damn, my foot hurts," said Morgan.

"I got something that will fix you up in no time. It'll make you feel like your foot doesn't even exist."

"What is it?"

"Marijuana."

"Marijuana? For my foot?"

"For the pain receptors in your brain. It'll reach your foot eventually."

"All right. I'm game."

Taking the proffered joint, Morgan imitated Doc and

sucked in the smoke, holding it in his lungs as long as possible. After several moments he exhaled, wheezing and choking on the acrid-tasting grass. Doc laughed and reached out to retrieve the joint.

Morgan had anticipated the rush of being stoned, but only felt drunk and slightly nauseated. He turned to Doc and asked, "What's the name of the street you live on back in the world?"

"Atwater. Why?"

"Just wondering," he said. His ears picked up the name of the street and pulled it into his head, where his brain circuitry transformed it into chemical and electrical forms. It seemed to Morgan that Atwater was the funniest word he had ever heard. He took another hit, then drank from one of the cans of beer, laughing so hard that the liquid choked his throat and snorted up into his nose.

Doc looked at him and said, "You're stoned, you know. It always hits you like this first time."

Laughing idiotically, Morgan could only nod as he reached for the joint and took another hit. In his mind he began thinking about the significance of Doc living on Atwater Street. He attempted to link that paved and calm street in Michigan to the dusty laterite street which ran through Dau Tieng. He linked Atwater Street to the country trunkline and connected this to the state highway. Reaching Chicago in his mind he called everything from there to Los Angeles, Route 66. A vivid picture the size of a television screen lit up in his head: Martin Milner and George Maharis driving their Corvette over the blacktop of Route 66, doing good deeds for people along the way.

"What a ride, man," he said.

"Some good shit, ain't it?" said Doc.

"Corvettes," laughed Morgan.

Doc looked at him quizzically. "What the hell are you talking about?"

"Jesus, Doc, I didn't know I was stoned until just now."

"Then have another hit."

"It's like there isn't anything between me and the moon. No clouds, no stars, no nothing." He stopped talking and stared at the moon, loving its thin crescent, and locked on a memory of Ginny, his former girl friend.

August 1965. He was lying with her on the couch in her living room, her parents somewhere else for the night, a muggy Michigan night in which the chirruping of crickets beneath the open window was laconic.

He faced Ginny and pressed tightly against her as she slept, her milk-sweet breath soft against his face. His left arm was under her neck and cramped; he ignored it in favor of not disturbing her sleep or their closeness. Every time he inhaled, he took in the aroma of Avon's Here's My Heart, the perfume diluted by time and perspiration.

Earlier in the evening they had made out after watching summer reruns on television while eating popcorn and peanut butter fudge. It had taken Morgan the better part of an hour—wordlessly cajoling her with a series of French kisses while his hands roamed gently over her Madras-print blouse and denim-clad thighs—until Ginny acquiesced and helped him undo the buttons of her blouse; she even shrugged her tanned shoulders in assistance as he fumbled one-handedly with the three hooks-and-eyes combination of her 36C cotton bra.

Morgan's face had gone hot as he moved his palms and fingers around the silky sides of Ginny's breasts, then cupped their full weight, his thumbs and forefingers tracing patterns over the pebbly texture of her brown nipples, pulling and pinching them lightly, kissing her deeply all the while.

So as not to awaken her, Morgan moved his head carefully forward and kissed her cleavage directly beneath the delicate chain which held a tiny gold cross. The perfume smell of her here, near the pulse beat of her heart, was stronger. He felt a stirring in his groin and pushed himself against her, his erection grinding into the sharpness of her pubic bone.

In her sleep Ginny responded. They dry-fucked in the predawn darkness and, at the moment of his orgasm, Morgan kissed her above the right eyebrow, tasting her salt on his lips. When he looked down at her face she was still sleeping, but her mouth wore at its corners the barest trace of a smile.

"You want to meet some of my friends?" Doc asked, rousing Morgan from his reverie.

"Sure. Why not?"

Doc Wrench led Morgan down to a sandbagged bunker near the perimeter wire. Four men were sitting on top of it, watching flares light up the sky in the west.

"Sit your ass down, Doc," one of them said. "Who's with you?"

"Buddy of mine from back home. Name's Morgan. Morgan, this is Kiss, Garrett, Craighead, and Angstrom."

"You Tropic Lightning?" asked Garrett, referring to the Twenty-fifth Division's motto.

"Nope, air force," said Morgan. The four soldiers laughed and jeered.

"What the hell's a flyboy doin' out here with us grunts?" asked Kiss.

"He came out to call up napalm on your asses if you keep acting rude," said Doc.

"Fuckin' zoomies," said Kiss, "they ain't so bad. Remember when we got assaulted at that laager site around Cu Chi, and we called in air to save our asses? Man, they were here in nothin' flat."

"You asshole," interjected Garrett. "They saved our asses, but that one flyboy came in too steep and crashed his Phantom right into the treeline, and you were cheering."

"I wasn't cheering," said Kiss, defensive. "I was thanking him for taking out the treeline like some fuckin' kamikaze pilot. Shit, the fucker missed it the first time with his bombs, so I just figured he was pulling a John Wayne."

"You remember the time we were high-stepping through those trees out by Hoc Mon," said Craighead, "and all of a sudden this hardcore motherfucker opens up on us with a machine gun. We all hit the dirt and started crawling, then this motherfucker's twin opens up with another machine gun. I can't go forward and I can't go back, so I hunch down in this little hole in the ground." The joint was passed around.

"I ain't firing back at the bastards—no sense bringing myself to their undivided attention, right? I'm thinking this shit might go on forever, so I light up a J and tune it out. I'm out there for more than an hour, grooving on two machine guns doing a triangulating, crisscrossing, son-of-a-bitching number right over my head, and I'm laid back, grooving on songs from Jefferson Airplane. Me and Grace Slick in a hole—can you dig it?"

Garrett said, "You remember the time we were dragging ass back here after that nothing hump, trying to make it to the wire before dark, and Doc sees this papasan riding a Honda down the road and hitches a ride with him?"

"Papasan didn't give him a ride. He was kidnapped," said Craighead. "Doc flagged him down with his fucking forty-five."

"Best part of the whole adventure was that Doc got his free ride, then turned the poor old bastard in as a VC. The fucking CO gave him a case of beer and a two-day pass to Vung Tau, and kept the motorcycle for himself."

"Fucking Doc," said Kiss, laughing.

"I don't know, you know?" said Garrett. "These peaceniks or whatever they're called—hippies—they're marching in the streets and hollering, 'Hell, no, we won't go.' Hell, no, they won't go because half of them are teenybop girls, and the other half got student deferments or rich daddies, and the other half are faggots."

"I guess they have the right to demonstrate," said Angstrom. "Freedom of speech and all that. Democracy."

"Shit!" Garrett said vehemently. "What's so god-damn democratic about running around San Francisco waving VC flags? Freedom of speech is one thing, but this other stuff is . . . it's treason. I mean, I don't mind some college kid shooting his mouth off about something he doesn't know nothing about. That's his business. But when they wave Charlie's flag and sing, 'Ho, Ho, Ho Chi Minh,' by God, that's something entirely different. Gimme a beer."

"I hear a lot of them are going to Canada these days," said Morgan.

"Fuck 'em," growled Garrett.

Angstrom changed the subject. "There's a story about Ho Chi Minh that goes back to the days when he was hiding in the hills and trying to organize resistance to the Japanese occupation force. The OSS heard about him and decided to help him set up an underground, like the French Maquis had. But since Ho was a communist, they didn't know how to go about it. They ran an intensive intelligence-gathering mission and found out he had an affinity for butterflies."

"Had a what for butterflies?" asked Garrett, calmer now.

"An affinity. A passion."

"Fucking Ho was queer for butterflies?"

"Well, not exactly. You see, Ho collected butterflies. He was a lepidopterist."

"I'll be damned. I can picture the dude running around the boonies chasing bugs with a net."

"Anyway," continued Angstrom, "the OSS assigned one of their operatives to compile a butterfly collection to end all butterfly collections, then parachuted him into Tongking with it strapped to his back."

"Where's Tongking?" Garrett asked, absorbed by the story.

"That's what North Vietnam was once called."

Garrett exploded. "Then why the hell didn't you just say North Vietnam? Tongking. Shit!"

Unperturbed, Angstrom said, "Did you know Ho was once a pastry chef in Paris?"

"You're shitting me now," said Garrett.

"No sau you. I have no reason to lie."

"I'll be damned. Old Ho over there in France. Oo-la-la." Garrett took a hit from the joint and held the smoke in his lungs for as long as possible. He exhaled amid a lot of coughing and choking. Smoke-induced tears rolled down his face, past the corners of his goofy smile. "This here is some good shit," he wheezed appreciatively, holding the joint out at arm's length.

"I wonder why they call him 'uncle,' " mused Morgan.

Angstrom picked at a scab near his elbow. "He's called uncle because it denotes the Vietnamese people's respect and affection."

"How come you talk so funny?" Garrett asked.

"I'm sorry. I didn't mean to sound pedantic."

"You don't. You sound more like a peanut ass," said Garrett.

"Can you imagine when God made Adam and Eve?" mused Kiss. "I mean, bizow, bizow, twice in the mud with a bolt of lightning, faster than a pom-pom gun."

"That was before my time," said Doc.

Kiss continued. "Zip, zap, and what? The beginning of mankind. Eden. The lion and the lamb."

"Is my head on?" asked Garrett.

"An' Adam's old lady ain't satisfied with having everything, so she lays a pear on him."

"An apple," corrected Angstrom.

"Hey, zipperhead, it's my story, dig it? So Adam's old lady lays a . . . fuckin' apple on him, and that's the end of Paradise. Fini and xin loi to easy livin'. Jesus, what a sorry bitch she must have been."

"You bumming out?" asked Garrett.

"Hell, no, just remembering my catechism, you know? Like raggedy old Noah pairing off all the animals for his boat. Two by two. That boat must have been bigger than the San Diego Zoo."

"Must have smelled bigger than the San Diego Zoo, too," said Garrett.

"Noah could have left the mosquitoes off," said Doc, slapping his arm.

"Leeches, too," asked Morgan.

"Roger that," said Garrett.

"Snakes," said Angstrom.

"Roger that."

"Viet Congs," said Craighead.

"Double roger that."

"He should have taken only blondes for women," said Kiss.

"Scandinavian blondes from Scandinavia," said Angstrom.

"Scandinavian blondes from Scandinavia with tight pussies," said Garrett.

"I'd settle for a baldheaded woman as long as she had a tight pussy," said Craighead.

Doc laughed. "I'd settle for a friendly water buff."

"Angstrom would settle for his hand," said Garrett, laughing cruelly.

"Would any of you settle for a gook whore?" asked Kiss.

"Only if I had to," responded Doc. "I'd rather find the water buff."

"I know where one's available. Not a water buff, a gook."

"Where?" Angstrom wanted to know.

"Fucking Angstrom," said Garrett. "You know you're keeping your cherry to donate to science. You just act eager so's you can tag along and be one of them peeping tom vouchers."

"Voyeurs," Angstrom corrected.

"See," chided Garrett, "you even know the right word for it. Yeah, Angstrom, you're one of them peeping tom voucher voyeurs."

Kiss spoke again. "Putting people on earth was God's

only fuckup. He should have been content with just the animals.''

"Why?'' asked Morgan.

"When's the last time you had a duck try to kill you because it didn't agree with your ideas about how the world should be run?''

"Never,'' said Morgan.

"That's my point. But man is an animal, too. Skin-deep civilized but bone-deep animal. Only thing that separates us from the rest of the animals is that our brains are bigger. We can think more. Maybe that's our problem.''

"Are we going to visit the gook whore?'' Garrett asked impatiently.

"In a minute, in a minute. Just give me time to figure this out. We're just animals with bigger brains, running here and there through the bush with weapons to kill other animals before they kill us. And if you're killed, you're the dead animal, but if you kill them, you're the live animal, but still an animal. That's all I wanted to point out. Give me a hit.''

The six men went quiet as they heard in the distance the thunder of a B-52 night raid.

"Custer would have had more than one last stand if he'd had our firepower,'' said Doc.

"Custer was an asshole,'' said Garrett, getting to his feet.

"Why?'' asked Angstrom.

"He was an officer, wasn't he?'' The men all laughed.

"Reefer madness,'' laughed Doc.

"There it is,'' affirmed Garrett.

Craighead stood up. "Let's go get laid,'' he whooped. "Lead the way, Kiss.''

Moon-obscuring clouds afforded the six men a measure of camouflage as they stumbled over hard clods of earth, their pants slicking wet from the thigh-high grass. They giggled shrilly.

"Shhh. This isn't a field trip," said Craighead. They slid under some barbed wire, catching their shirts and pants on the barbs and swearing when skin was lacerated.

The group was quiet and more alert now, thirty meters from a small, flickering fire. Beyond it they discerned the thatched roof of a hootch. At one side of the fire was a slim shadow—papasan, sitting motionless. Holding their rifles in front of them, they advanced and sheepishly greeted him. The old man stood and bowed, his wispy white beard waving in the breeze. A gold tooth gleamed dully when he smiled.

Garrett grinned evilly and rubbed his crotch. "I don't want a wet deck."

"Asshole," said Craighead. "Anybody who isn't first gets a wet deck." The men paid papasan and took turns. When it was Morgan's turn he declined, thinking of Tam.

Afterwards, the men were aloof from each other as they sat around the fire. Having shared the whore had pushed a temporary wedge of silence between each man; they sat gathering their individual thoughts.

Morgan watched the papasan watching him. The old man's wrinkled face resembled a heavily traced relief map of experiences, rich with pain, fear, and sadness. After a while the six Americans got up and made their way back to the sandbagged bunker on the perimeter at Dau Tieng.

Garrett, Angstrom, Craighead, and Kiss excused themselves and went to sack out. Doc told Morgan a story while they finished the warm beer.

"I don't even know where we were. A slick picked us up and dropped us at some LZ in the middle of nowhere. Our LT tells us to start humping, so we start humping. He keeps looking at his map and compass, and keeps changing us around. I start to feel like maybe we're at the North Pole and he can't get any bearings but South. Except it was too hot to be the North Pole. God, was it hot.

"We spent the night out in the bush, sitting back to back, nobody getting much sleep. Before dawn the LT tells us to saddle up and move out. Didn't even give us a chow break. We were eating dried rats on the run. He can kiss my ass anytime, but I'll have to die first because he got blown away a couple of weeks ago." Doc lit another joint and passed it to Morgan.

"Anyway, about an hour after sunup we see this helicopter smashed up in the jungle. The whole place stinks, so I figure we been sent to bring back the bodies. I'm thinking, well, why the hell don't they just send a Skycrane and lift the helicopter out?

"The LT looks around for a couple of minutes, then tells us, 'Don't bother with the bodies. Just find a little black box.' None of us could believe this shit, so we stared at him. He says all we have to do is find this little black box, set a couple of thermite grenades to burn the chopper, and then get the hell back to the LZ.

"Colucci—he's the squad leader—he asks the LT about the bodies. Like, are we going to bring them back with us or what? The LT says that as far as he's concerned there aren't any bodies. While he's saying this he's smiling and winking like he's gone jungle happy. Like, he's saying, 'What bodies? I don't see any bodies. Do you see bodies?' Hell, you didn't have to see them, you could smell them. Ain't nothing in the world smells like death.

"Frankie—he's our resident smartass, except he's back in the world with one less leg than he came over here with—he asks the LT what this little black box looks like. The LT gets pissed and tells Frankie it looks like a little black box, and that he ain't on 'What's My Line?' We were laughing and having a good time like we were having a party in some park back in the world instead of being out in Charlieland smelling bodies.

"Then we all get serious and start searching for the little black box and, check it out, Frankie finds it. He walks up to the LT with a dumb-shit look on his face and says, 'Is this the right one?' God, we about died laughing. The LT takes the box and sticks it in his pack, handling it like it was the Holy Grail and he was Sir Whoever. Colucci wires the chopper—it ain't got markings on it, no numbers, no letters, no nothing—then asks about the bodies again.

"The LT tells him that after the grenades do their number there won't be any bodies. So we blew the chopper and humped back toward the LZ. We chowed down about a klick from it while Colucci went ahead to make sure we weren't running into an ambush. After a while he comes back and tells us there's two roundeyes at the LZ wearing civilian clothes and sunglasses. Like fucking tourists, right?

"Also, and check it, the whole LZ perimeter is lined with badass-looking gooks. They're too big to be Vietnamese and two light-skinned to be Yards. Chinese, maybe.

"Anyway, we make a lot of noise coming in to the perimeter so they won't light us up, and this one civilian-type, the one with the French accent, asks the LT if he has the black box. The LT gives it to him, and the other roundeye says something into this little transmitter, and a couple of minutes later two slicks come in. Frenchy and the other dude climb into the first one and take off, and the second one lifts us out. I look down, and all them Chinese badasses around the perimeter have disappeared.

"A month later the LT gets the Silver Star, and the rest of us get bronzes. The whole fucking deal gives me the creeps. I mean, it was like being in the land of Oz, right?"

"What was in the little black box?" Morgan wanted to know.

Doc scratched his head. "Who knows?" he said. "Diamonds? Heroin? The Tin Man's heart?"

"I've got a better story than that," continued Doc. "Or a worse one, depending on your perspective."

"O.K., let's hear it," said Morgan.

Doc sighed and started. "We were humping through the bush toward a treeline, and all of a sudden a sniper opens up on our point man. The platoon just lays down in the grass while a couple of squads head out to flank the treeline. I crawl up to the pointman. He's got a through-and-through in the shoulder. It ain't that bad, so I give him some morphine and a cigaret and we lay there bullshitting.

"Then the LT tells us to get on line. We're going to assault the treeline. So everybody gets on line, and we charge. Everything but bugles, right?

"We get to maybe fifty meters from the treeline, and they open up with everybody they have. Heavy automatics, AKs, RPGs. They even had some bloopers.

"We got murdered.

"Both flanking squads ran into ambushes. The whole platoon is chopped up. Everybody's calling, 'Doc. Over here. Doc! help me.'

"I ran out of bandages. Then I ran out of morphine. I just didn't have enough stuff.

"Then Selbig got it. Selbig was my buddy. We were max tight. He somehow blew himself up with a willy peter grenade. Maybe a bullet hit it. I don't know.

"I've got wounded everywhere, and Selbig is still alive, screaming his head off. I mean he was so burned that most of his face was gone, and he didn't have any hands left. I crawled over to him and told him I didn't have anything to give him. He just kept screaming and screaming. He begged me to shoot him. He begged me, do you understand?"

"Jesus, Doc."

"I had to, Morg, I just had to."

"You don't have to go on if you don't want to."

"I'm O.K. I want to finish this."

"O.K."

"The rest of the company rolls in a couple of minutes later and pulls us far enough back so that air can take out the treeline. The medevacs came in and took out hurt, maybe twenty guys. We took our eleven KIAs back to this little dirt road where some trucks were. I carried Selbig out on my back. There was a truck, and I put him in it and it took him away."

"At least you got his body back," said Morgan.

"He didn't have a head. I blew his head off." Doc was crying softly now. "I can't go home. I have to find his head."

"Try to forget it. Finish your tour and go home."

"Can I do that?"

"You can if you want to."

"I don't know what I'd do back home. All I know is bandages."

"I think that's enough."

"You really think so?"

"I really do," said Morgan, patting Doc on the shoulder.

— 36 —

After Doc Wrench sacked out, Morgan remained on the bunker and watched as flares dropped from gun-ships. Occasionally a fiery burst of tracers would arc up into the dark sky, long fingers of beautiful, deadly light seeking airborne targets. Once he saw a vivid blossom of orange momentarily light up the sky—an hallucination

or an exploding helicopter. He swallowed the last of his
warm beer and immediately felt sick. He crawled off the
bunker and vomited in the dirt. Between retches he
wiped tears from his eyes.

He began crawling, not knowing or caring in which
direction. He heard noise to his right, stopped, and
squinted his eyes. Framed in the doorway of a barracks,
two black soldiers squared off against each other. One
held a bayonet in his hand and seemed ready to use it.
The other soldier stood in a crouch. Each man was
shouting angrily at the other to make the first move.

"Not my problem," muttered Morgan as he began
crawling again. He crawled until his forward motion
was halted by something that bit his nose. He backed up
a few inches and stared at the barb on the camp's wire
perimeter fence until he recognized it for what it was.

"Oh," he said dumbly.

Since he could go no further, he sprawled in the dirt
and fumbled in his pockets for a cigaret. After lighting
it he felt the urge to urinate. He unbuttoned his pants
and pissed without moving; stoned, he rather enjoyed
the sound of urine as it struck the dirt.

He puffed on the cigaret and closed his eyes. A picture of Ho Chi Minh flashed into his mind. Morgan saw
with clarity the hooded eyes, the full lips parted in sug-
gestion of a smile, the long and wispy hairs sprouting
from beneath the chin. Ho's image began undulating,
lost its features, and reappeared as a new face.

"LBJ, you old son of a bitch," Morgan said in recognition. "How's everything back in the world? How's
Luci?"

President Johnson's image didn't answer; instead,
the president raised his hands to his ears and pulled on
them sharply. His mouth opened, and he howled like a
beagle.

"You dumb shit," said Morgan.

The president opened his shirt, pushed up his T-shirt,
and grinned stupidly. Morgan saw the jagged incision,

pink and raw-looking, held together by sutures. He studied it and noticed that the healing scar had the same outline as that of North and South Vietnam.

"Jesus," Morgan said in awe. He felt himself suddenly rising up and away from the vision of LBJ's scar. Beneath him he saw the president grow smaller even as the scar grew larger, until it became the size of North and South Vietnam, until it *became* North and South Vietnam.

"I'm an angel," Morgan mused as he hung suspended over the seventeenth parallel.

He looked down at Vietnam and saw a column of tanks and troops cross the Song Ben Hai River which flowed through the no-man's land of the DMZ. Morgan broke into a cold sweat; the tanks and troops were North Vietnamese, headed south.

He swiveled his head and looked down at Hue, then at Danang, and saw that the road connecting the two cities, Highway 1, was clotted with fleeing civilians and ARVN soldiers. He squinted his eyes, which telescoped his vision.

"Aw," he said, "they've thrown away their weapons. They're giving it up."

Still above Vietnam in his hallucination, Morgan looked further south. More tanks and columns of North Vietnamese issued forth from Cambodia on Route 19, moving on Pleiku in the Central Highlands.

He looked beyond that. North Vietnamese and Viet Cong moved past the ruins of An Loc on Highway 13. Still more poured out of the Iron Triangle. Route 22 in Tay Ninh Province and the southern end of Highway 1 in the Parrot's Beak were similarly occupied. From Morgan's vantage point it seemed these roads, which led to Saigon, were long, writhing snakes, such was the profusion of men and material moving on them.

I need a cigaret, he thought, and then said aloud, "You stoned fucker—you got one in your mouth."

He puffed on it, but it had gone out. He found

matches and relit it, while continuing to watch the fall of Vietnam—a spectator at his own hallucination of an event that wouldn't happen for seven more years.

He looked down again and saw an armada containing junks, trawlers, PT boats, and sampans sailing in the South China Sea, forming a floating arc from Nha Trang to Cam Ranh Bay. The decks of the vessels were hidden under the crush of Vietnamese families and ARVN soldiers.

"Stand and fight," Morgan demanded weakly. "It's your country."

He looked again at Danang and telescoped his vision on the docks jutting out into the harbor. They were littered with the debris of a defeated populace—suitcases, guns, old and infirm people abandoned in panic by their fleeing progeny.

A baby cradle caught Morgan's eye. He saw that from under a thin cotton blanket projected an infant's arm and hand. The tiny fingers were curled into the palm of the hand. The fingernails, in death, touched the infant's short lifeline.

Morgan felt his chest tighten. His heart began hurting. "Oh, trip," he begged, "stop." He kept hallucinating.

He saw Saigon below him. He spotted the American Embassy on Thong Nhat Avenue. A helicopter lifted from the embassy's roof, and headed for the South China Sea. He watched until it landed on the deck of an aircraft carrier, then looked back at the city until he found Trung Ming Giang Street. He followed it north toward Tan Son Nhut until he saw the apartment he had lived in. Where Tam had lived with him.

"Tam," he said, her name on his lips a statement of loss.

Beyond the apartment, rolling smoke and flickering flames caught his attention. Tan Son Nhut, bombed and shelled by North Vietnamese vanguard units, lay broken and bleeding. Rows of American fighter-bombers and cargo planes sat unattended in protective revetments, like abandoned metallic birds. Morgan looked through the huge air traffic control tower windows. No air controllers sat behind the radarscopes; Paris Control was abandoned.

A movement caught his eye. A shadow in front of a hangar had moved slightly.

The hallucination was fading out; Morgan was coming down off the high. He squinted his eyes to the maximum as he tried to make out the figure standing in the doorway of the hangar. A drift of smoke from a burning C-130 momentarily obscured his vision. The smoke cleared. He saw a girl standing in the doorway. Long black hair covered her shoulders and disappeared down the back of her ao dai, which was white, the Vietnamese color of mourning. He tried to see her face.

"Tam?" he asked.

The oily smoke from the C-130 again blocked his vision, and Morgan crashed from his hallucinated vision of the future.

His head ached. He retched into the dirt, then grabbed at the barbed wire of the perimeter fence and tried to stand up. His legs would not support him. He lay back down in the dirt and felt a burning sensation in the palms of his hands. He looked at them and saw the cuts from the barbed wire oozing with blood. He removed his fatigue shirt and wiped the bloody cuts with it, then laid the shirt over himself like a shroud.

"Tam," he said before falling asleep, "was it you?"

Morgan returned from Dau Tieng and went to the Cherry Tree Bar.

"Mamasan, has Tam come back?"

"No."

"Do you know when she's coming back?"

"I expect that she isn't. She was supposed to return weeks ago."

"I wonder what happened to her?"

"Did you love her, American?"

Morgan paused. "Yes," he said, "I guess I did."
"Then remember her well. When all other memories of Vietnam die for you, you will remember her."
"I know."
"Good-bye, American."
"Good-bye, Mamasan."

— 41 —

June 1968. Demoralized by his vision of the fall of South Vietnam, Morgan spent the next few weeks flying mobility missions all over III and IV Corps. He shuttled from Cu Chi to Song Be, from Vinh Long to Can Tho, from My Tho to Chi Lang, doing what had to be done, numbly going through the motions.

After a month he said to Easy, "I don't think Tam's coming back, and I've had it with this goddamn war. Where's the most isolated place you can send me?"

"Let me think. I could send you back to Chi Lang. It's not very isolated, but it is quiet."

"I want isolated."

"How about Co Duc?"

"Where's that?"

"It's a Special Forces camp near the Cambodian border, up in the highlands. Nothing there but a Special Forces detachment and a Montagnard village nearby."

"It sounds right. Can you send me there?"

"Sure."

Morgan boarded the C-7A Caribou that flew him to the isolated outpost of Co Duc. There were fifteen Americans in the camp: twelve members of a Special Forces A team; SP4 Bloch, a weapons maintenance man; and Lieutenant Mack and Private Barry, weather operations personnel.

Captain Braux, the brawny leader of the Green Berets, showed Morgan around Co Duc, pointing out its defensive positions.

"What's that overgrown trail near the front gate?"

"The Old French Road."

"Where does it lead to?"

Captain Braux smiled and winked. "Old France, most likely, after a long detour through Cambodia."

Captain Braux led Morgan to a small barbed-wire cage that held a small Vietnamese youth who was clad in red shorts. "And this here is our prisoner. He's a small-time VC who's been checking us out. Grider and Foxworth caught him by the north wall one night." The VC prisoner stared dully at the two men.

Morgan was settled into the living quarters of the Green Beret medic, Sergeant Jesus Bighorse, a full-blooded Indian from Gallup, New Mexico.

"Would you like to go with me to Buon Sut sometime?" the medic asked Morgan. "What with only one resupply plane a week for you to work on, you're going to have a lot of free time on your hands."

"Sure. Thanks for asking me."

The weapons maintenance man, Bloch, walked up to Morgan. He had a mass of wiry hair that gave him an Art Garfunkel look. "Are you another hawk?" he asked. "It seems that all we have up here in this mountain resort are gung-ho hawks who intend to prosecute this immoral war to its fullest."

"I'm not a hawk or a dove. I'm just up here taking a break from reality."

"Well, I'm against the war, myself."

"So I gather."

"It's such a senseless waste of men's lives. Vietnam should have been left to the Vietnamese, don't you agree?"

"I don't know."

"Well, I know. We have no business being over here. Vietnam was an internal matter, and now we've barged in and made it the whole world's business."

"Listen," said Morgan, "I'll talk to you later. I've got to get ready for chow."

— 42 —

Sergeant Bighorse and Morgan walked the half-mile-long trail through thick stalks of towering bamboo to Buon Sut. Five roots, or thatched longhouses, dominated the village of ninety people. The Montagnards, nomadic agrarians considered to be savages by the lowland Vietnamese, had centuries ago claimed the highlands of Indochina for themselves.

Bare-breasted women, clad in brightly colored skirts, and naked children moved about the village. Bighorse approached a short, stocky man who was wearing a woven loincloth.

"Morgan, I want you to meet Truu. He's the leader of the village."

Morgan shook hands with Truu, who smiled, revealing black teeth that had been filed to points. Truu's earlobes were perforated and filled with silver discs. Around his wrists he wore several silver bracelets.

"And this is Baap," said Bighorse referring to another man, a wraithlike figure, who limped over to them. "He's the medicine man. We consult him on all cases." Bighorse pointed to another figure emerging from the jungle. "See that man with the crossbow? That's Kroong. He's the tribe's chief hunter. Truu wants us to go into his house and have soom rnoom."

"What's rnoom?"

"Fermented rice wine. It's kept in an earthen jar and sipped through a bamboo straw. Truu is honoring you with his invitation. To refuse would be an insult."

"I'm game," said Morgan, following Truu, Baap, and Bighorse into the cool, dark interior of the longhouse. The four men sat in a semicircle in front of a jar of rnoom and alternately sipped its contents. Morgan became slightly intoxicated. Truu kept smiling at him, and Morgan smiled back.

After a while, Bighorse stood up. "The formalities are over," he said. "I've got patients to attend to." Morgan followed him and Baap to a makeshift dispensary where half a dozen villagers waited, lounging in the shade.

Bighorse lanced a pus-filled wound on the leg of a little girl, smeared some ointment on the wound, and gave her a C-ration can of date nut bread. The little girl, apprehensive at first, smiled widely when she received the gift.

The next patient was an old man who had cut his leg on a wiah, or bush hook. He placidly smoked his brass pipe while Bighorse took several sutures in the wound and gave him an antitetanus injection. The medicine man, Baap, chanted in his native tongue and passed his hands over the bodies of the sick and injured.

"Does his brand of medicine work?" asked Morgan.

"It does if you believe in it," said the Indian medic. "Suggestibility plays a big role in medicine, whether it be up here in the hills or at the Mayo Clinic." He dispensed ointments and pills to the other four villagers, and was done for the day.

"Thanks for taking me along with you," said Morgan as he and Bighorse made their way back to Co Duc. "I think I'm going to like it up here just fine."

"If you're here long enough, maybe you'll get to watch the villagers sacrifice a buffalo or two. That's really something to see."

— 43 —

Morgan and Private Barry were lying on top of the command bunker's reinforced roof, tanning slowly under the noonday sun.

"I quit the seminary, joined the army, and volunteered to come over here ten months ago," said Barry.

"Why'd you volunter?"

"I wanted a firsthand look at the war. I've been to Cam Lo, Khe Sanh, Con Thien, and now here, and I've pretty much seen it all."

"Did you learn anything?"

"Only that man's inhumanity to man is still alive and thriving."

"You were at Khe Sanh? Weren't you scared?"

"I've never been scared over here."

"Why not?"

Barry smiled. "God isn't going to let anything bad happen to me."

— 44 —

"You see, the United States is over here propping up a democratic government that doesn't even exist," said Bloch to Morgan one afternoon.

"But we've been told that what we're fighting for is democracy for the South Vietnamese," countered Morgan.

"Democracy, shit. The Saigon government is a bunch of old men who've been corrupted by American values. They use power as an end in itself. They're more interested in maintaining the status quo than they are in creating a democracy."

"Americans aren't the only ones who have come to South Vietnam. How about all the North Vietnamese coming down the Ho Chi Minh Trail?"

Bloch laughed, a barking sound. "Ho Chi Minh didn't start sending large troop concentrations until after we landed here in force."

"Bloch, I give up. I don't know whose side you're on."

"I'm not on anyone's side. I just happen to believe that the struggle in South Vietnam was a civil war until we interfered."

"Then why the hell are you over here?"

Bloch laughed again. "Hell if I know. I volunteered for the army and was guaranteed three years in Germany. I was in Frankfurt for eighteen months, and then I got orders for this goddamned place."

"So much for army promises," said Morgan.

"The only promise I got left is the one I made to myself, and that's to finish my time over here without hurting anybody and then to go home."

"You're a weapons maintenance man. Have you ever fired your weapons at anybody?"

"No. I just fix them. I refuse to use them on anyone."

"You know what, Bloch? You should have applied for conscientious objector status."

Bloch laughed again. "What makes you think that I didn't?"

— 45 —

"Morgan, you want to see a buffalo sacrifice? The villagers are celebrating tonight."

"Sure. What are they celebrating?"

"Kroong killed a tiger last night. It had been prowling

ED DODGE

around the village for the past week, and he killed it
with an old M-1 carbine.''

The village was lit with torches. In front of Truu's
longhouse the buffalo was tethered, bedecked with a
headdress of woven grass. It pawed impatiently at the
ground. The village children were amusing themselves
by poking the dumb beast with pointed sticks.

After two hours of drinking rnoom and uttering in-
cantations to various gods and genies, the sacrifice
began.

Truu used a machete to hack through the tendons of
the buffalo's rear legs. The beast bellowed in pain and
fear. Raising the machete, Truu brought it down in a
series of blows to the buffalo's neck. A fountain of
blood spurted from the buffalo and sprayed everyone
with a fine, red mist. The dazed animal sagged and knelt
down on its front legs. Its tongue lolled from its gaping
mouth. Bloody foam frothed from its dilated nostrils.
The animal died slowly.

Even as it was in its death throes, Truu sliced the buffalo's belly open. Its entrails, steaming, slid out into the
dirt. The villagers picked them up and carried them to
the cooking fires, then began cutting the meat from the
body with long knives. Soon the aroma of broiling meat
filled the village. The children skittered here and there,
laughing and playing. The medicine man, Baap, with
blood on his lips, raised his bony arms toward the moon
and muttered a prayer. The men and women retired to
the longhouses for more pulls on the rnoom. The village
of Buon Sut was, for the time being, a happy place.

— 46 —

Morgan spent an increasing amount of time at Buon Sut playing with the children, flirting with the women, and drinking rnòom with the men. Occasionally he went on hunting trips with Kroong, who taught him how to kill monkeys with the crossbow. Once in a while he even spent the night in the village, sleeping in Truu's longhouse wrapped in a colorful blanket against the cold night air of the highlands. Morgan was happy again for the first time in a longtime, and the war seemed far away, a fading bad memory.

— 47 —

One day Morgan was returning from Buon Sut when he heard what sounded like a voice coming from the top of a small hill. Morgan followed the chanting sound until he crested the hill. Sitting naked in the middle of a clearing was Sergeant Bighorse, his anointed skin glistening with oil. He opened his eyes and looked at Morgan as if he were coming out of a trance. "Sit down," he said.

Morgan sat down. "What are you doing?"

"I'm preparing to die."

"To die?"

"I saw it in a vision last night. I will die here at Co Duc."

"How?"

"Two large beasts will attack the camp. I will die fighting them."

Morgan cleared his throat. "I really don't know what to say. Are you sure this vision of yours is accurate?"

"They always have been in the past."

"Were those words you were chanting a death song or something?"

Bighorse smiled sadly. "No, they were words to mourn the fact that I will never in this life see the Wakan Tonka."

"The Wakan Tonka?"

"The white buffalo. The old legends say that if one sees the Wakan Tonka, then one is graced for life. I shall not have the opportunity to see the Wakan Tonka in this life."

"I'm sorry," said Morgan. "Is there anything I can do?"

"You can wear this," said Bighorse, taking from around his neck a flat piece of bone that had the head of a buffalo carved on it. "Maybe you'll see a Wakan Tonka in your lifetime."

— 48 —

Morgan had been at Co Duc for six weeks when a mobility member, Welch, disembarked from a C-7A.

"Easy sent me up with your mail and to find out how you're doing," said the large airman who resembled a young James Arness.

"Tell Easy I'm doing fine. Tell him I'm getting a suntan and getting my head together. Ask him if he can send up some dancing girls."

"Speaking of girls, Morg, he told me to tell you that your girl friend hasn't come back yet." Welch lifted a heavy knapsack from the Caribou and handed it to Morgan.

"What's in here?"

"Booze. I thought you guys could use it."

"Thanks. You're stuck here for a week, Welch. I'll introduce you around."

— 49 —

Soviet PT-76 tanks 2711 and 2712 advanced slowly up the slope of the Old French Road, their tread noises masked by the steady hum of the generator at Co Duc. Strung out behind the two tanks in double file were three hundred NVA regulars.

Lieutenant Mack and Private Barry were in the weather bunker setting up atmospheric tests. Bloch, pensive, sat with his back against the 106 recoilless rifle. The perimeter was loosely guarded by a dozen Montagnards; the rest were at an all-night ritual in Buon Sut. Everyone else was partying in the command bunker.

In one corner of the dimly lit bunker four Green Berets were engrossed in a fast-paced game of blackjack. In another corner lay Mike the monkey. Wrapped in a towel, Mike's soft paws covered his ears as he mouthed simian obscenities at the circle of drinking loud-talking men in the center of the room.

"Damn, Welch," said Captain Braux, "if we'd known Morgan had a friend like you, we'da requisitioned your ass a long time ago." Welch raised his glass in a silent toast.

Above ground, Bloch grimaced. "Assholes just don't understand what I'm telling them," he muttered, passing a hand over his mass of wiry hair. "Dumb bastards are going to get wasted over here for nothing."

A Montagnard tribesman standing nearby ambled over. "You talk me?" he said.

Surprised, Bloch looked up. "No, but I might as well. They sure as hell don't listen to me."

"You talk me?" the Montagnard repeated.

"Sure," said Bloch, motioning for the man to sit down. "What would you like to know about Sartre?"

Both tanks halted less than seventy meters from the first tangle of concertina wire. The noises of their idling engines and the noise of the camp's generator meshed, each sound masking the other.

The three hundred NVA regulars were broken down by their cadre into platoons. The platoons dispersed and became squads which maneuvered noiselessly and with precision through the thick brush until they were within thirty meters of the north and west perimeters of the camp. Hunkered down and armed with an arsenal of AK47s, SKSs and several American M-60s, the squads

formed an interlocking, formidable field of fire. Fifty
NVA separated from the main group and made their
way toward Buon Sut.

Naked and camouflaged, sappers moved forward to
the concertina wire, carrying lengths of bamboo filled
with explosives; these crude but effective Bangalore
torpedoes would be used to breach the concertina wire
at several vulnerable spots. Other sappers carried satchel charges which they would throw into gun positions.

Morgan turned to Welch. "Let's go up to my hootch
and smoke some shit. The Beenies don't care as long as
they don't see it."

"I can dig it," said Welch, showing no indication that
he had downed six glasses of whiskey in the past hour.
He followed Morgan up the steps and through the
blackout curtain.

"Pretty up here, Morg. I can see why you want to
stay. Cool night air, no skeeters, and the Big Dipper lay-
ing low in the sky."

"That's only a small part of it," explained Morgan.
"It's the Yards. I know it sounds crazy, but I fit in with
them. Maybe I'm a throwback or something."

The two men ambled past Bloch and the Montagnard,
who had an intent look on his face as he listened to the
maintenance man.

"What are you doing, Bloch?" asked Morgan.

"Teaching this man comparative philosophy,"
gruffed Bloch.

"You'd be better off if you taught him comparative
hygiene," chided Morgan.

Bloch ignored him. "Now then, where were we?" he
said to the Montagnard.

"You talk me?"

"Ah, yes. We were discussing Socratic method-
ology."

Each North Vietnamese soldier tied tourniquets
around his extremities in order to slow the loss of blood
in the event he was hit during the forthcoming battle.
Adrenaline surged through each man's body as he strug-

gled with simultaneous but incompatible impulses to
either fight or flee. Vision narrowed and became more
acute. Breathing became rapid and shallow. Each man's
mouth filled with a brassy taste. Their ears filled with
the sounds of their pounding hearts. Disciplined by the
rigors of war, the soldiers rode along on their adrenaline
until it crested and was supplanted by the illusion of in-
vincibility necessary for men to face death willingly. In
their psyched-up state, the NVA possessed not only the
desire to face the enemy but also the ability to defeat
him. They rechecked their sweat-slicked weapons and
waited for the signal to attack.

The night suddenly lit up with a green cast as a flare
exploded over the camp. Welch, transfixed, stood with
his hands on his hips.

"Now ain't that a purty sight?" he said.

Morgan hit the ground and covered his head an instant after he heard the popping sound of the flare's
detonator. He grabbed Welch's leg and pulled him to
the ground. At first he did not understand the sound he
was hearing, and his brain worked furiously at culling
the information needed to identify it. When he realized
what it was, his skin first went hot and then cold.

"Tanks!" he screamed. Welch, who had tumbled to
the ground facing Morgan, looked into his eyes only
inches from his own and said, "You're bullshitting me,
right?"

Tank 2711 led the assault, followed closely by Tank
2712. It charged up the last seventy meters of the Old
French Road, its engine whining, and hit the first tangle
of concertina wire. It lurched briefly as its treads caught
in the wire, then tore it out of the ground, steel posts
and all. Sparks from the contact danced across the front
of the tank.

The Green Berets in the command bunker responded
to Morgan's scream. Weapons in hand, they headed up
the last few steps of the bunker.

"Ain't no goddamn tanks around here, Captain,"

assured the mortarman. "Ain't been no tanks since Lang Vei."

Tank 2711's gunner had been well briefed on his primary target. The first shell slammed into the command bunker near the entrance and exploded with a vengeance. Seven Green Berets were either killed outright or incapacitated. Down below, the radioman, scrambling toward his communication equipment, watched in disbelief as dead and wounded team members tumbled down the bunker's steps and sprawled in a bloody heap at the bottom. He cranked up his radio set. "Ah, Bravo Two, this is Moon Dog. We got a problem."

"Gawddamn," yelled Welch in response to the hit on the command bunker.

"Crawl this way," said Morgan, "toward my hootch." Instead, Welch began crawling toward the command bunker.

After firing its initial round, Tank 2711 came to a halt as the gunner inside searched out his next target. Tank 2712 idled impatiently behind its sister. The barrel of the first tank swiveled and sighted at Morgan's hootch, paused a second as if in consideration, then centered on the weather bunker. The gunner made several adjustments and fired. The shell slammed into the weather bunker with a deafening noise. The roof lifted several feet into the air, then collapsed. Fragmented metal and glass from the meteorological instruments showered the camp. Pieces of Barry mingled with them, for the religious soldier, curious, had climbed onto the roof to see what was going on.

The north and east perimeters of the camp came alive with a violence of their own an instant after the weather bunker had been reduced to rubble. The sappers guided their Bangalore torpedoes under the concertina wire, where they exploded. One detonated prematurely, killing its handler. Other sappers threw their satchel charges into the gun pits, killing the Montagnards who cowered under the unexpected onslaught. Two hundred and fifty NVA opened up as one with their weapons, pumping round after round into Co Duc.

Bloch, who had been mesmerized by the entire sequence of events, now acted. Beyond intellectualization of the immorality of war, he detachedly watched himself as he picked up a shell, slammed it into the 106's breech, took careful aim at the lead tank, and fired.

Tank 2711's driver felt a jolt. He throttled to his left and was surprised when the tank did not respond as it should; instead, it moved in a sluggish, pivotal circle, spewing up thick clods of dirt. Resigned to his fate, the tank commander ordered the gunner to keep firing.

The back flash of the 106 illuminated Welch as he crawled toward the command bunker. Morgan lay where he was and heard the 106 round explode. He heard a metallic sound and watched the lead tank divest itself of one of its treads, like a snake shedding old skin.

Bloch reloaded. He saw a silhouette to his right: Welch, upright, was running clumsily toward the command bunker, his bulk an easy target.

"Get down, you fat fucker," Bloch yelled as he sighted the 106 at the crippled tank. Welch dropped to the ground. Tank 2711's gunner lined up Bloch's position and fired at the same instant Bloch did. The young war protester disappeared forever in a slash of flame and smoke. The round he fired at the tank was low; it skittered into the ground beneath the tank, inexplicably ricocheted up into its vulnerable underbelly, and detonated. A thirty-meter fireball smashed into the sky like an angry red fist. Tank 2711 and her crew died instantly.

One of the Green Berets, grasping a .45, jumped out of the bunker and ran to where the VC prisoner squatted in his cage. The Green Beret took careful aim and shot the unblinking enemy between his black eyes. He then started to run for the south perimeter, seeking escape. A short burst from an AK47 sought him out. A first bullet puffed into the dirt inches from his left foot and ricocheted away. The second bullet tore into his calf muscle, gouging away fatty tissue. The third bullet drilled deeply into his left buttock. The fourth bullet smashed into his scapula, shattering it. The fifth bullet flew off the top of his head. The sixth bullet, missing, sped harmlessly into the night as the riddled American smashed to the ground like a puppet suddenly cut loose from its strings.

The explosion of Tank 2711 had been so awesome that soldiers on both sides were stunned for several moments. The NVA on the north perimeter had been preparing to assault when the tank was destroyed. Instead, they wavered momentarily, contemplating the destruction.

Welch completed his crawl to the command bunker and slid inside it, falling down the steps and onto the soft, bleeding bodies of the Green Berets who had been hit by the tank's first round.

Morgan continued his crawl along the south wall, stood up, and dashed for the east side. For all he knew he was the only friendly left alive, and his goal was a simple one: get through the concertina wire and make his way to Buon Sut. He knew he would be safe with the Montagnards. His people, as he thought of them, would hide him. The last thing he saw as he escaped from Co Duc seemed to be a surrealistic vision: Sergeant Jesus Bighorse, naked and carrying a grenade in each hand, was running toward the second tank. The sergeant's words to Morgan flashed quickly through his head, "Maybe you'll be luckier than me. Maybe you'll see a Wakan Tonka in your lifetime."

The NVA breached the north side of the camp. A small group of them ran up to the weather bunker, which was smoking from the direct hit. A small fire in one corner was feeding on torn sandbags.

Lieutenant Mack, wounded by shrapnel in half a dozen places and bleeding profusely, myopically searched the floor for his glasses. He heard the footsteps and the heavy breathing of the advancing soldiers. He squinted up at the shadowy figures. "Hey, guys, can you help me find my glasses? I think Barry needs help, but I can't find him." He neither heard nor felt the fusillade of bullets that killed him.

— 50 —

Morgan had not run far down the trail through the bamboo groves before he saw an orange glow above Buon Sut. He heard movement coming toward him and eased himself into the bamboo. About fifty NVA marched past, heading for Co Duc. Morgan remained hidden for the rest of the night and at dawn moved up the trail and entered Buon Sut.

A rooster crowed as Morgan looked at the ruins of the Montagnard village. What had once been sturdily built longhouses erected by the hearty tribesmen were now smoldering ashes. Small fires flared here and there; popping embers sent sparks flying. Thin wisps of smoke curled into the early morning sky. In the distance, a water buffalo moaned.

A charred body with its arms reaching for the sky blocked Morgan's path. He knelt next to the body, intently inspecting its unrecognizable face. Truu? he wondered. Baap? Kroong? He stood and walked on, passing the still, contorted forms of a dozen more bodies, some of them children's.

Finally, he sat down near the cooling ashes of one of the longhouses. Physically and psychologically numb, he never felt the pain as a live ember bit into the palm of his left hand. He stared at the sun as it rose above the devastated village and, overwhelmed by what he had seen, he closed his eyes for a long time.

When Morgan finally opened his eyes, he saw the carnage but didn't emotionally identify with it. He unfastened his canteen and drank deeply. His instincts told him that he should head south, out of the mountains. He replaced his canteen, stood, stepped onto the trail, and began walking.

The first day he worked his way over many acres of slashed and burned ground that the Montagnards had prepared for planting. At night he holed up on the bank of a stream and covered his body with mud to discourage mosquitoes. The mosquitoes buzzed around him all night, protesting his muddy armor, but found few chinks in it. He slept fitfully.

He descended the plateau in two days, arriving at a place where the jungle grew thicker. He drank his remaining water and stepped into the green. The noise of the birds and monkeys was raucous.

After two hours he came to a river. It was shallow and not very wide, and the water was brown. He filled his canteen and drank until he felt bloated. He knew that he would have to cross the river eventually, but for now he was content to lay at its grassy edge and rest.

A herd of barking deer, no larger than dogs, nervously skittered down to the river's edge. Spraddle-legged, most of the animals drank while several of them remained alert for potential danger. From out of the corner of his eye Morgan saw movement upstream; he watched what seemed to be a dark log undulating down the river.

Anaconda, he thought.

No, they live in South America, he corrected. It must be a python.

No, they live in Africa, he remembered.

Southeast Asian version of a python, he concluded, as the seventeen-foot-long reptile swam past.

From somewhere in the distance came the roar of a predatory carnivore. Morgan's heart pumped faster.

Tiger? he wondered.

What does it matter what it is? he thought. If it is hungry enough to eat me, what does it really matter? He flashed on the television program "Wild Kingdom" and heard Marlon Perkins say: "The jungles of South Vietnam are a beautiful but dangerous place."

Morgan crossed the river shortly after nightfall and holed up on the other side. He drank long from the water, then moved on into the jungle.

A troop of monkeys chattered overhead, scolding Morgan as he trespassed on their territory. Brightly colored parrots, disturbed by his passage, flew through the underbrush. Water dripped down from the leaves of one-hundred-foot-tall trees. Morgan persisted, concentrating on one step at a time, his head down, searching out firm footing on the tangled jungle floor.

I may be the first human being through these parts, he thought, until he smelled smoke. The odor of burning wood came from directly in front of him, but he couldn't tell how far away it was. He moved to his right in a wide, flanking movement. He crept stealthily, step by step, and dismissed the smoke smell as a reference point the moment he heard voices.

The rapid chatter of words was unmistakably Vietnamese. Villagers, VC, or friendlies, Morgan did not know. On his belly now, he crawled forward, every pore of his body alert, impervious to the stinging of fire ants. A camp stood in a clearing next to a small stream. From the stack of carbines and automatic weapons that were centered in the camp, Morgan knew the men were VC. He started counting them.

A skinny, ulcerated-skinned man tended the fire, occasionally turning the meat of a spitted turtle. Morgan, sixty meters away, could hear sizzling as turtle fat dripped into the fire. Two other men, who appeared healthy, were hunched over a sheaf of papers, talking between themselves. Another soldier, twelve or thirteen years old, lay asleep in a hammock which had been stretched between two trees at the edge of the clearing. Laughing voices and splashing from around a bend in the stream suddenly assailed Morgan's ears. Four in camp and two or three more swimming, he calculated. Six or seven in all.

A burning sensation on the back of his hand almost caused Morgan to cry out. He looked and saw the tail end of a blood-bloated leech as it burrowed into his skin. Morgan found a sturdy twig and jammed it into the leech, impaling it with a squelching noise. "Die, fucker," he whispered to the squirming parasite. New sounds suddenly came from only about fifteen meters away and on his side of the stream. Morgan tensed his muscles in preparation to jump and flee. Instead, he willed himself to relax. New sweat broke on his forehead and ran in rivulets down his face. He wiped his eyes, silently cursing the sting of salt, and stared at a thicket of bamboo from where the sounds issued— sounds of sex.

He heard a man's voice, high-pitched.

He heard a woman's voice, low-pitched and guttural.

He listened to the lovemaking for several more minutes, then heard what he surmised to be the man lost in the throes of orgasm.

The bamboo thicket rustled with movement. Morgan smelled cigaret smoke. He began to salivate uncontrollably.

The man and woman, soldiers in the National Liberation Front, emerged fully dressed from the thicket and casually waded across the stream toward the campsite.

The VC tending the fire watched their approach, a leer distorting his face. The lovers looked at him and laughed shyly. Three naked VC appeared from around the bend, carrying their freshly washed clothing. Talking animatedly while they dressed, they joined the others around the fire and dined on the roasted turtle meat.

Morgan pushed backward away from the edge of the stream, turned around, crawled two hundred yards on his belly, then stood, and in a wide arc moved away from the VC camp. As he did the night before, he crossed the stream after dusk and hid on the other bank. In the morning, he crossed a field of exotic variegated orchids, which transformed the jungle into a beautiful, benign place. Taking only a moment to admire their beauty, Morgan pulled many of the flowers from their stems and ate them. The petals, insubstantial and bitter-tasting, failed to halt the rumbling of his stomach.

After spending another day in the jungle, Morgan stumbled into a mountain valley which once had been cultivated.

— 51 —

Morgan plodded across the abandoned rice paddies. Sunbaked chips of mud crackled beneath his boots as he began the fifth day of his journey. He made directly for a village that sat on a raised area in the center of a maze of paddies.

Reaching the abandoned hootches, he began searching them. He sat down in a hootch that had served as a granary and patiently gathered a small handful of rice from the dust-covered dirt floor. He chewed several grains at a time. His teeth hurt as he crunched down on them.

A scrabbling sound caused Morgan to turn his head. A brown rat, skinny-ribbed but as large as a cat, peered through hard black dots of eyes at Morgan as it crouched in the doorway of the granary.

"Want some rice, rat?" Morgan asked as he overhanded a kernel at the naked-tailed rodent.

The rat, frightened by Morgan's sudden movement, retreated several feet. It watched Morgan for several moments; then, eyes glaring, it advanced on the rice, digging it out of the dust on the floor. It nibbled a kernel, making a staccato, grating sound.

Morgan's stomach growled at the same time that an idea flashed in his head. Maybe, he thought, I can get the rat close enough to kill it, and eat it.

Gastric juices spurted into his empty belly, causing a sharp pain to race across his abdomen. God, he thought, am I that hungry?

"Yes, you are that hungry," intoned a voice not his own but coming from inside his head. Morgan was puzzled by this new-toned thought of his, but not afraid. Must be from being tired and hungry, he explained to himself.

He turned his attention back to the rat and tossed another kernel. The rat shied away again; then, after a pause, it advanced on the grain of rice and devoured it. Morgan turned his palm over, allowing his supply of rice to fall to the dirt floor. The rat scarcely noticed.

With one hand he began tossing more rice to the rat. With his other hand he slowly unlaced one of his boots. The ravenous rat kept eating the handouts and ceased to flinch away as the grains dropped into the dust around it. Morgan used the toe of one boot to push against the heel of the unlaced one. The rat ceased eating and, now more curious than apprehensive, watched Morgan as he pushed the boot free of his foot.

The rodent started violently as he raised the boot over his head in slow motion.

Almost frantic, Morgan lofted several rice kernels. The rat stayed where it was, staring for a long time at the raised boot. Succumbing to its hunger, the vermin skittered closer and ate the offering.

Morgan became more confident. Taking a chance, he aimed at a spot eighteen inches in front of the rat and tossed four grains.

"C'mon, Pavlov," he silently urged the rodent.

The rat advanced, the ends of its long black whiskers coated with dust. It nosed around in the dirt, then used its curved claws to pull the grain to its mouth. Settling back on its haunches, the rat feasted on the abundance, occasionally stopping to peruse Morgan.

Morgan smiled encouragement at the rat, as he said to himself, "I hope you choke on it, bastard."

The rat, now four feet away, waited expectantly for the next tidbit.

Morgan coaxed the rodent forward: three feet, two feet, one foot. The arm holding the boot began to ache along the triceps. His fingers, bloodless in their tight grip, went numb. As the rat inched forward, he rewarded it with half a dozen kernels. The rat, after a brief and disdainful glance at his host, settled down to eat. Its pink tail rolled in the dust behind its mottled brown body.

Bring it closer? wondered Morgan. "Bring it closer," advised a voice not his own but coming from inside his head.

"What the hell is happening to me?" asked Morgan, suddenly feeling chilled.

He waited for this new voice to answer, but when it did not, he again focused total concentration on the rat, who was finishing off the last offering of rice.

Morgan used finger and thumb to pick up the kernels

at his side, palming more than a dozen. Ever so slowly he dropped the kernels of rice, one by one, onto his fatigue pants, just above the knee.

The rat, its eyes flashing greedily at this veritable feast, walked lightly over to the leg without once looking up at Morgan or the upraised boot, began eating.

Morgan experienced a rush of revulsion as he felt the rat's body brush against his thigh. Its twitching nose nudged against the rice on his leg. The rodent's claws made tiny scratching sounds against his clothing as it grasped the kernels.

Morgan's eyes fixated on the top of the rat's head. He swung the boot downward.

At the same instant, the rat had felt a tension gather in Morgan's thigh muscles. It started to jump away.

Morgan was faster.

Instead of smashing against the rodent's skull, the heel of the boot hit the animal a glancing blow where its body joined its neck, breaking one of its shoulders. The vermin, its upper teeth protruding to their maximum, yellowed length, hissed at him. Morgan leaped up and, his legs numb from lack of circulation, stumbled over to the injured animal. He retrieved his boot and relaced it, then sat down at some distance from the crippled rat.

After massaging blood back into his numb legs, he stood up and advanced. The rat, mortally betrayed, glared at Morgan's looming presence. Morgan lashed out a boot; the rat squealed as it dodged from the blow.

Looking for a vulnerable spot, Morgan began circling the animal. The rat, its black eyes glazed with pain as the shattered bones of its shoulder grated against each other, used its good leg as a pivot point and turned with Morgan, who feinted quickly. As the rat lurched in the same direction, Morgan moved swiftly to the other side and kicked the rat in the back of its head. Morgan lost his balance and fell to the granary floor. Fearful of revenge, he rolled hurriedly away from the rat. A wall of the granary halted his rolling. He looked over at the rat.

Stunned, it lay motionless in the dust.

Morgan got to his feet and walked over to the unconscious rodent. He squashed its head under his boot.

Dying, neural impulses in the rat seemed to cause it to come to life. The animal's rear legs dug at the dirt; the claws of both front feet extended reflexively as a final flicker of life coursed through the rodent's spine. Its back rippled convulsively underneath its brown pelt.

Morgan lifted his boot from the rat's ruined skull and cleaned the gore-covered heel by grooving it through the dirt floor of the granary.

"Sorry 'bout that," he eulogized, looking down at the dead animal.

"Let's eat," demanded a voice coming from the inside of his head.

"Who are you?" Morgan asked the voice aloud, waiting for an answer. When there wasn't one, he shrugged his shoulders.

"Let's eat," he said, reaching down for the cat-sized carcass.

Morgan sat cross-legged in front of the stone hearth of one of the abandoned hootches. The small cooking fire was dying out, smoke from it curling lazily toward the rotting thatch roof. A neat pile of small and delicate bones rested near his left knee. Morgan reached out and with grease-slicked fingers selected a tiny femur, which he snapped between his hands. He sucked the congealed marrow.

The rat had not been as meaty as Morgan had hoped. He discovered this after dressing the rodent, using a five-inch steel fragment from a rice knife that he had salvaged from one of the hootches.

"Fire's going to be a problem," Morgan had mused aloud. "If I have to eat a fucking rat at all, it will have to be a cooked one."

He had found the piece of rice knife, and carrying the rat by its tail, had settled down in front of the smoke-blackened hearth. Pulling several handfuls of thatch

from the wall, which he used as tinder, he struck the
steel fragment against the hearth's stones.

"Spark, blow, spark, blow," he advised himself.

After more than an hour of trying to create a fire, his
diaphragm aching from compression as he bent over his
work, Morgan threw the steel fragment against the
hearth.

"It doesn't work," he said disgustedly.

He got to his feet and walked over to the window.

"I hope you motherfucking Boy Scouts freeze to
death in a blizzard!" he shouted. His words carried
across the dried rice paddies.

"Fuck you, Norman Vincent Peale!" he raged, mis-
taking him for Robert Baden-Powell, the founder of the
Boy Scouts.

Morgan kicked blindly at the rat's skinned carcass.
He missed, and the toe of his boot struck against the
hearth, causing one of the mud bricks to crumble. Surprised, Morgan looked at the broken brick and saw a
ragged edge of plastic.

"What the fuck?" he asked, then pulled at the
plastic.

A plastic sandwich bag appeared. Something was in
it, but dirt adhering to it obscured whatever was inside.
He undid the rubber band that secured it and turned it
upside down. A brass hash pipe, a small amount of plastic explosive, and a book of matches dropped to the dirt
floor.

Morgan stared unbelievingly at the treasure trove.
Ignoring the other items, he picked up the book of
matches and opened it. The book contained four paper
matches.

"Ohio Bluetips!" he exclaimed.

The hunger in his mind for something familiar in this
alien and hostile terrain overrode the hunger in his
stomach. He read each word on the matchbook's inside
cover. It was an advertisement for a correspondence
school.

"Oh, hell, no problem at all," said Morgan. "Send me the course on hotel/motel management."

He looked around at the deteriorating hootch.

"Hell, I've already got the buildings." He let his train of thought carry him away.

"Hell, yes! Send me the course, and I'll make this place into a Howard Johnson's. I'll put in a big parking lot for the tracks and tanks, and a paved LZ for the choppers. Instead of having mamasans for maids, we'll import roundeyes."

He laughed as a vision of mini-skirted, frilly-aproned girls flitted through his mind.

Morgan's stomach grumbled ominously, reminding him of his hunger.

"And," he added, ending his reverie as he touched a match to the tinder, "the specialty of the day is rattus barbecueous."

After his meal, Morgan wanted a cigaret. The rat meat, lean and stringy, had tasted to him what he could only describe as "gray." He needed a cigaret to cover the taste which now cloyed on his palate.

"I will not," he ordered himself, "become sick."

Gagging a few times as he pondered what he had just eaten, he remembered the hash pipe that had fallen out of the bag. Although only dusk outside, the interior of the hootch was awash with darkness. He used his fingers to search out the pipe, found it, put it into his mouth, and sucked through the stem. He struck the second match and held it to the bowl, inhaling deeply. A small amount of hash residue puffed into his lungs. Shit, he thought, not enough to buzz a midget. The match burned his thumb.

Swearing, Morgan reflexively dropped the match and sucked at his blistering thumb. He waited until he was sure the pipe bowl was cool, then inserted his tongue into it. The hash residue burned acridly.

Morgan put the pipe into one of his pockets, saving it for a souvenir. For when I get out of here, he told himself.

"If you get out of here," said a voice not his own but coming from inside his head.

This time the voice was only a whisper. Morgan ignored it and settled in for the night.

— 52 —

Morgan awoke several hours before dawn on the sixth day of his journey. He molded the remaining C-4 explosive into a small ball, lit it with a match, and warmed himself with its intense heat.

He was hungry again and cursed himself for his gluttony in eating the entire rat the night before.

The C-4 burnt itself out. Morgan left the village and entered the dried rice paddies again, continuing eastward.

The dawning of the sun was spectacular. First there was a false rising, a half hour in which scudding clouds turned from black to gray and then to royal purple, the purple becoming tinged with pink. The sun, a fiery orange ball, glittering bright yellow at its edges, appeared and ascended slowly into the sky. The clouds burned away, leaving only wisps of white streaking the sky.

The dry rice paddy beds yielded up whatever traces of moisture they still contained. Morgan's throat became parched and constricted, while the top of his head itched as it burned.

Morgan plodded past abandoned villages that shimmered like mirages in the brutal Vietnamese heat. He heard a helicopter approaching, but couldn't see it because the blinding sun was at its back. He stood unsteadily, and waited to be rescued.

Suddenly, the parched earth around him erupted from the impact of machine gun bullets. Incredulous, Morgan watched the helicopter clatter past him, the door-gunner's face an impassive blur.

"You're gonna kill me after all I've been through?" he railed.

The gunship climbed into the cloudless sky, wheeled about and hovered briefly while the pilot fixed the defenseless sergeant's position, then began its deadly descent.

Morgan began to hyperventilate. He ran in the direction of the sun, not able to see the approaching chopper but facing its sound.

The noise of the gunship's rotors preceded it. Morgan listened for the change in engine pitch which would let him know that the pilot had leveled off, thus affording the gunner a steady firing platform.

The engine pitch changed slightly. Morgan took one more running step, then hurled himself headlong against the base of a paddy dike. Bullets thudded into the top of the dike, then passed over Morgan as he huddled in the fetal position. Too exhausted to move or evade the gunship anymore, he lay there and waited to die.

"Stand up!" exhorted the voice in his head that had first made its presence known back in the abandoned village.

"Die like a man," it continued harshly.

Morgan uncurled his limbs, willing his arms and legs to work. Like a crab he scuttled up the side of the dike, then stood erect on trembling legs.

He heard the gunship begin its third run. Morgan

squinted his eyes against the solar intensity, which enabled him to briefly discern a black insect-like dot flying toward him.

When the engine pitch changed this time, instead of trying to escape, Morgan raised his clenched fists high over his head.

The thunder of the helicopter as it bore down on him was deafening. He closed his eyes and waited to die. Instead, he was perplexed to find himself still alive. He opened his eyes. At some distance from him the helicopter hovered above the paddies, a maelstrom of dust churning up beneath its whirling rotors. Morgan watched the door gunner as he watched Morgan, for what seemed an interminable amount of time.

Am I supposed to know some fucking password? Morgan asked himself.

"New York Yankees," he shouted, trying the words he had heard in countless war movies.

The door gunner continued studying him.

"Mickey Mouse?" he ventured next.

The door gunner continued scrutinizing him.

"Chieu Hoi?" he yelled, raising his open hands above his head as he mouthed the Vietnamese words that the VC used when they surrendered or defected.

The door gunner remained unmoved.

Morgan gave up.

"Fuck ya, then," he said as he flashed the peace sign. "I'll walk out of here."

At Morgan's movement, the gunship edged its way closer to him until it stood off at a few dozen meters. Morgan was enveloped in dust. He protected his eyes with his hands and through his fingers saw the door gunner waving him forward.

Crouching against the force of the rotor wash, Morgan stumbled over to the gunship.

The door gunner, his eyes hidden behind sunglasses and his mouth tightened in a thin line, stood up from behind his gun, reached out his gloved hands, and yanked Morgan into the helicopter.

The door gunner spoke a few words into his mouthpiece. The gunship, after first tilting to one side,
gathered power, raised into the sky, and headed back
into the sun from which it initially came. Morgan lay on
the aluminum floor of the chopper and reveled in the
coolness of the air streaming in from the gunship's open
sides. The door gunner tapped his shoulder, then
slipped headphones over his ears.

A static crackled through Morgan's ears. He watched
the door gunner's mouth work.

"What the hell were you yelling at us back there?"
the gunner asked, his voice a thick Georgian drawl.

"Chieu Hoi," Morgan said into his mouthpiece. "I
was giving up."

The gunner looked at him, laugh lines around his eyes
suddenly creasing.

"Shit, boy, you ain't no VC," the gunner chuckled.

"You couldn't prove it by the way you were putting
smoke on my ass!" Morgan shot back. "I'm glad
you're a poor shot."

"Negatory," the door gunner said, coolly. "I was
just playin' before I put you away for keeps."

The helicopter carried Morgan to Ban Me Thuot,
where he was fed, cleansed, and debriefed by Fifth
Special Forces before being put on a C-130 and flown
back to Tan Son Nhut. He checked in with his squadron
and promptly ran into Welch.

"I thought you died at Co Duc," said Morgan.

"I thought the same thing about you, except you were
listed as missing in action."

"Tell me what happened to you, and I'll tell you what
happened to me."

"Well, I got down into the command bunker, and a
tank rolled up and sat right on top of us. We were in
there the rest of the night, but about ten in the morning
our air force came in on a bombing run. They cleared
out the gooks pretty good. After that they brought in a
new Special Forces team and some mercenaries by C-
one-twenty-three and relieved us."

"How many of you made it out?"

"Three. Captain Braux, who was pretty well shot to shit, the radioman, and myself."

"You're lucky. What about Sergeant Bighorse?"

"He's still listed as missing in action. Now tell me what happened to you."

Morgan told him the story of his escape and went to the Harem to rest.

— 53 —

July 1968. Despondent about the loss of the Green Berets—particularly Sergeant Bighorse—and the Montagnards at Buon Sut, Morgan brooded for a week, drinking heavily. When he sobered up he realized there was nothing to do except to continue working and survive the war. He went to Easy and requested a mission.

Morgan and the other team members landed at Phouch Vinh an hour before the transport planes would arrive to lift out an army battalion. The other team members sat down to wait, and Morgan walked around aimlessly.

He was moving along a line of jeeps filled with soldiers, head down, when he felt an impulse to look up. His skin crawled, and he was filled with horror at what he saw: Sitting in the jeep in front of him were Sergeant

Bighorse, Lieutenant Mack, Barry, and Bloch, and standing behind them were Baap, Truu, and Kroong. They all wore grim expressions as they stared at Morgan.

"You're all dead," Morgan said, his voice quavering. The seven men smiled sardonically.

Morgan's mind began shredding itself, like a machine left running but unoiled. He heard a plane land. He quickly turned away from the seven-man apparition and hurried toward the unloading area. The ground beneath his boots felt insubstantial, and his knees were rubbery.

He was twenty feet from the plane when its ramp lowered and soldiers began filing off. Morgan looked from one soldier's face to another's and realized with a shock that each face resembled that of men he knew who had been killed in combat. His heart beat wildly, and he had to lock his knees to keep from collapsing. The smell of death filled his nostrils. He gagged and tried to swallow, but couldn't. He shook his head violently, trying to shake off the illusion.

He chanced another look at the soldiers filing off the plane, and this time he saw that they were staring at him, smiling. Morgan shuddered and turned away, standing like a statue while he tried to compose his thoughts. A C-130 lumbered past him and pulled into the parking area, leaving its inboard engines running.

The plane's propellers attracted Morgan's attention and held him in an hypnoticlike trance.

Suddenly, the dormant voice inside Morgan came to life, all but overwhelming the young airman with terror.

"Well, there it is, Morgan," the voice said seductively. "The answer to all your troubles. All you have to do is to run through the propeller. It won't hurt you a bit. I promise."

Morgan trembled. He moved two steps closer to the plane, his eyes fixated on the whirling propeller.

"That's right," the interior voice soothed. "Keep going."

Morgan was torn. His body wanted to run through the propeller, but in some remote chamber of his mind that still harbored a sliver of sanity he knew that the moment he encountered the propeller he would explode in a bloody welter of minced flesh.

"No," he shouted. "I'm not going to do what you tell me to."

"But I'm only you," the interior voice said. "We can do it together."

"No," Morgan shouted again. Using his last reserves of willpower he forced himself from the plane and stumbled to the edge of the loading area where he sat down shakily near his rifle and pack. He was panting like a thirsty animal.

As if in a dream, Morgan watched his hand reach for his canteen. He grasped it, but his trembling fingers could not unscrew the cap. Giving up, he let the canteen fall to the ground. He then drew up his knees, rested his head on them, and closed his eyes.

The interior voice shouted at him: "Look out! Look out! It's coming!"

Morgan snapped his head up and looked around frantically. Across the runway he spotted puffs of red dust kicking up from the ground in a straight line that was heading directly at him, and he knew instinctively that the puffs of dust were caused by machine-gun bullets.

"Oh, Jesus, when does this stop?" he moaned. The bullets advanced on him, seeking his body. He struggled to get up, to escape, but his legs refused to work.

When the bullet hit, it dealt Morgan a bone-shattering blow to the left side of his jaw. His head snapped back violently, and his mouth filled immediately with a hot, burning wetness. He spat, and saw a copious amount of his blood spatter the dust.

I am hit, he thought, numb with shock.

"Hit bad," the interior voice noted. "Hit real bad."

Morgan tried to yell for help, but no words came out. His throat was filled with blood, slowly strangling him.

He knew that he needed to stanch the flow of blood, and his fingers tore frantically but futilely at the knot in his camouflage scarf.

A helicopter clattered low overhead and hovered fifty feet away. Morgan perceived the helicopter to be a prehistoric flying reptile come to devour him. He had to kill it. Disregarding the hallucinated bullet wound, he reached for his M-16. As his hand gripped the weapon's sun-warmed stock, dizziness overwhelmed him. Morgan's hand slipped from the rifle, and he fell on his side, his arms and legs jerking convulsively.

Morgan watched an ancient Buddhist monk appear from nowhere and sit in the lotus position a few yards away. The monk raised a jerry can above his head and doused himself with gasoline. When the jerry can was empty, the monk set it aside, struck a match, and calmly touched it to himself. The gasoline ignited with a whooshing sound. Greasy black smoke darkened the sun. Orange and blue flames swirled greedily around the monk, consuming his saffron robe and creating a fiery dancing halo above his shaven head.

Morgan smelled the sickly-sweet stench of burning flesh as the bonze's skin first glowed cherry-red, then blackened and hung in charred strips from his fingers and chin. His ears, nose, and lips melted away. His skull was exposed.

The monk closed his eyes and toppled over. The flames encircled him; his stubs of arms and legs drew inward as the fire bit into ligaments.

Morgan closed his eyes and moaned, and when he opened them again, the monk had disappeared. In his place were three cheerleaders, identically dressed in short blue skirts and sweaters, and holding red, white, and blue pompons.

"One, two, three, four," they chanted in unison, kicking up their long legs, "we don't want your fucking war." In a flash they were gone.

Morgan had endured enough. He felt blood pumping

from the wound in his jaw. He felt his heart slowing to a
standstill. His stomach contracted in a long wave of
nausea. He vomited.

He rolled onto his back and stared at the sky.

"This is the way I die?" he asked weakly.

"This is the way you die," the interior voice said
blandly.

"I'm thirsty," Morgan said.

His vision dimmed.

"I'm thirsty," he pleaded.

Darkness enveloped him and, mercifully, Morgan lost
consciousness.

— 54 —

When Morgan woke up it was dark. He was
dizzy and his body ached. But mostly he was thirsty. He
went into the small terminal and drank deeply from the
water cooler. Dazed, he lay down and slept fitfully
through the night.

The next morning he caught a ride to Bien Hoa, then
a flight to Tan Son Nhut.

He did not confide in anyone what had happened to
him at Phouch Vinh. The next two weeks he experienced
disorientation and paranoia as he completed mobility

missions to Song Be, Bu Dop, and Bao Loc.

The symptoms increased in intensity and duration daily, until he was suffering for hours at a time. He needed to get away from everything for a while, he thought, and then he would be O.K. again. He put in for his R 'n' R.

— 55 —

The jet carried the GI's through the night and landed at Darwin shortly before dawn. An area of the terminal had been cordoned off for them and they drank Foster's Lager while they waited for the plane to be refueled. At last they landed in Sydney and were taken on buses to a hotel, where they were briefed before being turned loose.

Morgan took a room in the Chelsea Hotel in King's Cross. He spent the first day in Sydney in his room, listening to rock and roll music on the radio. That night he went to a bar and got drunk.

The next day he walked through the park and spent a lot of time at the War Memorial, a beautiful monument to Australian and New Zealand war dead. That night he got drunk again.

The next day it rained, and Morgan spent the afternoon in a coffee house, sipping espresso and brooding

over his illness. That night at a discotheque he met
Erica, a nurse who worked at Prince of Wales Hospital.
She went to his room with him, undressed, and lay in his
arms. Morgan discovered that he was impotent, and he
was filled with shame and rage.

"Relax, Morgan. It happens to everyone, sometime
or other." Her words failed to console him, and he saw
her to a taxi.

The next night Morgan, drunk and walking through
the red-light district, was accosted by a prostitute who
stood in the lighted doorway of a building.

"Come on in, luv," she said. "It's a bit brisk out
tonight."

Morgan briefly considered going with her, then declined. "No, thanks," he said. "I guess I'm just not in
the mood."

"Sort of makes you feel like you're in kindergarten
without a sandbox, doesn't it, luv?" she said, a sad
smile on her face.

"Sort of," he agreed.

The next day Morgan stayed in his room nursing a
hangover, and when he came down from his room that
night he witnessed a street demonstration. Young members of the Socialist Party were snake-dancing through
the streets of King's Cross, chanting, "Kill the third
Kennedy." Incensed, he went into a pub and stood at
the bar.

"Excuse me," said a tall man on his left. "You're a
Yank, aren't you?"

"Yes, I am," said Morgan.

"Then let me buy you a brew. Did you just arrive
from Vietnam?"

"Yes."

"You know, mate, I fought against the Malaysian
communists in the fifties. I believe that what you Yanks
have to do is to go into the bush in small units—that's
the way we did in Malaya. Battalion-size operations
won't get the job done, and artillery is only good for

guarding the cities. Your air force is only making noise and killing monkeys. No, mate, if it was me, I'd go after the bloody Cong one at a time.''

"Thanks for the advice," said Morgan, not feeling inclined to talk.

"We had some times in Malaya," sighed the tall man.

"I'm sure you did."

Drunk again, Morgan weaved his way through the streets back to his room and spent the rest of the night sick, with his arms wrapped around the base of the toilet. He ate a solid breakfast the next day and felt somewhat better, although his overwhelming feeling of isolation still persisted.

When he boarded the plane back to Vietnam, he had four weeks to go.

Filling out medical papers in preparation for his return to the States, Morgan requested to see a psychiatrist. He was flown to the huge hospital at Cam Ranh Bay where he checked into a transient barracks. One of the men in the barracks, a soldier from Arkansas, was also awaiting a psychiatric review. He told Morgan his story.

"When I got leave from A.I.T., I went home and married Vonette. Three months after I got over here she sent me a letter telling me she was pregnant. I applied for a compassionate change of duty stations, and they turned me down. I applied for a leave, and they turned me down. I tried to go AWOL, and they found me. Then one night I just decided to shoot myself." He took off his shirt and showed Morgan a small entry wound just below his left nipple. "The bullet missed my heart and really messed me up," he said, turning around; the middle of his back was a mass of puckered scar tissue. "I'm waiting now on this here psychiatric review. Maybe they'll send me home. I hope so, because if they don't, I'll kill myself again."

Morgan saw the doctor, an army major, the next day. He explained his symptoms of anxiety and depression but left out the hallucinations he had experienced at Phouch Vinh.

"You've got a case of postadolescent adjustment," the doctor told him.

"What's that, sir?"

"You have some growing up to do. Nothing serious. Time will take care of it." He gave Morgan a bottle of Librium and dismissed him, and Morgan returned to his unit.

— 56 —

Flim-Flam Man showed up at Tan Son Nhut and asked Dandreau if he would like to accompany him and Millie to a Special Forces' camp.

"Millie's putting on her own private USO show, if you know what I mean," Flim-Flam Man said, winking.

Dandreau smiled. "Sure, I'll go with you."

Twenty miles up the road, an armored personnel carrier blocked their way.

"ARVN roadblock," explained Flim-Flam Man, slowing the jeep to a halt.

An ARVN lieutenant carrying an M-16 spoke to Flim-Flam Man in Vietnamese.

"What's he say?" Dandreau wanted to know. Millie looked at herself in a compact mirror and combed her hair.

"Says there's a VC ambush about a mile up the road. Wants us to turn back."

"If there's VC a mile up the road, why the hell ain't he a mile up the road kicking their ass?" muttered Dandreau.

Flim-Flam Man smiled. "ARVN don't fight unless they absolutely have to." Flim-Flam Man said something to the ARVN lieutenant, who shrugged his shoulders and ordered the armored personnel carrier out of the way. Flim-Flam Man shifted the jeep into first and let out the clutch.

"Ah," began Dandreau apprehensively, "you're taking us through the ambush?"

"No sweat, Dandreau. I've been through them before. You just smile while I give them a few piasters and some cigarets."

The jeep with its three occupants was moving along at thirty miles an hour when the command-detonated mine exploded under the right front wheel, tearing Dandreau with shrapnel. The jeep leaped two feet into the air and overturned. Small arms fire began peppering it.

"Hey, Flim?" Dandreau's voice was barely audible.

"Yeah?" Flim-Flam Man was sitting behind the jeep, slowly shaking his head.

"Flim, I'm all bloody."

Flim-Flam Man crawled over to his friend. "What?"

Dandreau's eyes were wide open and staring. His face was pale, his lips cyanotic. A thin line of blood trickled from his mouth.

"Ah, I think I'm dying."

Flim-Flam Man searched Dandreau's body. His fingers slid into a slippery hole on the left side of Dandreau's rib cage and touched bone. "Christ, Dandreau."

A burst from an AK-47 punched into the ground in front of the overturned jeep. Several bullets ricocheted off the chassis with a whining sound.

Flim-Flam Man looked at Dandreau's wound and discovered another one just below it. "You dumb shit," he said despairingly, covering the wound with his other hand.

"It doesn't hurt," mewled Dandreau. Flim-Flam Man saw another wound just above the collarbone, welling blood.

"I'm all out of hands, Dandreau," he said apologetically. Dandreau's blood flowing across his hands was warm.

Dandreau's eyes dilated and lost their ability to focus. "I can hear the ocean in my ears," he murmured. He began shaking uncontrollably, as though locked in the grip of malaria. His teeth chattered.

"Flim," he said, "hold me."

Flim-Flam Man removed his hands from Dandreau's wounds and cradled his head in his arms. Dandreau's breath now came in shallow gasps. His lips pursed as he sucked air into his lungs. He exhaled and went limp in Flim-Flam Man's arms.

Flim-Flam Man put his lips on Dandreau's and breathed. Dandreau's chest rose with the resuscitation. Flim-Flam Man repeated this three times, then took his mouth away. His lips were smeared with arterial blood. His breath leaked out of Dandreau's lungs, which remained deflated. Tears blurred Flim-Flam Man's vision as he balled his fist and slammed it against Dandreau's chest.

Dandreau's heart began beating again. He sucked in a chestful of air. His breathing was tortured. The expression on his face was one of confusion as his glazed eyes swept across Flim-Flam Man's features.

"Mama?" he asked plaintively.

Flim-Flam Man hesitated momentarily, then said, "Yes, Dandreau?"

"Mama?"

"It's O.K., Dandreau," crooned Flim-Flam Man. "I'm here."

Dandreau nodded his head slightly and died. Flim-Flam Man gently rocked the dead man in his arms.

Millie, knocked unconscious when the mine exploded

under the jeep, regained consciousness. She crawled over to Flim-Flam Man and began beating on his head with her fists.

"Bloody damn Yanks," she railed hysterically. "Bloody damn Yanks."

The VC ambush squad warily advanced on the jeep, their rifles ready. Two of them pilfered Dandreau's body for valuables, even taking his jungle boots. With curt nods of their heads and poking them with their rifle barrels, they prodded Flim-Flam Man and Millie to their feet and led them into the vast jungle which swallowed up the sounds of Millie's weeping forever.

— 57 —

Morgan walked into the Harem and saw Easy standing at the open window and looking down on Trung Ming Giang Street.

"You O.K.?" asked Morgan.

Without turning, Easy spoke. "It's over, Morg."

"What do you mean, 'over'?"

The sergeant shrugged his shoulders. "I can't send any more guys out; I can't do my job anymore." Then he added, his voice cracking, "I can't."

"Hey, Easy," tried Morgan, "you're out of here in —what?—three, four more weeks? You can hang on that long, can't you?"

"Don't want to," replied Easy, still looking out the window.

Something in the tone of his voice warned Morgan to proceed cautiously.

"Well, whether you want to or not, you're going back to the world soon, and all of this bullshit will be behind you."

"It'll never be behind me."

"Well, Christ, Easy," said Morgan. "I'm more than half crazy and getting worse, but I'm going home. Fucked up or not, I'm walking out of this place and going home. You're going home, too, unless you're crazy enough to pull an extension."

"I did," he said, his voice a whisper.

Morgan lit a cigaret, walked over to his friend and handed it to him, then lit one for himself.

"No shit, Easy? You extended?"

"Roger, rog."

"Christ!"

During a silence in which they both smoked, Morgan agitatedly regarded his friend.

"Easy, that doesn't make sense. You tell me you can't send us out anymore, and then you tell me you extended. What the hell kind of sense does that make?"

Easy looked at Morgan, and Morgan saw in his friend's eyes the same thing he had been seeing in his own for the past two months: the glazed look of the half-crazed, the same haunted look an animal has in that split-second interim between the time it hears the click of a trap's release lever and the steel-toothed bite. Morgan suppressed a shudder.

"Aw, Easy," he said softly, "when did you go crazy?"

The tall sergeant smiled wanly at Morgan and replied, "At exactly twenty-two forty last night."

"Why? How?"

"We lost a bird and everybody on it over Cambodia last night. One minute we were in radio contact, the next we weren't. We scrambled Rescue and Recovery, but they didn't find anything, so now we're working through diplomatic channels. I logged the bird down at twenty-two forty.''

"What the hell were they doing over Cambodia?''

"What does anybody do over Cambodia?'' parried Easy as he squashed out his cigaret on the windowsill. "What the hell does anybody do anywhere?''

"Who was on it?'' asked Morgan, rubbing his suddenly tired eyes.

Easy shrugged, "Didn't know the crew, but we lost a bunch, Morg.''

"How many?''

Easy's voice cracked. "Sixteen.''

Morgan was stunned. Using the butt of the last cigaret, he lit a fresh one, then laid the pack on the windowsill.

Easy pulled one from the pack, lit it, and stared out the window.

Feeling very old and tired, Morgan walked over to the refrigerator and pulled out four bottles of Biere '33,' then went back to Easy and put the beers on the window ledge. He opened two, then stood beside Easy and stared out the window with him.

"Who?'' he asked.

Through clenched teeth Easy carefully enunciated each syllable of the dead men's names.

"Edgewater, Hinkle, Hitchings, Clayton, Coates, Boudrealt, Swissensmith, Parker, Malachowski, Andrews, Cripp, Dutton, Keaton.''

"Easy, I've never heard of any of those guys. They ours?''

"They were,'' corrected Easy. "All new guys, less than two weeks incountry.''

"Fuck 'em,'' exhorted Morgan, trying to snap his friend out of his dangerous state of mind. "When we got down to fifteen we all agreed that that was it, that we were a club, that we wouldn't get to know any of the new guys. We took them out and broke their cherries, but we didn't get tight with them. We started with seventy, remember? Easy, we thought we were bad-asses.'' Morgan was rambling in an effort to reach his buddy.

"We went out on those missions and kicked ass, then came back and strutted into the Enlisted Men's club. Nobody fucked with us, remember? We were so cool, and we even got blown away cool. Remember how Britt was at Khe Sanh, stuck in that hole while they were getting shelled? When he saw the Bird get kissed he just stood up and said, 'Fuck this shit,' and walked toward the strip until he got kissed, too. You remember all the villagers we pulled out of those places? You remember stealing chow and taking it up to where it was really needed? We were cool, Easy.''

Easy still stared out the window, smoking and drinking the '33.'

"Easy, listen to me! So we started with seventy guys, and now there's only five of us left. Everybody we started with is either blown away or rotated the hell out of here. The five of us are going to rotate, too. Crazy, fucked up, whatever, we're going to rotate the hell out of here, too! So now we're down to five. Only five alive out of seventy, plus a few others who are back home already. The rest are dead. Fuck all of them, Easy. There's nothing we can do for anyone except the five of us, and we're all finally going home!''

Easy said, "You might make it home, Morg, but I've extended.''

Morgan suddenly felt sick.

"Easy,'' he started, already knowing the answer before he asked the question, "where's Fisher and Jacques and Zeke?''

"Morg, you already know where they are; I named only thirteen of our guys that went down in Cambodia, but I told you sixteen were on board.''

"Jacques, Zeke, and Fisher were breaking their cherries,'' mumbled Morgan, envisioning his three friends lying dead somewhere in the mountainous jungles of Cambodia.

Now, out of the original seventy in the Seventh
Mobility Task Force, there were only Easy and Morgan
left in Vietnam.

They stood at the window together, staring out at
Trung Ming Giang, smoking cigarets, and drinking '33,'
as tears rolled silently down their cheeks.

The sun set over Saigon, and Easy and Morgan stood
in the darkness of the Harem staring at the black
silhouette of the city. Both were drunk on the formalde-
hyde-laced '33.'

Finally Morgan spoke.

"Hey, Easy, we're out of beer—let's go get some
more."

"I can't, Morg."

"What do you mean, you can't? You don't want any
more, or what?"

"I need more, but I can't move. I'm"—he searched
for the correct word—"stuck."

"You sure?" Morgan asked.

"I'm sure."

"Then I'll go get us some and come right back. You
just stay here."

"I have no choice but to stay here," replied Easy.

Morgan left and walked down Trung Ming Giang
until he came to a bar. He went inside and ordered a
dozen beers; on impulse, he sat down and opened one as
he pondered. He thought, Easy has only three or four
weeks left incountry—or at least he did have until he
extended for an additional year. Easy says he can't go
home, and I don't have anything to go home to—no
woman, no job, no friends, no house. He laughed
aloud. The Vietnamese bartender shot him a quizzical
look. Morgan ignored him.

So, if Easy can't go home, Morgan concluded drunkenly, and if I'm going home to no home, I'll extend and
stay here with Easy. He smiled and dropped a five hundred piaster tip on the bar, then picked up the beers and
started back to the Harem.

He walked along Trung Ming Giang, tired, drunk,

and relieved that his decision had been made so easily. He was anxious to tell Easy as soon as possible, but he also wanted to "taste" the street. He walked past a huge mound of garbage which towered over the sidewalk. A horde of Vietnamese children scurried all over the refuse, tat-tatting at each other with stick "rifles" as they played "war." He watched as first one, then another child clutched at the front of his body and fell onto the garbage as a "bullet" hit him. At the bottom of the garbage hill, old mamasans picked through the refuse, searching out anything that might be used, sold, or added to their diets.

Morgan walked past doorways that were dimly lit by brazier fires, over which meals were being prepared. He nodded at each clustered family that squatted around their meals; they in turn either nodded back or else turned away.

He walked past a heavily barred and shuttered window. From inside he heard music. The sorrow of a dieu nam tune was being played on a don huyen, a single-stringed guitar of ancient origin. Accompanying the music was the soft and sad voice of a young woman. He stopped beneath the window, opened another beer, and stood drinking it as he listened. He imagined the song to be about a young husband and father who being patriotic, becomes a soldier in order to defend his country against intruders. After exhibiting courage in countless battles, the soldier dies heroically. The sad ballad would be sung by his widow, Morgan knew. Although the music and singing were sad, they were also laced with a delicate touch of beauty.

Finishing the beer, he carefully set the bottle on the sidewalk and continued up the street toward the Harem.

"Hey, GI," the ten-year-old pimp began as he tugged at Morgan's sleeve, "you wan' numma one girl?"

"No, thanks," Morgan affably told him as he continued walking.

The street urchin persisted.

"You wan numma one boy?"

Morgan laughed.

"You wan' numma one ticky-tock?" the child asked, his free hands suddenly displaying half a dozen Seikos.

"Not anymore," Morgan told the boy who kept pace with him. "I don't need to know what time it is anymore." Then he added, "Or what time it isn't."

"Dope?" asked the child, becoming frustrated.

"Nope."

"You fucky-sucky chicken?" he asked, now openly contemptuous of the uninterested American.

Morgan laughed and continued walking. The boy stopped, watching Morgan, then yelled, "Sometime you die, GI."

Morgan whirled, a beer bottle held over his head as if he were going to throw it at the boy, who flinched but stood his ground.

"Sometime we all die," Morgan said.

Then, with an underhanded motion, he lofted the beer at the boy, who easily caught it and then disappeared into an alley.

Morgan turned again and noticed the flashing red light of an army ambulance up the street near the Harem.

"What the hell would they be doing down here?" he mused as he walked toward it.

Then, as he realized the ambulance was parked directly in front of the Harem, he began walking faster, becoming more sober with each step.

The Canh family huddled in the doorway of the house. Morgan looked at them and noted they were all staring at the back of the ambulance. Several army personnel milled about, talking among themselves.

Mr. Canh, his black eyes glistening, saw Morgan.

Sympathetically, he said, "Mr. Morgan, I sorry for you. I very sorry for you."

"What the hell . . .?" mumbled Morgan.

He stopped and looked into the rear of the ambulance. A filled body bag rested on a stretcher. At the end closest to Morgan, two sharp points pushed out at the rubber of the bag. Morgan knew unmistakably that they were the tips of Easy's cowboy boots. Comprehending, he just stared.

"You knew him?" asked a burly MP, his black-lacquered helmet glistening as it reflected the ambulance light.

"We lived together upstairs," Morgan answered, looking up at the empty window and seeing the sill lined with empty beer bottles.

"Excuse me," he said to the MP as he started for the doorway.

"Ah, I wouldn't go up there if I were you," the MP warned. "It's kind of messy."

Morgan stopped and turned.

"How did he do it?"

The MP grimaced as he answered, "With a forty-five."

"He would," Morgan said absently.

The MP studied him, then said, "What do you mean by that? Did you know he was going to kill himself?"

"No," Morgan said. "It's just that Easy never did anything halfway."

"Do you know why he did it?"

"Yeah, I know why," replied Morgan as he looked straight into the MP's eyes.

"He got 'stuck.' "

— 58 —

Morgan spent his last night in Vietnam drinking heavily at a bar near the Harem. He went back to the apartment at dawn, packed his bags, and caught a ride to the airbase, where he waited several hours in the terminal. At last his flight number was called, and he boarded the plane without once looking back. He studied the backs of his hands as the jet cleared the runway and lifted into the sky.

The 162 men disembarked the jet in Japan while it was being refueled. In the snack bar were 162 young soldiers on their way to Vietnam. One of them, pale and nervous, walked over to Morgan who was sitting alone drinking coffee.

"What's it like over there?" the young soldier asked.

Morgan looked into his eyes and saw the innocence and apprehension there. He tried to think of something to say that would console the youth, but couldn't. He sighed, then said, "You'll have to find out for yourself. That's the best I can tell you. Nobody's story is the same. Good luck."

— 59 —

October 1968. The jet glided down through the mist on its final approach. Most of the men on board were lost in the regenerative sleep they desperately needed. A few, including Morgan, sat with their noses pressed against the windows, intently peering out through red-rimmed eyes and waiting to experience the moment when the freedom bird would cross the Pacific's eastern shoals and enter California airspace.

Morgan looked down through gaps in the mist and saw tiny pinpoints of light shining in a sea of darkness, as though thousands of diamonds had been haphazardly thrown onto a carpet of black velvet. He rubbed his knuckles into his aching eyes. "Tired," he said. With his fingertips he rubbed the dark skin beneath his eye sockets. "Home," he said. He yawned, feeling the hinges of his jaws almost dislocate. "Shit."

These were not the same 162 men who had shared the Saigon-bound flight a year ago. Of that original group, thirteen had been killed in action and nineteen had been wounded severely enough in large- and small-scale actions, ranging from the Ben Hai River in I Corps all the way down to Camau in IV Corps, that they had been medevacked out earlier.

There were other casualties from the original group —those listed as either killed or injured as a result of nonhostile actions. These included an Eleven Bravo from Guam who simply dropped dead one day while fording a nameless stream west of Saigon. Still another was a Wyoming youth who, while on R 'n' R in Singapore, had injected himself with a too-pure hit of heroin. A maid had found his body face up on the floor of his room, a needle embedded in a vein, a rubber tourniquet bound tightly around his arm. The young man's face in death was frozen in a visage of ambivalent joy.

There was also a soldier from West Virginia who had

been accidentally shot and killed by his buddy while the two of them were on a kangaroo hunt in the outback of Australia, and a warrant officer from Utah who had been stabbed to death by a roving gang of Danang orphans.

Casualties also included a corporal from Louisiana who had been captured near Kontum; a door gunner from Maine who had inexplicably unhooked his safety harness while two thousand feet above the Plain of Reeds, had given a thumbs-up to the startled chopper pilot, and then stepped out into the sky; and a soldier from New York City who, under surveillance by the Criminal Investigation Division for drug trafficking, deserted and disappeared in the maze of Cholon, the Chinese section of Saigon.

— 60 —

Morgan deplaned at Travis Air Force Base. Twelve hours later, honorably discharged from the United States Air Force, he was on a bus bound for San Francisco International Airport. The young soldier sitting next to Morgan offered him a drink from a pint bottle of whiskey. Morgan saw tears on the soldier's cheeks. There was a wild glint in his eyes.

"You just get back from Nam?" the soldier asked nervously.

"Yes," affirmed Morgan.

"Me, too. I'm glad that shit is over. I guess I'll always have dreams about Song My."

"Song My?"asked Morgan. That was the name of the village Tam had gone back to and from which she had never returned.

"Yeah. Song My, Pinkville, My Lai, or whatever you want to call it. I thought the slaughter would never end. We wasted all the gooks, even the kids. And when we ran out of people to kill, we wasted the pigs and ducks and chickens. It was a total massacre. We had this weird-ass lieutenant named Calley, and he was gunning them down right along with the rest of us." The soldier drank from his pint bottle and shuddered.

"You wiped out a village called Song My? In Quang Ngai Province?"

"That's a roger. We wasted everything that moved. I can still see those kids lying in the ditch. I'll never get over it."

Morgan slumped in his seat. He now knew the reason that Tam had not returned to him from Song My. He rode the rest of the way to the airport in silence, listening to the soft whimpering coming from the drunken young soldier next to him.

— 61 —

In a daze, Morgan flew from San Francisco to Chicago and changed planes for the short hop to

Michigan. He had called ahead, and his father had met
him at the airport. He had been driven to his father's
and stepmother's home, where he had eaten supper and
gone to bed.

The next day his father took Morgan to a car lot
where he put a down payment on a used car. Morgan
thanked him and drove off in the car, aimlessly driving
around town. The next day Morgan rented an old
house.

Home less than a week, Morgan sat on the dilapi-
dated couch and haphazardly threw playing cards at his
upturned bush hat, which sat in the middle of the floor.
The dim light from a small lamp gave the room a
twilight cast. A disconnected telephone, its cord coiled
snakelike, sat over a worn spot in the carpet. The radio
was tuned to a rock and roll station. Richard Harris was
singing "MacArthur Park."

Morgan finished throwing the cards, got up, and went
into the kitchen. He opened the refrigerator, pulled out
two beers, opened them, and stood in front of the sink
as he drank.

"Something, ain't it?" he said. "This is really something." He chugged the last of the first beer and picked
up the second, then turned the faucet on and put his
head under it. The cold water failed to do anything for
him. He turned the flow off.

"There ain't nothing here for you," he said. He finished the beer, pulled one more from the refrigerator,
and went into the bedroom, where he stripped off his
clothes, lit a cigaret, and crawled under the covers. He
sat in the darkness, drinking and smoking and listening
to the voice in his head as it said over and over like a
broken record, "Shoulda died, Morgan. Shoulda died,
Morgan. Shoulda died."

— 62 —

In addition to the continuing presence of the voice, Morgan was experiencing ever-lengthening periods in which he felt dazed and disembodied. During these spells his vision would narrow markedly, his ears would go deaf, and his mind would become very confused. His chest and face would feel hot, and he had to quell a strong compulsion to flee whatever environment he was in when the spells hit.

He became reclusive, venturing out of the house only to buy beer and canned food. He drank steadily all day long and until dawn, when he would turn off the radio and stagger off to bed. The drinking quelled the voice somewhat but failed to drown it out completely.

"Soon, Morgan," it said. "Soon."

His dreams were filled with broken and bloody, wailing wraiths that ran through his mind. He got little rest from his encroaching mental illness.

He got a job as a stock picker at a local automobile factory but quit after three days; the disorienting spells were becoming stronger and lengthier.

At his father's insistence, Morgan moved back into his father's and stepmother's house. The nightmares continued.

In one dream Morgan was running across bare and cratered terrain, a moonscape containing no place to hide. He had been running for centuries. Above him a flying saucer tracked him, and he knew that soon a laser beam from the flying saucer would incinerate him in a blinding flash of light.

The laser beam flashed. Morgan's retinas burst from the light's brightness.

"Time to get up, Morg," said his father, who had just turned on the overhead light in the bedroom. His father went downstairs, and Morgan dressed himself with trembling fingers, then sat on the bed and smoked a cigaret.

"Morgan, breakfast," his stepmother called. "Are you going to eat with us today or not?"

He finished his cigaret and put on his field jacket. He walked down the stairs and into the kitchen. "I'll eat something later," he said as he quickly left the house. It was early morning on December 21; the shortest day of the year would prove to be one of the longest for Morgan.

He started his car and, without waiting for it to warm up, pulled out of the drive and onto the main road leading north out of town. He cut west and drove onto the interstate that bisected the length of Michigan. He drove at a steady seventy-five miles an hour. His mind was confused, and he felt as if he were dreaming. He shook his head vigorously in an attempt to wake up.

He looked in the rearview mirror and saw flashing lights approaching him. He pulled over onto the shoulder of the road and waited for the police car.

As the state trooper walked over to him, Morgan rolled down the window and offered his driver's license. The trooper spoke to Morgan, but Morgan couldn't understand the words; instead, he simply nodded his head. The trooper filled out a speeding ticket, gave it to Morgan, and left.

Morgan started his car and moved back onto the highway. Suddenly, the train appeared. Consisting of three black, steam-fed locomotives, it was on his left side, one hundred feet away.

Morgan accelerated and sped from forty-five to sixty miles an hour. The train kept pace, soundlessly paralleling him. He broke into a sweat and accelerated until the car was doing eighty. The train kept pace with him. He looked into its cabs and saw no one.

Morgan jammed on the brakes and slid onto the shoulder of the road. Fighting the steering wheel, he managed to turn the car around and start back for home. He chanced a look out the right window, and to his relief the train was not there. Something to the left of him caught his eye. The train was there, still pacing him. Morgan's hands trembled so badly that the steering wheel wobbled. He wanted to scream. He pulled to the side of the road again. He tried to light a cigaret, but the matches kept going out in his shaking hands. His fumbling fingers found the cigaret lighter, and he lifted it to his cigaret. He looked in the mirror again and saw the locomotive only inches away from the rear of the car. With an animal cry he threw the transmission into low and jammed the accelerator to the floor. The car threw twin rooster tails of dirt into the air as the tires squealed back onto the pavement. He was racing blindly now, grateful that the highway was straight. He pushed the car to fifty before he shifted into Drive. He gripped the steering wheel tightly as he approached ninety miles an hour.

He glanced at the rearview mirror. The train wasn't there. The reflcted sight of his own eyes held him hypnotically. His thinking became fragmented. He was losing sanity so rapidly now that he failed to recognize his eyes as his own. He blinked at them. They blinked back. He pulled his gaze from the mirror and back onto the road. He screamed when he saw the train charging toward him down the centerline at ninety miles an hour, but he did not have time to bring his arms up to his face in defense as he met the hallucinated train head-on.

— 63 —

It was snowing lightly as Morgan's father drove him to the Veterans' Administration hospital. Morgan slumped against the car seat with his eyes closed. His arms were wrapped around himself as if he had been gutted and was trying to hold his entrails in. He muttered something inaudible.

"What?" his father asked. "What did you say?"

"Hurry," begged Morgan.

It was just after dark when Mr. Preston drove up to the hospital. Morgan looked out the window and saw a gathering of old, two-story, brick buildings.

Mr. Preston stopped the car in front of the admissions building, and he and Morgan got out. Mr. Preston opened the door of the building and held it for Morgan. The hallway was dim and quiet as they followed an arrow, painted on the wall, to admissions. Presently they came to a small office. A nurse sat at a paper-cluttered desk.

"I'm Samuel Preston, and this is my son Morgan. I think you received a phone call that we were coming?"

"Yes," said the nurse, reaching for a sheaf of papers. "I'll just get a little information from your son, and then he'll be taken to a ward. Would you like to have a seat?"

Mr. Preston looked uncomfortable. "Well, I've really got a long drive ahead of me, so I'd better get going."

"I understand," said the nurse. Mr. Preston turned to Morgan and hugged him.

"Good luck, son," he whispered, holding Morgan close. Mr. Preston then left the hospital and wearily began the long trip home.

The nurse politely asked Morgan questions about his military history and health problems. After the brief interview she picked up a phone and punched three numbers. It rang for a moment, then she spoke into it. "Mr. Preston is ready." She hung up.

Minutes later a black orderly dressed in white appeared. "You're Mr. Preston?" he asked, smiling.

"Yes."

"Follow me, please."

Morgan followed the orderly down a long, winding, dimly-lit hallway. The orderly stopped at a solid oak door with a small, reinforced-glass window in it and selected a key from about a dozen that were affixed to a brass ring.

"Is this a locked ward?" Morgan asked, apprehensive.

"Sure is."

"But I'm not violent," Morgan protested. "I'm just sick. I don't belong on a locked ward."

The black orderly smiled soothingly. "Maybe you do and maybe you don't belong on a locked ward, Mr. Preston, but this is Friday night, and there ain't any doctors to evaluate you."

"When will I be evaluated?"

"When the doctors come back."

"When's that?"

"Monday."

Morgan sighed. "Then I've got to be here for three days."

"At least three days, Mr. Preston," the orderly said, turning the key in the lock. "At least that, and maybe more." The orderly pushed the door open and motioned for Morgan to precede him.

I can take it, thought Morgan. After Vietnam I can take anything. He walked through the doorway and entered the ward. The very first thing he noticed was the stench of stale tobacco and perspiration that assailed his nostrils.

A tall, pathetically emaciated man with crazed eyes stopped his pacing in the hallway and peered down at Morgan.

"Do you have a mother-in-law?" the tall man asked in a guttural voice.

"No, I don't," replied Morgan.

"Well I do!" raged the tall man whose name was Gibbons. "Aw, God, I've got a mother-in-law, and she's got warts in her eyes!" He abruptly resumed his harried pacing.

The orderly led Morgan to the nursing station where he was told to strip. He was given blue pants and a lighter blue shirt, both garments too big for him; he held the pants up with one hand. They took away the buffalo head pendant that Sergeant Bighorse had given him.

The orderly led Morgan into the dayroom which was filled with milling, mumbling bodies, about thirty in all. High on one of the institutional-green painted walls was a television set. Sitting in front of it was a group of patients. A fat black man dressed in white sat at a small table in the middle of the room, playing solitaire with a worn deck of cards. His face wore a frown, and he continually glanced around the room, his eyes missing nothing.

A black Buddha, thought Morgan, as the orderly led him over to the seated figure.

"Mr. Preston, this is Mr. DeLance. He's your ward supervisor."

Black Buddha took Morgan's hand and smiled. "Is this your first time in a place like this?"

"Yes," said Morgan.

"Well, why don't you just have a seat and relax? Medications will be served soon, and after you get yours you can go to bed. Just try to relax and be cool."

"O.K.," said Morgan, finding an empty chair near the television. Next to him in a massive chair sat a porcine young man whose head had been completely shaved. The young man had his eyes fixed on the television and was chanting, "You goddamned pig! You no good, goddamned, oink-oink pig!"

"Excuse me," said Morgan. "Who are you talking to?"

The fat young man's eyes never left the television. "To myself, if it's any of your goddamned business!"

Morgan got up and moved to another chair. He pulled out a cigaret but did not have any matches. He did not know what to do. Black Buddha said, "I've got a light. I carry the matches on this ward." Morgan went to him, got a light, and thanked him. He moved to the back of the large, smoke-filled dayroom and stood near the pool table.

A ghoulish-looking individual approached Morgan. He was slump-shouldered, and his forehead wrinkled and unwrinkled constantly in time to whatever hallucinations he was experiencing. His eyes under bushy black brows were piercing and full of paranoia. The front of his shirt was a mosaic of food stains.

"You got an extra cigaret?" he asked Morgan. Morgan started to pull his cigaret pack from his shirt, but before he could do it, the man growled and began choking him. Morgan's eyes bulged with surprise and terror. He struggled weakly.

Black Buddha—Mr. DeLance—had moved quickly in spite of his bulk. He broke the man's grip from around Morgan's neck and threw the man aside. "Are you all right, Mr. Preston?" he asked solicitously.

"I think so," said Morgan.

Black Buddha turned to the man he had thrown aside. "Any more out of you, Perkins, and you're going into the time-out room. Do you understand me?" Perkins slunk away.

Morgan took a seat next to an ashen-faced man who was strapped to a chair. The man's eyes were closed. His head lolled. Spittle drooled from his mouth onto his chest.

A bespectacled man in his sixties walked into the dayroom from the bathroom. He wore a black watch cap and three plaid shirts, over which he wore a tattered black sweater. All four of the sweater's pockets bristled with pens and pencils. A large wooden crucifix, tied to a knotted piece of string, dangled from his neck. Rosary beads were tied to each belt loop on his tweed trousers and rattled when he walked. He carried a well-thumbed Bible in the curled palm of his left hand. This apparition spotted Morgan and walked over to him. Standing above Morgan, he made the sign of the cross in the air with his right hand and mumbled something in Latin. He stooped and put his mouth to Morgan's ear. "Welcome to Bedlam, brother," he said. "Peace be with you." The man straightened and shuffled away.

I don't belong here, thought Morgan. I don't know where I belong, but it's certainly not here.

"Medications," shouted a nurse as she rolled a medication cart into the dayroom. The patients assembled and shuffled into a haphazard line. Morgan joined them.

Coming to him, the nurse said, "Mr. Preston, this is for you." She held out a paper cup containing a yellowish-colored liquid and another cup containing a purple liquid.

He hesitated. "What am I getting?" he asked.

"Thorazine, honey. And a little grape juice to wash it down." Morgan swallowed the medicine. It burned his throat. He gagged and hurriedly downed the juice, then dropped the empty paper cups into a wastebasket.

"O.K., gentlemen," said Black Buddha, "The sleeping room is open. Don't forget to shower first. Mr. Preston, if you'll come with me, I'll show you your bed." Morgan followed the man into the sleeping room.

A half hour later, as he was lying in bed, the Thorazine hit him. He felt his arms and legs tingle and then go numb. His confused and ravaged brain became even more confused as the psychotropic drug wended its way through his brain. He felt dizzy, and tried to lie perfectly still.

The voice was back. "I told you it would be soon, didn't I?" it said mockingly. "And this time I brought company." Morgan sat upright in bed, his eyes widening with fear.

"Hi, Morgan," said a baritone voice.

"Hi, Morgan." This voice was feminine.

"Morgan!" shouted a chorus of voices. "Are you ready for us?"

Morgan suppressed a groan.

" 'Cause if you're not ready, we're going to take you over. You won't exist anymore."

Morgan shuddered.

"Shoulda died, Morgan. Shoulda died, Morgan. Shoulda died," said the feminine voice. Morgan closed his eyes and fought against the auditory hallucinations. "You're not real. I am," he protested weakly.

"Bullshit," roared a deep and angry voice. "You're not real. We are."

"No. You're just sick parts of me," he said. He was trembling. His forehead beaded with sweat. Perspiration dropped from his armpits and rolled down his sides.

"Face it, Morgan. You're nothing," said the baritone.

"You're nothing," chorused a half-dozen voices.

The original voice spoke. "We can't leave you alone, Morgan. We're all that you have. Without us, you're nothing."

"I am me," said Morgan desperately. The voices laughed in unison.

"You little prick," thundered the original voice. "We're done fucking with you. You can fight us all you want, but we'll outwait you."

Morgan cringed.

"You can't stay awake forever, and when you fall asleep, we'll get you."

"Get you. Get you. Get you," murmured the chorus.

"Sweet dreams, Morgan," said the original voice.

Morgan bolted from his bed. On shaking legs he hurried down the hallway until he stood at the nurse's station where the nightshift nurse sat at the desk reading a paperback novel. She looked at Morgan quizzically. "Yes?" she asked.

Morgan, perfused with Thorazine and fear, tried to

explain. His words came out slurred. "My brain is eating itself."

The nurse frowned and put the book down on the desk. "Now, Mr. Preston," she said, her tone that of a parent patiently speaking to a wayward child, "your brain couldn't possibly 'eat' itself. You just go back to bed, and on Monday you can talk to one of the doctors about it." Dismissing him, she picked up the book.

"I can't go back in there," persisted Morgan. "They're waiting for me."

The nurse sighed, put the book down, and took off her glasses. "Mr. Preston, there's no one waiting for you in the sleeping room. All the patients are asleep. Now I want you to go back to your bed and go to sleep."

Morgan was defeated. He staggered back into the sleeping room and lay down on his bed. He kept his eyes open and breathed shallowly as he waited for the voices to return. It wasn't a long wait.

"See, Morgan," hissed the original voice, "no one's going to help you." Morgan fought to stay awake. The Thorazine in his body worked against him. He began counting numbers, first forward and then backward. He tried to name every color in the spectrum. He named every aircraft he had seen or flown on in Vietnam.

"Play all the games you want," said the baritone voice. "We can wait." Morgan named the names of all his relatives, living and dead. He named all the saints he could think of, petitioning each of them in turn to help him.

"It won't work, Morgan," said the feminine voice. Morgan's eyelids drooped over his drugged eyes. His head filled with a rushing sound as the voices yelled, "We're coming, Morgan." He snapped his head up, forcing himself awake. His heart beat wildly and thudded in his ears.

The voices laughed. "Just fucking with you, Morgan." He used his fingers to hold his eyes open.

"Shit," sneered one of the voices. "That won't

work." Morgan's eyes watered. He had to blink and did. "Told you," said the voice.

"Soon, Morgan," said the original voice, whispering now.

Morgan's eyes closed involuntarily. His mind emptied of all thoughts as he fell into sleep.

The sound of a voice laughing maniacally inside his head jolted him awake. "Got you," it rasped triumphantly.

To keep from screaming aloud, Morgan bit deeply into his lower lip. The taste of his own salty blood was his last sensation before he lost consciousness.

It seemed an eternity for Morgan, but Monday finally came and with it the psychologist Dr. Beckwith, a short man with a crewcut and a cherubic face. His fingernails, Morgan noticed as they sat across from each other at the table in a small room, were bitten to the quick.

For more than an hour Dr. Beckwith asked questions and Morgan answered them as best he could, telling about his childhood, adolescence, sexual encounters, and experiences in the war. When he told Dr. Beckwith about his hallucinations and voices, the psychologist frowned and gnawed at a thumbnail.

"Well, I guess that wraps it up for now," Dr. Beckwith said. "Do you have any questions?"

"Two," Morgan said.

"Shoot."

"When do I get off this ward, and when do I get well?"

Dr. Beckwith pursed his lips for a moment, then said, "I'd like to keep you on the ward until the medication stabilizes you."

"How long will that take?"

"Oh, I think two to four weeks."

Morgan sighed.

"As to when you will get well," Dr. Beckwith continued, "that's entirely up to you."

"What do you mean?"

Dr. Beckwith spit out a piece of cuticle. "Well, Mr.

Preston, since you were the one who allowed yourself to
get sick, it's up to you to allow yourself to get well." He
grasped his briefcase, stood, and left the room, leaving Morgan, perplexed by his last statement, alone to
ponder it.

— 64 —

Christmas Eve 1968. In a Thorazine-induced
stupor, Morgan sat in one of the large chairs, staring at
the cracked paint on the wall. The television set on the
wall to his right was a blizzard of white and black; none
of the half-dozen patients who stared at it seemed to notice or care.

To Morgan's left, in a shadowed corner, sat a
scraggly Christmas tree, already drying out and drop-
ping needles in the hot and stuffy dayroom. The top of
the tree was crowned with a tissue-paper angel that was
missing one of its wings. The rest of the tree was devoid
of decorations, as the staff had deemed any plastic or
glass baubles to be potential weapons.

Lying on his back on the floor in front of the tree, a
man was singing "Jingle Bells," the two words intoned
emotionlessly over and over.

Black Buddha sat at his card table playing another
hand of solitaire. His small black eyes missed none of
the activity in the dayroom as he shuffled the torn and
greasy cards.

In the connecting hallway between dayroom and sleeping room, Gibbons mouthed obscenities. He paced back and forth, his long, bony fingers running through unkempt hair, as if he were trying to calm the voices inside his head.

The deranged man who had tried to strangle Morgan on his first night in the hospital walked up to the metal full-length mirror near the doorway, grimaced at himself, then spat a large gob of phlegm on his reflected image. His eyes glazed, and laughing in a way eerily reminiscent of the man in the asylum in the original Dracula movie, he slunk off to the sleeping room.

After a while, Morgan, dizzy, got up and slowly made his way down the corridor to the bathroom. He crossed the tile floor and stood at the window, ignoring the patient who stood in front of one of the sinks and drank continuous drafts of water from a Styrofoam cup as he chanted some kind of mystical incantation.

The window in the bathroom was open. Morgan pressed his nose against the heavy gauge screen and pushed against it until the thick vertical bars on the outside of the screen stopped his advance. He breathed in; the cold air made his nostrils ache. He raised his palms and rested them on the screen. He watched the snow fall quietly from the night sky.

When I get out of here, he thought to himself, I'm going to go down to the river, take off all my clothes, and freeze to death. He had heard that this method of dying was relatively painless, that you first became numb, then fell asleep before falling asleep forever.

"Psst! Psst!" a voice from behind him beckoned.

Morgan turned and saw a beer-bellied man standing in front of one of the sinks. The man wore a red flannel shirt and a brown cotton duck-hunting hat with a pair of crossed guns embroidered above the bill. The ear flaps were pulled down.

"C'mere," the man said conspiratorially.

Morgan walked over and stood next to the man, who was now staring at a naked light bulb above the sink.

"Listen," he whispered to Morgan, not looking at him. "You want to go on a trip?"

"Where to?" asked Morgan, his own voice a whisper.

The man beamed. "Zylar."

"Where's that?"

"Well, I can't tell you exactly, because they won't clue me in. All I know is that for the last three Christmas Eves, these Zylarians fly their spaceship through the lightbulb and take me with them for the holidays."

"How do you fit on their spaceship?" Morgan wanted to know.

"They got this beam they shoot me with, sort of a blue light. It don't hurt none, and it makes me small enough to climb aboard. In fact, one of them says that to me, just like a train conductor. 'All aboard.' " He laughed gleefully, then turned serious again. "You want to go?"

"I don't know," Morgan said. "I've only been here a few days, and I don't feel too good."

"Well, you're gonna miss out on a good Christmas dinner. The slop here ain't nothing compared to what the Zylarians fix. They've got turkey and stuffing, and cranberry sauce, sweet potatoes, homemade bread—the works! If you decide to go, we'll be leaving at midnight."

Morgan walked back into the dayroom, hugging the corridor wall in order to maintain his balance, as well as to avoid the rapidly pacing Gibbons.

"Aw, Gawd," Gibbons moaned as he suddenly stopped and bent his long neck down, peering at Morgan.

"Do you have a mother-in-law?" he asked.

"No," Morgan said.

"Aw, Gawd!"

Morgan heard the buzzer on the door go off. One of the staff left the nurse's station, twirling the keys on their chain as he went to admit whoever was buzzing. After a pause Morgan saw an old lady wearing a Red Cross hat. Her snow-white kinky hair twisted out from under the hat. She was carrying what looked like a mail pouch, and from this she extracted a tissue-wrapped parcel and handed it to Gibbons as he paced past her. He tore at the tissue paper. Pieces of it fell to the floor, littering the length of the corridor. The gift was a comb and brush set. Gibbons, still pacing, held them up to the light, examining them, and when he reached the bathroom doorway he tossed them in.

"Aw, the motherfuckers!" he said as he wheeled around to complete another circuit.

The Red Cross lady came into the dayroom and handed each of the patients a similarly wrapped gift. Most of the men shyly accepted their gifts, while a few murmured thanks as their eyes avoided hers.

She stood in front of Morgan. He looked up.

"Hello," she said. "Merry Christmas to you."

She handed him a tissue-covered oblong object. Embarrassed and drugged, he simply held the gift in his hands and tried to return her greeting, but it came out of his slack mouth something like, "Mare . . . miss . . . to . . . you."

She left him and went over to where the man was lying near the tree singing "Jingle Bells."

"Hello, Merry Christmas," she addressed him.

"How nice," she admired, cocking her head to one side as she nearsightedly looked at the singer, who had not acknowledged her presence.

"Do you know any other Christmas songs?" she ventured.

"I know 'Silent Night'! the man snapped, sounding as though he not only knew the song but owned it and kept it hidden away.

"Will you sing it for me, please?" she requested.

"Silent night, silent night, silent night," he sang, as monotonic as he had "Jingle Bells."

"Surely you must know the other verses," the old lady declared.

The prone man sang, "Holy night, holy night, holy night."

The attendant, swinging his keys, accompanied the Red Cross lady to the door and unlocked it to let her out. Keys still swinging, he disappeared back into the nurse's station and buried his head in the Christmas issue of *Playboy*.

Before long, all the patients had gone to bed except for Morgan and the hatted man. Both of them sat in the dayroom watching the clock. The only sounds were the hiss of steam from the old radiators and an occasional riffling of cards as Black Buddha marked his time with solitaire.

At 11:00 P.M. the shift changed. The incoming nurse and two attendants shivered as they shook the snow from their coats. Over cups of coffee, the outgoing nurse briefed them. The transition made, the group of employees bade each other holiday pleasantries. The swing-shift employees left, while the grave-shift attendants checked the patients in the sleeping room with flashlights, then entered the dayroom.

"What you gentlemen still up for?" one of them asked the hatted man and Morgan.

"We're going to Zylar," the older man confidently informed him.

"Ummm," noted the attendant, rubbing his chin, affecting seriousness, "how many trips will this make for you?"

"Oh, only three," he replied. "But—" he leaned forward confidentially—"they trust me now. There's talk that they'll take me on Thanksgiving. And Easter, too!"

"You be a regular commuter, you don't watch yourself," admonished the attendant.

He turned to Morgan. "You be going with him, Mr. Morgan?" he asked.

Then, seeing the tissue in Morgan's lap, he said, "Mr. Preston, shame on you! You haven't even opened your present yet."

Morgan looked down at his lap. His numb fingers

worked slowly at the tissue. It came apart in his hands, revealing an imitation leather travel kit. Unzipping it, he saw a plastic comb, fingernail clippers, and a miniature plastic bottle of English Leather.

"Whoo!" exclaimed the attendant as he confiscated the fingernail clippers. "Now you be all set for your trip with Mr. Simpson."

The hatted man grinned and said, "Zylar, here we come."

Now Morgan was even more confused. He knew that he was crazy. Although he was not in condition to judge accurately, he was fairly sure that Simpson was crazy, too. But the attendant isn't supposed to be crazy, he thought. He puzzled over this a few minutes, then concluded that perhaps, just perhaps, there was going to be a trip to Zylar for Christmas dinner. To him, it all added up: Simpson's invitation to join him on the journey through the lightbulb; the Red Cross lady's gift of the travel kit; and a presumably sane attendant telling Morgan that he was now prepared to go.

The attendant had left the room. Mr. Simpson, smiling, watched the wall clock as its large black hands, now at 11:28, moved inexorably toward midnight.

"Hey," slurred Morgan, "you sure this beam that makes you small doesn't hurt?"

"Nope," said Simpson, his face alive with anticipation. "It sorta makes you feel like you do when you've just finished servicing a woman."

At 11:50 Simpson nudged Morgan. Rubbing his bleary eyes, he looked up questioningly at the jovial man.

"It's time," he whispered.

Morgan frowned, confused.

"Zylar," Simpson prodded. "It's time to go to Zylar."

Morgan stood up, the sudden move causing his blood pressure to drop. His heartbeat thudded in his ears as the room went black around him. He held onto the wooden armrests for several moments.

"Was that the beam?" he asked Simpson.

"Nope, that was the medication," he replied. "The beam will come in the bathroom, soon's the spaceship comes through the bulb. C'mon."

Morgan followed him down the hallway and into the bathroom. The two of them stood at either side of the sink and watched the lightbulb. The silence, except for an occasional dripping sound from a leaky shower head, was suspenseful.

"Eleven fifty-eight."

"Eleven fifty-nine," Simpson said with bated breath while Morgan fought to stay awake.

"Bingo!" breathed Simpson.

Morgan held his breath.

At 12:08, Morgan mumbled good night to the still-waiting Simpson.

"Maybe," Morgan said, trying to be helpful, "they had car trouble."

"No, that ain't likely 'cause they're not in a car. They're in a spaceship."

"Then maybe they had trouble with that. Maybe," Morgan mumbled on, "they have something on spaceships that's like a flat tire on a car."

Simpson, who had been looking worriedly out the bathroom window, suddenly snapped his fingers. "That's it!" he exclaimed. "That's it! The snow! It's snowing so hard out that the Zylarians are having trouble with their radar. They'll just be a little late, but they'll be here."

Morgan mumbled good night again and felt his way along the wall into the sleeping room.

Simpson poked his head into the corridor. "You're going to miss the time of your life," he called after Morgan.

Morgan paused a moment, his hands against the wall for support, and said, "Bring me back a doggy bag."

"I can't!" hissed the perturbed Simpson. "There ain't no dogs on Zylar."

"Aw, God," mumbled Gibbons as he continued pacing down the hallway.

Morgan, surrounded by two dozen snoring mental patients, soon fell asleep.

— 65 —

New Year's Eve 1968. The ward was relatively quiet. Most of the patients had drifted off to their beds and Thorazine dreams. Black Buddha sat at the card table playing another interminable hand of solitaire.

Fat Parker slouched in a chair, swearing at himself as his porcine eyes absorbed "Hawaii Five-O" on the television.

"You goddamned pig," he growled, his teeth grinding out the words. "You goddamned oink-oink pig."

Morgan stood near the pool table, idly rolling the cue ball against the torn felt cushions. Near him a jowly, unshaven man strummed an out-of-tune guitar and sang in a clear voice as tears rolled down his ravaged cheeks.

Quist, who was from Kentucky and wore his hair in a greasy pompadour, stood in front of one of the dayroom's windows looking out through the glass and mesh, and intently nodding his head.

"Hey, Morgan. Come over here, man," he said.

Morgan walked over to him.

"Hey, man, you know I've got to get outta here. You know that, don't you?"

"Yes," said Morgan.

"Gotta take care of business down in Memphis."
Quist looked around the room warily, then whispered,
"Elvis is waiting for me, dig?"

"Why?" asked Morgan, playing along.

"Me and Elvis, we grew up together. We was kids
together. He told me to break out and get my ass down
to Memphis. He's got some chicks waiting for me. Real
hot numbers, you know?" He winked at Morgan.

"Did Elvis tell you all of this?" asked Morgan.

"No, man, he's cool, you know?" Quist scratched his
nose. "He can't let on that he knows me or else they
might catch him and lock him up, too."

"Then how do you know he's waiting for you in
Memphis?"

"JD told me," said Quist.

"JD?"

Quist was exasperated. "James Dean, man, James
Dean." Quist's eyes were glittering. He looked out the
window and pointed at a thick grove of pine trees.
"Yeah, old JD comes every night. He hides out in them
trees and keeps me hip. He uses a flashlight. We got
special codes and everything."

Morgan looked out the window. "If he's out there
tonight he'll freeze his ass off." He headed for the
sleeping room. As usual, Gibbons was pacing in the hall
corridor, his emaciated body looking even thinner as his
aberrant mind compelled him toward exhaustion. His
dry, cracked lips burbled incoherent words.

"How's your mother-in-law, Gibbons?" asked Morgan.

Gibbons stopped pacing. His eyes rolled up into their
sockets, and a grimace twisted his mouth. "Aw,
Gawd," he moaned, "she's got warts in her eyes."

Morgan walked into the bathroom. An old man was
sitting on one of the commodes, rocking slowly and
steadily, a human metronome. The old man's eyes
watered. His forehead was wrinkled quizzically, as

though he were trying to understand something that he
once had understood very well. There was a timeless
quality to the old man, as though he'd been sitting on
the commode forever. It was as if the hospital had been
built around him.

Morgan flushed the urinal and looked down at the old
man, who reached up with both hands and rubbed them
across two identical red scars high on the sides of his
forehead. His lobotomy scars seemed to be bothering
him.

"Good night, old timer," Morgan said softly. The
old man continued rocking.

Morgan undressed and climbed into bed. Just before
he fell asleep he heard strange snuffling sounds coming
from the dayroom.

"Hey, gimme a hand!" he heard one of the attendants shout. "Mr. Parker be rooting at the chairs. Poor
motherfucker think he a pig!"

Morgan dreamt that he was in a tunnel under the
hospital. He crawled on his hands and knees for what
seemed miles and finally saw a dim shaft of light ahead
of him. He exited the tunnel and stood up in a large
room. Three men were sitting at large television screens,
their backs to Morgan. He crept up behind the first man
and looked over his shoulder.

On the television screen a black limousine convertible
was moving slowly in a motorcade. A man and a woman
were in the back seat of the limousine; the man was waving and smiling broadly at the knots of people lining the
street. Suddenly the man's head snapped forward, and
his hands went to his throat. The woman stood and
clambered onto the trunk of the limousine. Everything
was chaos.

Morgan looked at the man who was watching this
scene. The man was John F. Kennedy.

Morgan moved to the second man who sat in front of
a television screen. On the screen a man was lying on the
upper walkway at a motel, surrounded by several other

men, one of whom was trying to stanch the fallen man's flow of blood by pressing a bloodied towel against his neck.

Morgan looked at the man who was watching this scene unfold. The man was Martin Luther King, Jr.

Morgan advanced on the third man who sat in front of a television screen. The picture on the screen showed a man lying on the floor, his eyes open and glassy, a pool of blood encircling his head like a crimson halo.

Morgan looked at the man who was watching this scene. The man was Bobby Kennedy.

Loudspeakers mounted in the corners of the room suddenly filled with the intonations of Walter Cronkite's voice as he said over and over, "And that's the way it is. And that's the way it is. And that's the way it is."

— 66 —

It took the Thorazine three weeks to dispel the voices and paranoia that tortured Morgan. He was transferred to an open ward where the patients exhibited little bizarre behavior.

Morgan got to talk with a staff psychiatrist once a week for a half hour. The rest of his time he spent at the occupational therapy shop where he made leather belts and wallets, and assembled the plastic Buddy Poppy flowers that were sold each spring by veterans' groups. He had a lot of time on his hands, and he waited impatiently for the day he would feel well enough to be released from the hospital.

Morgan's father and stepmother visited him every weekend. The three of them would sit on the cracked vinyl couches in the visitor's room, ill at ease with each other. His father would ask how he was, and Morgan would say fine. Morgan would ask his stepmother how she was, and she was always fine. From there the conversations would degenerate into discussions of the weather, the prospects of the Detroit Tigers for another pennant-winning season, and whether Fords or Chevys were better cars.

The truth of the matter was that his father and stepmother were trying to treat Morgan normally while they harbored a deep suspicion that he was not in the least normal, and Morgan was trying to act normal for them while in reality he felt alienated and alone.

The three of them went off-grounds once, to a restaurant. They had eaten their meals in silence, and Morgan had felt extremely uncomfortable, thinking that the other diners were surreptitiously watching him, all of them knowing that he was a mental patient, different from them, strange and, maybe, violent.

He had hated going to bed at night because he would more often than not dream about Vietnam. The dreams were vividly real and cruelly bloody, filled with the torn and bleeding bodies of Americans and Vietnamese. He dreamt about a village called Song My and about a beautiful girl named Tam who had died there along with hundreds of other men, women, and children at the hands of a platoon of Americans led by some lieutenant named Calley, as Morgan had been told on the bus by the drunken, conscience-stricken soldier. When Morgan awoke from the dreams in the morning, he was covered with sweat and felt exhausted.

He played pool with other patients, sat in the coffee shop by the hour, and walked around the hospital grounds, his collar turned up to ward off the February chill.

— 67 —

In April, seemingly without reason, Morgan started getting sick again. His relapse began as a general feeling of uneasiness which, in the course of several days, progressed to a specific physical and psychical restlessness, as though some form of speed were coursing through his body.

He reported his symptoms to one of the ward nurses, and she in turn informed the ward psychiatrist, who prescribed a different kind of medicine. Instead of helping, the new medication seemed to enhance Morgan's symptoms, causing severe trembling.

Unable to sit still, he would leave the ward for hours at a time and wander the hospital grounds. Walking rapidly over the melting remnants of the last snowfall of the year, he would mutter aloud to himself, "Hold on. Hold on. Hold on."

It was a Friday night, and the regular ward staff had gone home for the weekend. Stammering, Morgan had told the weekend nurse that he needed something because he felt as if he were going to explode. She smiled maternally at him and scribbled something on his chart, but said nothing.

Several hours later the nurse summoned Morgan to her station. "Doctor Phelps has prescribed a new medication for you. Which hip do you want it in?"

"What kind of medicine is it?" he asked.

"It really doesn't matter, Mr. Preston, whether you know the name of it or not as long as it helps you to get better," she said, the syringe poised in her hand.

He acquiesced and pulled down his trousers.

A half hour later, whatever had originally set off his relapse was now aggravated to an intolerable intensity. The synergistic action of the medication and mental illness were driving him out of his mind.

Whimpering, he crawled under his bed in the darkened room and groveled on the cold tiles.

"God, help me!" he pleaded.

"Will somebody help me?" he yelled, writhing under the bed, his mind on fire.

He did not hear the attendant approaching but squinted as the man's flashlight beam speared his eyes.

"Help me," shrilled Morgan.

"What'sa matter, Mr. Preston? You having a nightmare?" asked the attendant.

"I can't stand it. I'm going to explode. Help me. Lock me up. I can't . . ." Morgan's mind began to give way at the edges.

"Can't hear you, Mr. Preston. Don't you think you'd be more comfortable in your bed instead of beneath it?"

Morgan had gone completely rigid.

With an inhuman shout he came to life, arching his back and heaving upward. The bed raised off the floor amid a flurry of sheets, blankets, and pillows.

Men in the beds on both sides of him sat bolt upright and began swearing.

Morgan lunged for the attendant. Before the startled

man could react, Morgan was upon him, clawing frantically at the front of the man's shirt.

"Please lock me up! Please. I can't hold on much longer. I can't control myself."

"O.K., Mr. Preston. Why don't we go down to the nurse's station and see what she says?"

"Yes. Oh, God, yes. C'mon, we gotta hurry. I can't control it."

The nurse at the duty station took one look at Morgan and called the duty doctor.

While waiting for the physician to arrive on ward, Morgan ate cigarets. Totally beyond the ability to execute lighting and puffing, he jammed two and three cigarets at a time into his mouth, filters and all. He ground them between his teeth and swallowed the bitter mess.

The attendant, inured to the idiosyncrasies of the insane, just watched him. "You take 'em like that, you'll run out of your monthly ration, Mr. Preston," he said without sarcasm.

"Can't help it!" said Morgan through chattering teeth. "It's not me doing this. I'm not me. I'm sorry."

"Shoo, don't apologize to me, Mr. Preston," soothed the attendant.

The doctor arrived and gave Morgan an injection that he could hardly stand still for. The nurse and the attendant had to hold him at the waist. He never felt the needle penetrate the skin of his buttock but groaned as the cold medication shot into him.

Two more attendants arrived and led him away between them.

"You gonna put me back on the locked ward?"

"That's what you wanted."

"Thank you. Thank you."

The attendants led him down a hallway, unlocking doors in front of them. Reaching the hall elevator, they stopped while one of them inserted a key into the door's mechanism.

Morgan stiffened.

"This isn't the way to the locked ward. Where are you taking me?"

Both men turned to watch him warily while one of them moved around behind him.

"Hey, man, there's more than one locked ward in this place."

"But I want to go back on the one I came from. They know me there. They know how to take care of me."

"Shit," replied the attendant with the key, "there ain't no takin' care of you crazies. They's just keepin' you in line." His voice took on an ominous tinge. "An' you gonna keep your ass in line."

The two attendants entered the elevator with Morgan sandwiched between them. The door closed behind them. The elevator lifted silently two floors, then stopped. The door rattled open; the three men stepped out and walked down a short corridor until they stood in front of a massive wooden door.

"Here's your new home," the first attendant said as he inserted a key into the lock.

The attendant behind Morgan said softly, "This motherfucker must be crazy. Onliest one I ever heard of who *wanted* to be locked up."

Vertigo hammered at Morgan. He began falling and reached out, grasping the shirt on the back of the first attendant. The burly man whirled and smashed an elbow into Morgan's ribs.

"Don't you go grabbing me, motherfucker," he raged.

Morgan caromed off the hallway wall and fell to the floor.

"I can't see right," Morgan whimpered. "It's not you. I just can't see right."

His vision was shattering. Strobelike and prismatic, he was seeing hundreds of particulated images in rapid and random patterns, sometimes sideways, sometimes upside down. The effect was terrifying.

The attendant who had elbowed him squatted down and waved his fist in front of Morgan's face. "See this, motherfucker? You grab at me again, and you ain't gonna need to see nothing. Now get your ass up and inside.''

"Help me," pleaded Morgan.

"Help your own ass," retorted the attendant. "You the one who got it here."

Morgan crawled toward the doorway. In actuality he was crawling toward several since his vision remained fragmented. His hands found the opening, and he scuttled inside the room.

The attendants came in after him, locking the door after themselves.

"Now you just stay there and be a good boy," ordered the first attendant.

Morgan lay to the right of the door. He tried to sit up but couldn't. He rolled over on his side. He buried his face in his arms and wished he could cry. This ward was a locked ward similar in size to the one he had initially been admitted to when he had come to the hospital four and a half months previously. The only significant differences were that this ward had a kitchen built right into it so that the patients never had to leave, and all of the patients were old men, unshaven and unkempt, who wandered aimlessly in gray bathrobes.

In one corner of the room Morgan saw an old man sitting on the floor, his hands working at mounding up something like clay. Morgan squinted until his eyes were horizontal slits. He realized that the man was molding shit. With that recognition, Morgan's nostrils flared with the assaultive stench of feces, urine, and unwashed bodies. Gorge rose in his throat. He forced it down and looked again at the man compiling his feces. This time, because of whatever was wrong with his vision, he saw six men.

I'm in hell, he concluded.

A moment of crystalline lucidity flashed across Morgan's mind: If this is all an hallucination, then I should be killed because I cannot take any more of it. And if this is really happening, then I should be killed because I cannot take any more of it.

"KILL ME!" he screamed. No one came to kill him. Instead, he lay there and suffered.

He was aware of harsh breathing near him. Turning his head, he saw a yellow-fanged monster contemplating him. The monster growled as it extended a claw toward Morgan's shoulder.

"Hello," said the monster, a smile on his face. His hand dropped gently on Morgan's shoulder. "What's your name, sonny?"

Morgan recoiled at the monster's touch.

"I'm . . . I'm . . ." And then with terror Morgan said, "OGODIDON'TKNOWWHOIAMANYMORE!"

"That's O.K.," comforted the monster, patting his shoulder. "You'll find out again."

"Will I?" pleaded Morgan. "Will I really?"

"Sure," soothed the monster. "Everyone knows who they are sooner or later."

"When will I know?" Morgan asked frantically.

"You'll know when you know, sonny," he said, shrugging. "That's all any of us know."

"Thank you," said Morgan.

"You're welcome," affably replied the monster. "But when you find out who you are, then you owe me a favor."

"What's that?"

The monster smiled sadly. "You'll have to help me find out who I am."

— 68 —

A mistake had been made. Morgan had been led off to the wrong ward. Realizing this, the two orderlies came for him and took him to the proper locked ward.

"Please tie me down," he begged the nurse. "I think I'm going to get violent."

"If you do, we'll tie you down for sure," she told him. He wandered around the ward for a while and then, not able to hold out from his encroaching madness any longer, he picked up a chair and hurled it at a window.

Two attendants grabbed him and carried him to the seclusion room. He lay on the bed while they secured leather restraints around his wrists and ankles. He thanked them as they left, closing the soundproofed door behind them.

Morgan looked at the wall and saw a shape forming. He began screaming as he watched the Devil separate from the wall and crouch in the corner, his long barbed tail sweeping sinuously across the tiled floor.

Still screaming, Morgan fought against the leather restraints. The Devil stood up and on cloven hooves slowly advanced on him, his white horns gleaming. Standing eight feet tall, he smiled, revealing upper and lower canine teeth glistening with saliva. Morgan began praying for his own death. He prayed that his heart would burst, ending this unendurable horror. Blood dripped from where the leather restraints chafed him. As the world went black around him, the last thing he heard was Satan's mocking, triumphant laughter.

— 69 —

Morgan was spoon-fed by a black woman who spoke calmly to him, and he was given around-the-clock injections of medication. The abrasions on his wrists and ankles were cleaned, smeared with ointment, and bandaged.

Two attendants came into the room and removed his restraints. They helped him to his feet and ushered him into the dayroom. He held onto them for support. He squinted against the harsh sunlight which shot through the ward's windows.

"How do you feel?" asked a doctor.

"Everything's too real," replied Morgan. "The people and furniture seem to be glowing. It's been a long day, and my throat hurts."

"It has been three days, Mr. Preston. You screamed continuously for the first two. You need some rest now." The two attendants helped him shuffle back to the seclusion room, but this time they did not put the restraints on him.

— 70 —

The new medication made Morgan pace involuntarily.

He put on his coat and went out the dayroom door to the patio. The bare concrete floor of the patio and its steel-meshed walls gave it the appearance of a cage. He began pacing the length of the patio.

Snow was falling outside, and he watched the huge flakes slowly settle to the ground. The temperature was near freezing.

His feet swelled up and blistered, after pacing for about two hours. He removed his shoes and continued pacing, trying to force his mind to forget where he was and what he was doing. His socks quickly became soggy on the wet concrete. He paused, pulled them off, then continued pacing. Like an animal, he thought, like some poor dumb animal in a zoo.

The cold of the concrete floor worked up through the soles of his feet, numbing them. His teeth began to chatter.

He continued pacing.

The blisters on his feet broke. He tried to ignore the pain. Then the foot that had been wounded in Vietnam began to ache; Morgan limped and kept pacing.

How long? he asked himself.

The balls and heels of his feet began bleeding; smears of blood marked the circuit of his pacing. The bloody trail became more distinct with each step.

The ankle on his bad foot gave way; Morgan pitched forward and grabbed the mesh wall in order to keep from falling. He supported himself as he looked out into the dusk of yet another endless night. Snow was still falling.

Fifty yards in front of him stood a line of tall, old trees, their branches stark and fragile-looking. He wanted to walk over to them and touch them, and press his cheek against their cold, rough bark that girded them.

He pushed himself away from the wall and began pacing again. The injured ankle slowed him considerably, but he continued until an orderly came to the door and told him to come inside for the night. Morgan complied, first picking up his shoes and now-frozen socks.

The track of blood he left behind on the concrete floor congealed, then froze.

Inside the ward Morgan continued pacing long after lights out. He walked barefoot up and down one side of the corridor between the dayroom and the sleeping area, while Gibbons, muttering frantically to himself, paced the other side of the corridor. Both were locked in the grimness of their journeys which led them nowhere except around and around.

— 71 —

June 1969. Morgan paced continuously for two weeks, stopping only to sleep, and then he slowed down and began recovering again. In short order he was returned to an open ward where he resumed his routine of occupational therapy, sitting in the coffee shop, taking long walks around the grounds, and playing cards with some of his fellow patients.

In mid-June he was summoned to the psychiatrist's office. He sat across the desk from the doctor, a tall man in his sixties who wore wire-rimmed glasses.

"Well, Mr. Preston, how do you feel?"

"Fine."

"Are you still hearing voices?"

"No."

"Seeing unusual things?"

"No."

The doctor leaned forward. "Do you feel you're ready to leave and get on with rest of your life?"

"Yes," Morgan said. "I've already been here too long."

"Some things take time," the doctor murmured. "And time heals."

"I've always been impatient," Morgan said.

"Remember, Mr. Preston, after you leave it is still important for you to take medication. It will help keep your thoughts from becoming confused. Also, I think it would be wise for you to find employment as soon as possible."

"I'll do that," promised Morgan.

"Good. Do you have any questions?"

"More of a complaint, actually."

"And that is?"

"I'm still having nightmares about the war almost every night." The doctor dropped his chin to his chest momentarily, then raised his head. "Your nightmares may last only a few months or perhaps a lifetime. Unfortunately, we don't know much about dreams. You'll simply have to put up with them."

"Dr. Parrish, I have another question."

"Yes?"

"Will I ever get sick again? I mean, is it over or will it happen again?"

The doctor pursed his lips for several seconds, then said, "To be perfectly candid, Mr. Preston, there's no way of telling. But I have the feeling that in your case, if you continue taking your medication regularly, go easy on the beer, and abstain from drugs, you'll make out adequately."

"How about sex?" Morgan asked, smiling. "Do I have to abstain from that, too?"

The doctor cackled heartily. "Mr. Preston, considering your age and hormonal composition, I shall be happy to write a prescription ordering sex for you, PRN.''

"What's PRN?"

"As needed," Dr. Parrish said. Morgan joined him in laughter.

Three weeks later, after having been hospitalized for more than six months, Morgan was released.

— 72 —

During the drive home from the hospital, Morgan's father and stepmother insisted that he stay with them, at least until he found a job and got his feet back under him.

Morgan did not do much except eat, sleep, and watch television during the first week at his father's home. Late at night he would slip out the back door and walk for hours, with no particular destination in mind, then return to the house, climb into bed, fall asleep, and have nightmares: faces of dead soldiers, American and Vietnamese; napalmed bodies; helicopters plummeting to the ground; voices murmuring, babbling, crying, shrieking, begging. When he woke up in the morning from these tortured dreams, Morgan was so tired that he felt he had not slept.

On his second Saturday night home, Morgan decided

he was ready to venture out. He showered and shaved, used his father's Right Guard and Old Spice, put on a blue shirt, jeans, and shoes, and went out to his car.

The town he lived in was not very large, so he arrived at the bar in less than six minutes. He turned off the ignition and sat with his hands tightly gripping the steering wheel. I can do it, he told himself. I'm no different from anyone else. I can do it.

He got out of the car and walked to the bar. When he reached the door he noticed his hand trembling slightly. He took a deep breath and opened the door.

The bar, complete with brass rail, ran the length of the right side of the room. To the left were tables, and a few of them were occupied by groups of three or four people. At the far end of the bar three young men sat on stools. Morgan walked up to the bar and sat on the nearest stool. The barmaid took his order for a draft beer, drew it, and set it in front of him.

Morgan sipped his beer, savoring its taste and coldness as it went down his throat. So far, so good, he thought. I don't feel as self-conscious as I thought I would.

"Hey, Morgan," someone at the far end of the bar shouted. "Morgan Preston."

Morgan looked at the three men seated at the bar. One of them waved at him. It was Duane Arnold, a gregarious jock with whom Morgan had graduated.

"C'mon over, Preston," Duane yelled. "I ain't seen you in a coon's age."

Morgan grabbed his glass, got off the stool, and walked up to Duane. They shook hands. Duane's face was flushed from too much alcohol.

"How the hell you been?" he asked.

"Fair," said Morgan. "How about you?"

"Shit, things couldn't be better. I got an old lady and two rug rats, and the construction business is booming."

"That's good to hear," Morgan said. He noticed that

Duane's two companions were staring at him, and he felt uncomfortable.

"Who are your friends, Duane?"

"Oh. Sorry. I should have introduced you when you came over. Morgan, meet Jack and Barney. Guys, this is Morgan. He just got out of the nut house because he wanted to kill people when he came back from Vietnam."

The silence following Duane's statement was crushing. Morgan's face turned crimson. He saw Jack and Barney looking at him with a mixture of shock, fear, and suspicion. He turned to Duane. "Where'd you hear that?" he quietly asked.

"Shit, man," Duane said, "you know how you hear things in a small town. When I first heard it I figured, what the hell, anybody's bound to come home a little fucked up from Vietnam."

"I never came home wanting to shoot anybody, Duane."

Duane shrugged. "I'm just repeating what I heard."

"You heard wrong. I did have to be hospitalized for a while, but it didn't have anything to do with violence." Barney and Jack listened intently to the conversation.

"It's nothing to feel ashamed about. Hell, I feel like shooting my old lady about twice a year," Duane said, laughing.

Morgan set his glass on the bar. "I gotta go," he said.

"What's the rush?" Duane asked. "We're just getting started."

"I just gotta go."

Duane shrugged. "If you gotta, you gotta."

Morgan looked at Barney and Jack. "Nice meeting you guys." They said nothing and refused to meet his eyes. Morgan turned and walked to the door, feeling the three men's eyes on him all the way.

— 73 —

Morgan drove to Flint and parked outside one of the auto plants. A security guard gave him directions to the employment office.

In the outer office a middle-aged woman with a bee-hive hairdo gave him an employment application. He sat at a long table and filled it out. When he was finished he got up and handed the papers to the woman. "Have a seat," she said, then disappeared into an office whose door bore the sign: Personnel Director. The woman returned to the outer room and sat behind her desk, filing her nails.

Ten minutes later the personnel director appeared in the doorway. He was about thirty-five and wore wire-rimmed glasses.

"Mr. Preston," he said. "Please come with me." Morgan followed him into the office.

"I'm Mr. Buehler," the man said, shaking hands with Morgan. "Why don't you have a seat right there?" Buehler went around his desk and sat in his swivel chair, then picked up Morgan's application papers. He leafed through them slowly, his lips pursed. Finally, he said, "I see that you pumped gas while you were in high school, then served in the army."

"Air force," Morgan politely corrected.

"Ah, yes. The air force. Off we go and all of that, right?"

"Something like that."

"Mr. Preston, the only discrepancy I see here is a lack of employment from October 1968 to the present. That's, ah, nine months. Seems like a mighty long vacation to me."

"I was in a mental institution," said Morgan.

"Oh," said Buehler, licking his lips. "Well, I see." He squirmed uncomfortably in his chair.

"I thought if I told you about it straight out, we could

get it out of the way," explained Morgan.

"I see," said Buehler. "I certainly do admire your forthrightness."

"Thank you. I figured that if I lied about it and put some phony job down to cover those months, you'd hire me. But if you found out later that I had lied, you'd boot me out the door."

"Well," said Buehler, "we certainly don't like falsified applications. As much as I appreciate your honesty, Mr. Praxton . . ."

"Preston."

"Of course, Mr. *Preston*. As I was saying, as much as I appreciate your honesty, I cannot hire you."

"Why not?" Morgan asked.

Buehler's face turned red. "That ad in the paper was supposed to be pulled a week ago. All our positions are filled."

"The security guard at the gate said you hired more than twenty guys yesterday," said Morgan.

Buehler cleared his throat. "That was yesterday, Mr. Preston. Today is an entirely different matter. I'm afraid there's nothing here for you." Buehler stood and extended his hand to Morgan. He rejected it and left the office without saying a word. Buehler then took Morgan's application form, tore it in two, and dropped it in the wastebasket.

— 74 —

For the rest of the week Morgan hunted for a job. Some prospective employers turned him down simply because he was unqualified for the positions offered, but the majority rejected him because of his psychiatric record.

His last interview, on a Friday afternoon, had been with an obese, chain-smoking man who read Morgan's application and then told him that he could not hire him.

Morgan thanked him and stood, ready to leave. The fat man leaned forward in his chair and in a confidential voice said, "I was never in the service myself, but tell me, how many of those gooks did you kill?" His eyes glittered with anticipation.

Morgan stared into the man's piggish eyes, recognized his need for a vicarious thrill, and felt overriding contempt.

"I've never killed anyone," he said.

The man seemed to deflate and leaned back in his chair. He looked at Morgan with a mixture of disappointment and disgust.

"Not even one? What the hell kind of a soldier were you?"

Morgan pondered the question for a moment. "An honorable one," he said, and left.

That night, discouraged, Morgan went to a bar at the edge of town. He found an empty stool and perched on it. The band's music was loud, insistent, sexual. All the tables were occupied, the dance floor was crowded. Everyone seemed to be enjoying themselves, laughing, talking, yelling; healthy young people raising a little hell.

"What are you having?" asked a cute blonde barmaid.

"Hi," he said. "Just a draft." She smiled, revealing one front tooth that slightly overlapped the other. "Coming up," she said and disappeared. She returned with the beer and placed it in front of him. When he paid her she flashed him another smile. He smiled back.

Maybe she likes me, he thought. Or maybe they taught her to smile at bartender's school. Or, he concluded, maybe she just likes to smile.

When his glass was three-quarters empty, she returned. "Ready for another one?" she asked. Again the smile.

"Sure," Morgan said. The band was on a break when she brought the beer. He paid her, but she did not move away; instead, she studied his face intently, then said, "nice eyes."

"What?"

"You have nice eyes. Dark brown and piercing. I bet you can look right into someone's head and tell what they're thinking."

"Not really. I only see the things that other people do."

"How old are you?" she asked.

"Twenty-one."

"Your eyes look a lot older. They look like they've seen a lot of things."

Morgan shrugged. "A few."

"You're a mysterious dude. What's your name?"

"Morgan Preston. What's yours?"

"Carol Bisalkis."

"Nice smile."

"This?" she said, pointing to her mouth. "I'm saving my tips to get braces. I have the smile of a beaver."

They both laughed.

Morgan finished his beer. "You up to another one?" Carol asked.

"Sure."

She went off, drew the beer, and returned to him. "It's on the house."

"Thanks."

"Are you from around here, Morgan? I've never seen you before."

"Born and raised here, but I've been away for about four years."

"To a mysterious place, I'll bet."

"Vietnam."

"Oh. What a bummer."

Morgan shrugged.

"You married?" she asked.

"Nope."

"Engaged?"

"Nope."

"Good."

"Why's that?"

"Because if you're single, I can ask you out."

"You can ask me out?"

"Sure. Geez, you have been away a long time. You ever heard of women's liberation?"

"Rings a dim bell."

"Well, that's what's happening. Even Dear Abby says its O.K. to ask a guy out."

"And I don't have anything to say about it?"

"Honey, all you have to say is yes, then show up on time."

Morgan laughed. "Yes, I'll take you out, or let you take me out, or however it works."

"Now you're talking, Morgan. Let me give you my address." She took a pen and wrote on the back of a napkin, and handed it to him. He read the address and tucked the napkin into his pocket.

"When do we do it?" he asked.

"I'm off tomorrow night. Why don't you pick me up around eight?"

"Where should we go?"

"Any place where we can talk; I want to get into your mysteriousness."

"And what do I get into?" he asked mischievously.

Carol laughed. "With me you'll probably get into trouble."

"Good trouble or bad trouble?"

She smiled sexily. "Hey, we'll talk about it. But right now I've got to get back to work."

"I'm about ready to leave anyway," he said.

"That's cool. Eight o'clock. Don't forget. Bye."

Morgan left the bar and drove, but he didn't go home. It was too early, and he was too elated. A date, he thought. Contact. A girl with whom to talk, to touch and, perhaps, to make love. An end to loneliness.

Slow down, he told himself. You haven't taken her out yet. And when you do, and if you get involved, sooner or later you'll have to tell her about the hospital, and then what? Would she understand? He thought about this for several minutes, then concluded that anyone who had such a great smile and personality as she had would understand just about anything.

The night was warm and muggy; Morgan grew thirsty. He stopped at a mom and pop store, and bought two six-packs of beer.

He drove slowly on the country roads, loose and happy, drinking beer and listening to the radio. He swerved once, spilling beer on his shirt, when a possum waddled across the road.

After four beers his mood changed; he did not know that alcohol was a depressant. His thoughts of the cute lap-toothed barmaid were supplanted with the rejections by the employment personnel during the past week. He thought of the fat man who had asked him how many Vietnamese he had killed, as if killing men was the epitome of masculinity. I probably would have been hired, he thought sardonically, if I had told the asshole that I killed so many I lost count.

And that dumbshit Duane, he thought, telling me that it's all over town that I came back wanting to kill people. How can I defend myself against a rumor like that? Take an ad in the paper telling everyone that I'm

not a killer? That I'm just lonely? That I have nightmares? That I need love?

He knew that a lot of people in small towns loved
rumors, the juicier the better; that they got a cheap thrill
out of the tiniest bit of gossip. He stopped the car, got
out, and relieved himself.

"Fuck 'em," he murmured, zipping up. He returned
to the car and drove on.

— 75 —

Saturday, 7:55 P.M. Morgan stood on the porch
and rang the doorbell. Carol Bisalkis opened the door.
She wasn't smiling, and her eyes were wary. She crossed
her arms.

"Hi," Morgan said. "You ready to go?"

"We're not going anywhere," she said, her voice flat.

"Are you sick? Maybe we could make it another
night."

"You're the one who's sick," she said.

"What are you talking about? I feel fine."

"I'm talking about the dishonorable discharge you
got."

"What?" Morgan was incredulous. "What dishonorable discharge?"

"You know. The one they gave you for being a sex
pervert."

"I don't believe this."

DAU 239

"I do, because my mother told me when I got up this morning. I mentioned to her that I had a date with Morgan Preston, and she told me the whole story. She heard it from one of her friends."

"Well, it's a lie," Morgan said. "I've got my DD Two Fourteen right in my wallet. It's a copy of my separation papers. I can prove that I have an honorable discharge." He pulled out his wallet, found the paper, and held it out to her.

Carol made a face of disgust. "I don't even want to touch anything that belongs to a pervert."

"Just look at it, will you?" Morgan pleaded.

"I'm not interested," she said. "And I'm not interested in talking to you anymore, so why don't you just leave?"

"You won't look at the paper?"

"Man, I don't even want to look at you. I don't know what your perversions are, but I hope the cops keep a close watch on you."

Morgan gave up and put the paper back into his wallet. He looked at her and tried to smile. "Good-bye, Carol. I'm sorry you won't believe me."

She shrugged indifferently. "And another thing. You're no longer welcome at the bar. If you show up, I'll have you bounced." With that she closed the door.

Morgan walked woodenly to his car and got in. His face burned with humiliation. Another rumor, he thought. No one gets the story straight, but they sure do love the rumors, and it's costing me. He started the car and slowly drove away.

— 76 —

Two weeks later, on a cool September evening, Morgan loaded the last of his possessions into the trunk of his car and slammed it shut. He walked over to his father and stepmother.

"You're sure we can't talk you into staying?" his father asked worriedly.

"Let me think," Morgan said. "I've applied for fourteen, no, fifteen jobs, and I've been turned down fifteen times. I'm living in a small town where some of the people think I came back from Vietnam wanting to kill people and where other people think I got a bad paper discharge for being a pervert. Oh, yeah, I don't think you've heard the latest one. I'm now putting heroin in my arm and selling drugs to support my habit. They've got me pegged as a drug-crazed Vietnam vet pervert who's going to shoot up Main Street." He laughed bitterly. "No, Dad, I really don't think you can talk me into staying."

"You don't know a soul in Los Angeles," said his stepmother.

"And no one there knows me. At least I'll have a clean start." He hugged his stepmother, kissing her on the cheek, then turned to his father. They started to shake hands but ended up hugging each other tightly.

"I love you, son. I don't like to see you hurt like this."

"That's exactly why I'm leaving," Morgan said. "To escape the pain. I had enough of it in Vietnam and in the hospitals. If I had come home with an arm or leg blown off, people would say, 'Oh, he was in Vietnam.' But since my wound doesn't show, they can't understand it. They fear it. They think it might rub off on them."

He got into the car and started it. His stepmother waved.

"Take care," said his father.

"I will," Morgan said. "I've got to." He backed the car down the driveway and swung into the street. Minutes later, when he passed a sign marking the city's limit, he didn't bother to look into the rearview mirror.

•   •   •

Morgan reached Los Angeles in three and a half days. His first impression of the sprawling megalopolis, with its multitude of pedestrians and countless cars on the multilaned freeways, was that of an overturned human anthill; frenetic, disorganized activity.

He bought a Thomas Brothers Guide to Los Angeles County, then a newspaper, and turned to the apartment rental pages. In a short time he was inspecting a studio apartment near Wilshire and Western. The tiny apartment didn't have air conditioning, but it was clean and furnished, and the price was right. Morgan paid the manager, a jovial Greek named Kokkinakos, first and last month's rent plus a security deposit, and moved in.

Exhausted, he turned in early, sprawling on the sofa bed. The air in the apartment was sweltering; his body became sweat-slicked. He tossed and turned restlessly.

A dream formed in his mind. He was in a landing craft heading for an enemy-held beach. In his hands he cradled an M-60 machine gun; the belt of ammunition attached to it was ten or twelve feet long. The landing craft's ramp opened. Enemy bullets hit all around him, ricochets whining away. He aimed the machine gun at the beach and began firing as he advanced. The water was thigh-deep, and as he moved forward the ammunition belt entangled his legs. He tripped and fell headlong into the water. Salt stung his eyes. He needed air; his lungs ached. He tried to struggle to his feet, but the ammo belt prevented him from rising. He could hold his breath no longer. His mouth opened in a desperate search for oxygen; water filled his throat, drowning him.

Morgan woke up choking. After a few minutes he

calmed down, smoked a cigaret, then took a long cold
shower. He returned to the sofa bed and stared at the
ceiling. Two hours and many cigarets later he managed
to fall asleep.

•   •   •

Morgan spent the next week learning his way around
the city; then he went looking for work. The first place
he tried was the City of Los Angeles Municipal Department.

"I don't care if you spent six months in a nuthouse or
an outhouse," the burly personnel manager told him
gruffly. "As long as you do a man's work, you'll be
paid a man's wages. You like to work outside?"

"Sure," Morgan said.

"Good. I'll put you in the Parks Department. When
do you want to start?"

"Tomorrow's fine."

"Be at the observatory in Griffith Park by eight.
Your supervisor's name is Larry Gerard. He'll tell you
what to do. Now give this paper to my secretary, and
she'll give you some forms to fill out."

Morgan took the paper, rose, and shook the man's
hand. "Thanks for the break," he said.

The manager brusquely waved off Morgan's gratitude. "You know," he said in a soft voice, "my son was
in Vietnam. He was a lieutenant in the infantry."

"Oh, yeah? Does he live in LA?"

The manager's voice regained its gruffness. "He's in
Forest Lawn Cemetery. Now get out of here. I've got a
lot of work to do."

— 77 —

Morgan enjoyed working in the Parks Department. He was assigned to a crew of six men whose job it was to mow grass, trim weeds, pick up trash, prune trees, and monitor the irrigation system. Every week or so the crew moved to a different park, performing the same tasks. There were also daily euchre breaks; Gerard, the crew supervisor, proved to be the most enthuiastic player.

Although Morgan engaged in the crew's bawdy banter and joined in the card games, he kept himself emotionally aloof. He missed the camaraderie he had had in Vietnam, and he felt somewhat ill at ease among his co-workers, whom he considered to be good men but civilians: people who could not begin to understand what Morgan and other soldiers had experienced and were still experiencing as the war continued unabated. When Friday evenings came the crew picked up their paychecks and went to a nearby bar for several hours of drinking and bullshitting.

Morgan never went with them. Instead, he would go to Korrey's Klub on Beverly Boulevard and drink alone while listening to the jukebox. After a few hours he would leave, eat a couple of burgers, return to his apartment, and watch television until he fell asleep.

Nightmares continued to plague him.

Morgan reserved his weekends for the beach at Santa Monica. On a warm afternoon in December he was stretched out on a blanket, face up, lazily engaged in a semi-erotic daydream while his body absorbed the sun's tanning rays. Nearby, two girls chattered amiably as they tossed a Frisbee between them.

Suddenly, something slashed painfully across Morgan's right eye and the bridge of his nose. He instantly sat up, his hands covering his injured eye.

"Are you O.K.?" asked a feminine voice. Morgan

looked with his good eye and saw kneeling at his side a cute young woman with long chestnut hair, freckles across her nose, and concern in her green eyes.

"My eye won't open right now," he replied, "but I think it'll be O.K. What hit me?"

"My Frisbee," she said. "I'm really sorry. You'd better let me look at it." Her slender fingers pulled at his hands. He resisted.

"I'm a nurse," she said. "I'd really like to look at your eye. It could be serious."

Morgan relented, and while she expertly probed the injured area, he used his good eye to survey her petite, bikini-clad body.

"You're eye is O.K.," she said, "but the upper lid is swelling. You should have some ice on it."

"I don't have any ice."

"I'll get some at the concession stand. It's not far. I'll be right back."

Returning shortly with a Styrofoam cup containing shaved ice, she had Morgan lay down and applied the ice to his injury.

"You said you were a nurse," Morgan began. "What hospital do you work at?"

"Hollywood Presbyterian," she answered. "I work on the OB ward."

"What's OB?"

"Obstetrics. Babies and mothers. What do you do?" He told her, then said, "I think we should introduce ourselves. I'm Morgan Preston."

"Hi, Morgan. I'm Rhonda Galloway." She smiled warmly. "You're going to have pain for a while. I think you should go home and take it easy for the rest of the day."

"Whatever you say," Morgan said, sitting up. "What do I owe you?"

Rhonda looked puzzled. "Why should you owe me anything?"

"Because you're a nurse, and you treated me."

She smiled. "I was the one who hurt you. If anything, I owe you."

"O.K.," Morgan said. "If that's the way you feel, then go to a movie with me tonight. Or out to dinner. Or anywhere."

Rhonda paused. "I don't think so."

Morgan looked crestfallen.

"What I mean is, I really do want you to rest your eye." She smiled. "And if you feel better tomorrow, give me a call, and we'll take it from there. I'm in the Glendale phone book."

"Great," he said. "You can count on the call." He picked up his blanket and car keys, ready to leave. "Thanks for the first aid."

Rhonda shrugged, smiling. "My pleasure." Morgan said good-bye and headed toward the parking lot.

— 78 —

Sunday night, Morgan and Rhonda took in an early movie, then went to the Flower Drum, a Chinese restaurant on Hollywood Boulevard that specialized in Yunnan cuisine. The young couple's conversation was light and animated, and punctuated with laughter, particularly when Morgan futilely tried to teach Rhonda how to use chopsticks.

When they had finished eating, their hostess gave them hand towels, and placed on the table a dish holding a pair of fortune cookies.

"Open yours first," suggested Morgan. Rhonda crumbled the cookie and plucked out the piece of paper. "It says, 'Kindness in giving creates love.' " She smiled. "That's a nice sentiment. I'm going to keep it. Now it's your turn."

Morgan cracked his fortune cookie open like an egg; the paper dropped to the table. He picked it up and read, "A long journey awaits you."

"Sounds mysterious and exciting," mused Rhonda. "Where do you think this long journey will take you?"

He furrowed his brow for five seconds, then said, "Disneyland."

Rhonda laughed. "Disneyland? That's only forty miles from here."

Morgan shrugged. "It's long enough for me."

"You're crazy," she said, laughing. Her words made him flinch internally, even though he knew she had said them in jest.

He smiled cryptically. "That's what they all say." He picked up his glass, downed the beer, and signalled for the check.

When they arrived at her apartment, Rhonda invited him in. He sat on the couch in the neat, spacious living room while Rhonda disappeared into the kitchen. She returned with glasses of iced Amaretto laced with cream. She gave him his drink and turned on the radio. Soft rock music filled the room. She came to the couch and sat next to him, her legs tucked under her.

"Is that K-O-K-O?" he asked, referring to the radio station.

"Yep. I listen to it mainly to hear the dee-jay."

"Tommy Wallace?"

"Right. He has the most mellow voice on the coast. I met him once."

"What's he look like?"

"A Viking. Tall, with red hair and a red beard. And glasses."

"What kind of Viking wears glasses?" he bantered.

Rhonda shrugged. "A nearsighted one, I guess." They laughed together.

For the first hour or so, Morgan and Rhonda talked about inconsequential things and sipped at their drinks, which Rhonda regularly freshened. As the night wore on their conversation became more serious. Bit by bit they revealed personal things about themselves: Rhonda related how she had grown up in a small town in central Wisconsin and had moved to Los Angeles three days after receiving her degree in nursing. She told Morgan that she enjoyed working in obstetrics and had a special affinity for premature babies.

"They look so helpless," she said, "but they're real fighters. Sometimes I want to bring them all home with me."

Morgan told her that he had also come from a small town and had served in the air force. He did not mention Vietnam. He asked for another drink. She brought it to him, then sat down and put her hand on his knee. He looked into her eyes; they were gentle, and the green was flecked with gold.

Morgan put down his drink. His hands went to her shoulders; his fingers touched the warm nape of her slender neck. Their lips met in a soft and lingering kiss. When it ended they held each other for a long time, each luxuriating in the other's touch.

"I think we've started something," Morgan said, running his fingers lazily through her long hair.

Rhonda smiled. "That's O.K. by me. How about you?"

His answer was another kiss, more passionate than the first.

Rhonda looked at her watch. "It's past three. We both have to work in the morning. I hate to kick you out, but . . ."

"One more drink," he said. "Please fix me one more drink, then I'll go." Rhonda fixed the Amaretto and gave it to him. "Thanks." He gulped it down.

Rhonda walked him to the door. After a final kiss she touched his cheek and looked at his eyes searchingly. "You know, your eyes were the first thing I noticed about you at the beach. Or, rather I should say your eye, because the other one was swollen shut. They're so dark and intense. Where did you get them?"

"I'm part Indian," Morgan explained.

"Well, they're beautiful. And bloodshot. And a little glazed. Are you drunk?"

"Just a slight buzz," he said, smiling.

"It was that last drink. You're supposed to sip them, not guzzle them like a a barbarian. Can you drive?"

"No problem."

"I really enjoyed being with you tonight. Call me tomorrow?"

"Count on it."

"Good night, Morgan."

" 'Night."

Not far from his apartment Morgan was pulled over by the police. Officer Janet Dedic, five-foot-two and incredibly tanned, asked Morgan for his driver's license. She scanned it briefly with her flashlight, then looked at him.

"Mr. Preston, I stopped you because you were weaving. How much have you had to drink?"

"Three or four Amarettos," he admitted.

"You're sure that's all you've had?"

"Well, maybe five. You see, I was with this girl tonight, and we talked a lot and did a little drinking. I don't think I was weaving because of the booze but because I was thinking about her. She's something else!"

"Sure," Officer Dedic said skeptically.

"You don't buy that?"

She laughed. "After being a cop for eight years, I don't buy much of anything. I should give you a courtesy ride to the drunk tank, but I see by your license that you're only two blocks from your residence. So I'm going to give you two choices and leave the decision to you. Sound fair?''

"Yes," said Morgan. "I guess."

"Kid," she said, "either go home or go home."

Morgan grinned. "I'll do both."

"Smart move," said the woman cop, handing him his license.

Morgan started his car and drove away carefully. Officer Dedic approached her partner, Wayne Rendie, who had been trying to light his pipe for the past five minutes without success. "What was his story?" he asked, striking another match.

"Five drinks and a case of the hots." She slid behind the wheel of the patrol car. Rendie was still on the curb fussing with his pipe.

"Wayne," she said wearily, "get that damn thing lit. We gotta go nail some shitbirds."

— 79 —

After their initial date, Morgan and Rhonda became virtually inseparable. In the evenings after work they went out to movies or restaurants or to the Carnation Building, which served the best banana splits in town. Weekends they went to the beach, sometimes as early as dawn; they would walk along the tide line watching sandpipers dart ahead of the incoming waves and taste the salt carried on the morning mist. After a day at the beach they would go to Farmers' Market and sit in the plaza sipping frothy fruit drinks.

Some evenings the couple simply stayed in Rhonda's apartment, talking, having a few drinks, and becoming more mentally and physically intimate. They discovered how many interests and aspirations they shared—and how well they complemented one another. Gradually, inevitably, Morgan and Rhonda fell in love.

One of their favorite places to go was Sarno's, an Italian restaurant on Vermont Avenue where the patrons were entertained nightly by a succession of amateur and professional opera singers accompanied by a pianist. The mood in Sarno's was usually lively and sometimes bordered on the raucous.

One night at Sarno's, Morgan and Rhonda were listening to the singing while they sipped wine and nibbled cheese. Rhonda turned to speak to Morgan and noticed that he was lost in concentration; his face appeared troubled.

"What's wrong, honey?" she asked.

Morgan sighed. "I need to talk to you. Can we get out of here?"

"Sure," she said, puzzled.

They drove to her apartment in silence. Inside, Morgan sat on the sofa, his tension palpable. Rhonda sat next to him and took his hand in hers. She searched his eyes and saw pain and apprehension.

He cleared his throat. "I should have told you about this before we became so involved, but I couldn't. I thought I'd lose you, and after you hear this, I probably will."

She squeezed his hand. "Morgan, nothing you could say would drive me away. I love you too much."

"This might change your mind."

She smiled. "Try me."

Morgan took a deep, ragged breath and said, "I was

in Vietnam. I got sick. When I came back I had to be hospitalized in a mental institution. Now you know." He watched her eyes intently, expecting to see fear and rejection. Instead, he saw compassion and love.

Rhonda embraced him tightly. "Oh, Morgan, Morgan. You must have been so lonely. It must have been awful."

"No one knows how bad it is except for the people who've been through it," he said. "There's no such thing as a Funny Farm."

Rhonda looked at him; tears glistened on her cheeks. "I still love you," she said fiercely. "And I always will."

"And I love you. I wanted to tell you about my past so that if you didn't throw me out, I could ask you something."

"What?"

"Will you marry me?" he asked solemnly.

Rhonda began crying again, but she was smiling. "Yes," she said. "Yes, I will." They hugged; their lips met tenderly. After a few minutes, Rhonda stood, grasped Morgan by the wrists, and whispered, "Come."

She led him into her bedroom. They undressed wordlessly and moved toward each other. Moonlight filtered through the window, bathing their bodies in a lustrous glow. Rhonda reached out and ran her fingernails lightly through Morgan's chest hair. He cupped one of her breasts, teasing a thumb over the erect nipple.

Hand in hand they moved to the bed. Their bodies joined, sealing with flesh the bond they had already made with their hearts.

• • •

Three months later, in June 1970, Morgan and Rhonda were married in a simple ceremony that was attended by Rhonda's friends from the hospital. After the wedding reception in Chinatown, the newlyweds set off on their honeymoon.

They drove up the coast to Monterey and set up a tent high in the quiet, deeply-forested hills above the bay. Early afternoons they drove to the ocean and picnicked in meadows near the jagged, rocky coastline, laughing at the antics of otters frolicking offshore. Evenings they dined at the Hog's Breath Inn, lingering over wine, arousing each other with eyes and words and discreet touches until, inflamed and engorged, they would return to their tent and make love.

After an idyllic seven days, Morgan and Rhonda reluctantly returned to Los Angeles and settled into Rhonda's apartment. Since they both worked during the day, the nights belonged to them: candlelight dinners at Marina del Rey; Dodger ball games; concerts at the Greek Theater, where they listened to Joni Mitchell, Jose Feliciano, Johnny Mathis, and Crosby, Stills, Nash, and Young. Sarno's was still their favorite spot, and they often returned to the Flower Drum, the site of their first date. Sometimes late at night they would drive up the winding road to the observatory in Griffith Park and stare down at the myriad lights of the city, their arms around each other, standing in the same spot where James Dean had in *Rebel Without a Cause*. Invariably their nights out were capped with bouts of intense love-making. And, naturally, they spent weekends at the beach, lost among and oblivious to tens of thousands of other sun-worshippers.

— 80 —

In September, Morgan had his first nightmare in months. It was uniquely different from past ones in that it contained no fighting or gore, but distinct faces; Easy, who had committed suicide; Dave Bruckner, who had been killed by a VC sniper; and Tam, who had been murdered at My Lai.

The three faces gazed at Morgan, their dark eyes filled with inexpressible sorrow. They said nothing. They waited.

"No," cried Morgan, thrashing wildly. He woke and sat up. His face and torso were beaded with cold sweat; his hands shook uncontrollably.

"What is it, Morg?" asked Rhonda, who had been awakened by his shout and now sat next to him, her hand on his shoulder.

"A nightmare," he said shakily, lighting a cigaret.

"Do you want to talk about it?"

He shrugged. "It was some faces of people that I knew in Vietnam. They were . . . friends."

"They're dead, aren't they?" said Rhonda, offering more of an intuitive statement than a question.

He nodded.

"I'm sorry. Do you want to talk about it? Maybe it would help."

"No," he said, extinguishing his cigaret. He lay down. "I just want to sleep. And forget."

Rhonda lay next to Morgan, stroking his chest for a long time, trying to soothe him. Eventually she fell asleep, but Morgan couldn't. He lay quietly, staring at the darkness, sweating profusely, and earnestly praying that the ghosts of his two friends and lover would never return.

His prayers were in vain. Either God did not hear his petitions or chose to ignore them. For Morgan, although unaware of the fact, the appearance of the faces signaled the beginning of a long journey—a journey that a fortune cookie at the Flower Drum had foretold months ago. It was best that Morgan did not know what awaited him. Had he known in advance the agony that was to follow, he might have crumbled before venturing a single step.

                          •   •   •

At first Easy and Dave and Tam appeared in Morgan's dreams once or twice weekly, their faces always the same and their eyes filled with unbearable sorrow. They never spoke, yet they seemed to be waiting for something.

Morgan's response to the nightmares was always the same; shouting himself awake, being covered with a sheen of cold sweat, trembling hands fumbling for a cigaret. Rhonda was always there, to offer him soothing words and touches. She gently prompted him to talk about the dreams, but he would only mutter, "Faces. Just faces." Eventually the couple would lie down to sleep, but Morgan just stared at the darkness, full of despair. Finally he would sleep, averaging four or five hours before the alarm clock awakened him to another day.

In a month's time the faces appeared almost nightly. One night, after what was becoming a tortuous ritual, he got out of bed and dressed.

"Where are you going, Morg?" The concern on Rhonda's face was hidden by the darkness.

"Out," he said.

"Out where? It's late."

"Just out," he said irritably. "For a walk. For a drive. For a beer. For the hell of it."

"Well," Rhonda said hesitantly, "be careful."

He walked to the bed and kissed her.

"I wish I knew what to do for you," she said sadly.

He held her tightly. "Just be here." he said and left.

Morgan walked the streets of Glendale hoping the

cool night air would calm him. When that failed he went
to a bar. He sat on a stool, lit a cigaret, and ordered a
beer. Drinking it quickly, he ordered another, downed it
rapidly, and asked for a third.

He was oblivious to the other patrons, but a few of
them noted his grim visage and wondered at the haunted
look emanating from his eyes.

Although Morgan had never been a problem drinker,
this night he drank like one—too fast and too much,
and for the same reason: to anesthetize psychic pain or
at least to reduce it to a tolerable level.

He was drunk when he entered the apartment.
Rhonda was sitting in the living room. He kissed her. "I
think I can sleep now," he said, smiling crookedly.
Rhonda said nothing; she followed Morgan into the
bedroom and got into bed. He undressed, fumbling with
the buttons on his shirt, and lay down heavily. In a few
minutes he fell asleep, snoring loudly. The ghostly faces
of his friends did not appear, but something else was
different: Now it was Rhonda who could not sleep. She
stared at the darkness, filled with fear and apprehension, wondering what the future held in store for her
and her tormented husband.

Easy, Dave, and Tam continued to make their nightly
appearances, and to counter them Morgan continued to
go out and get drunk. Rhonda was always waiting for
him when he returned home. She pleaded with him to
stop; he told her he couldn't. She reasoned with him;
her words fell on deaf ears. Finally her concern and pa-
tience gave way to anger, and she argued with him.
That, too, failed.

Morgan continued his nightly drinking, but Rhonda
no longer waited up for him. They became more civil
than loving toward each other. Their sex life waned.
Their nights out together dwindled, and the beach was
forgotten.

Morgan's nightmares persisted despite his drinking.
He began bringing beer home after work, hoping that
going to bed intoxicated would obliterate the faces. It

didn't work. He began showing up late for work and became sullen and irritable.

One night Morgan came home more drunk than he had ever been.

He stumbled through the darkened apartment past the sleeping form of his wife and into the bathroom. He knelt in front of the toilet, his arms embracing the bowl, and vomited forcefully.

When his stomach was empty, he continued retching, his body wracked by spasms of nausea. He tasted bile as it spewed from his system. Still, he could not stop retching.

"Rhonda," he gasped weakly, "I need you." There was no response.

He forced air into his lungs. "Rhonda! Help me!"

The bathroom light switched on. Rhonda stood in the doorway looking down at him, her arms crossed. "What do you need me for? You've got your booze," she said coldly.

He retched again. "I can't go on like this. It's killing me."

"No shit," she said.

"Help me. *Please*." He reached for her. Rhonda hesitated, but as she looked at the drunken, pathetic man on the floor, she saw something she had never seen before: tears in the corners of his eyes, albeit small ones. She had never seen him cry.

Deeply moved, she took Morgan's hand and knelt beside him.

"I'll help you, Morg," she said, tears welling in her own eyes. "We'll get through this together."

"How?" he asked, wiping his mouth.

"Maybe therapy will work. Are you willing to try it?"

He retched. "Oh, God. I'll try anything."

"I'll ask around the hospital tomorrow for a referral to a good therapist."

"Thanks," Morgan said. They stood. Rhonda waited while Morgan rinsed his mouth and brushed his teeth, then she helped him to bed.

— 81 —

Morgan drove to the psychologist's office in Coldwater Canyon and then sat in the waiting room. After a few minutes a young woman came out of the office, dabbing at her eyes with a Kleenex.

A man appeared in the doorway. He was about thirty-eight years old and had curly brown hair, thoughtful blue eyes, and a neatly-trimmed mustache. "You're Morgan Preston?" he asked.

"Yes."

"I'm Jack Danielson. C'mon in."

Morgan entered the spacious office. The walls were painted in pastel colors. A Navajo rug dominated the parquet floor.

The two men shook hands. "Have a seat, Morgan," Jack said, motioning to two chairs arranged around a table that held an ashtray and a box of Kleenex.

When they were settled, Morgan said, "So, you're the man who's going to solve my problems."

Jack smiled. "No. I'm the man who's going to help *you* solve your problems."

"How long will it take?" Morgan asked, lighting a cigaret.

The psychologist shrugged. "Depends on what your problems are."

"Where do I start?"

"Start by telling me what's going on in your life at the present, and we'll go from there."

Morgan sighed, leaned forward, and began. He told about the relentless nightmares containing the faces of Easy and Dave and Tam, about his drinking, and about the increasing alienation between himself and Rhonda.

After Morgan's litany there was a silence of several minutes. Finally, Jack spoke. "It's an interesting story, Morgan. It must cause you a lot of pain, and you told it in a monotonic voice."

"What's that mean?"

"There weren't any feelings connected to your words. How do you feel?"

"Right now?"

"Yes."

Morgan thought for a while before answering, then said, "Empty."

"There's a lot more than 'empty' going on inside you. Have you ever heard of survivor's guilt?"

"I don't feel guilty about surviving."

Jack lit a cigaret. "Maybe. Maybe not. But survivor's guilt has to do with anger and sadness. When was the last time you got mad?"

"Really mad?" Morgan asked.

"Really mad."

Morgan shrugged. "I can't remember."

"When was the last time you cried?"

"I never cry," he said fiercely.

Jack looked at his watch. "Time's up," he said. "If you're willing to work on this stuff, make an appointment for next week, same time."

"I'll be here," Morgan said. Jack walked him to the door. "There's one thing I want you to do between now and our next meeting."

"What's that?" Morgan asked.

"Stop drinking. It will destroy you and your marriage more quickly than anything else."

"Cold turkey?"

"The colder the better," Jack said.

"I'll try."

"Don't try. Just do it. I'll see you next week."

Morgan drove down the Hollywood Freeway, excited about the way the first appointment had gone and apprehensive about the next one. Jack Danielson had said that resolving Morgan's problems would be hard work, and Morgan did not know if he wanted to go through the probing of painful memories—bringing them into the open and being forced to confront them.

He wanted a beer. He pulled off the freeway and
found a bar. The bartender approached him, wet rag in
hand.

"What'll it be?"

Morgan needed a beer. His hands trembled slightly.
The bartender waited.

"A . . . Coke," Morgan said. The bartender got
one and set it in front of Morgan. He took a sip and
grimaced. This cold turkey business, he thought, is
going to be a bitch.

Rhonda met him at the door. "How did it go?"

"We talked."

"I know that. Did you get anything accomplished?"

"I quit drinking."

"What?"

"I gave up drinking. After I left his office I wanted a
drink, so I went to a bar, but all I had was a couple of
Cokes."

"That's great, Morg," she said, hugging him. She
caressed his chest. "Would you like to get something
going tonight?"

Morgan paused. "I'm not up to it. I'm sorry. What
I'd like to do is take a shower and just go to bed and
hold you. If that's all right?"

"Fine," she said. "I'll settle for that, for now."

The next few therapy sessions went nowhere. Jack
tried to prod Morgan into connecting his thoughts to
feelings, and Morgan did his best to avoid this by asking
irrelevant questions and playing dumb.

"We're not getting anywhere," Jack said one night.

"I'm trying," Morgan offered lamely.

"Bullshit, you're screwing around."

"What the fuck do you want from me?" Morgan
flared.

"That."

"What?"

"That anger. This is the first time you've shown
any."

"All right. I've got enough anger in me to probably blow up LA. But I'm afraid to let it out. I don't know what would happen."

Jack shrugged. "I don't know what would happen either, but by holding it all in, you're tearing yourself apart."

Morgan sighed. "Sometimes I think I should just shoot myself. Sometimes I just want . . . blackness."

"Suicide's an alternative, Morgan, although not one I'd recommend. You check yourself out of this world, and Rhonda lives the rest of her life tormented by the thought that she somehow failed you. You get rid of your problems and stick her with them. How very fucking thoughtful of you."

"I didn't say I'd do it," said Morgan. "All I want is some peace inside my head."

"Then get off your ass and work for it. Face the dragons."

"What dragons?"

"The dragons in your mind—the nightmares and the anger and the sadness."

"I can't face them alone," Morgan said between gritted teeth.

"I'm with you, Morgan," Jack said. "Hell, my nickname is Saint George."

— 82 —

"Let's talk about Vietnam in general," Jack said.

"In general," Morgan began, "I thought we were doing the right thing, saving a bunch of people from communism and all that. But somewhere along the line I realized that the average Vietnamese farmer just wanted to grow rice and raise his family and didn't really care about politics as long as he could live in peace. So what happens? We burn their villages down and make refugees out of them.

"The civilians were always getting caught in the crossfire, and they took more casualties than the armies did. You ever see a little girl with her leg blown off and her face burned to shit by napalm?"

"No," Jack said softly.

"I have," Morgan said, just as softly.

"Keep going," Jack prompted.

Morgan felt anger rising in him. "It was waste this or zap that. Napalm and flamethrowers and willy peter. Tanks and tracks, howitzers, 106s, B-52s and Cobras and Puff the Magic Dragon. Claymores and M-16s. We killed Viet Cong and North Vietnamese, but mostly civilians got blown away." His hands were balled into fists.

"Like Tam at My Lai?" Jack said.

"Tam," he said softly. "Calley," he muttered contemptuously. "You know what I'd like to do to him?"

"What?"

Morgan told him in one scathing sentence.

Jack rose from his chair and walked over to a closet. He returned with a two-and-a-half-foot-long piece of plastic shaped like a baseball bat with a handle at the tapered end. He held the bat out to Morgan.

"What's this?"

"A bataca bat. You use it to express anger. Just go

over to that footstool and start hitting it. The words that go with the feelings will come to you.''

Morgan shook with rage. ''I'll do it,'' he said, taking the bat, ''but not in front of you.''

Jack shrugged. ''I'll wait in the reception room.'' He left. Morgan approached the footstool, bat in hand. For several minutes he stood, paralyzed. A picture of Calley flashed through his mind; a picture of Tam lying dead in a ditch flashed through his mind. He raised the bat above his head with both hands and brought it down on the footstool softly. He tried again; the impact was more substantial. Each successive blow was more powerful than the last until Morgan was beating the footstool rhythmically. ''Calley,'' he roared, his face distorted with hatred. ''Calley, Calley, Calley . . .'' The words gave way to animalistic sounds that tore from Morgan's throat. Totally immersed in primal feelings, he smashed the footstool until his arms were too tired to raise the bat. Red-faced and spent, he sat on the floor panting.

Jack quietly entered the room. ''How'd it go?''

''It worked,'' Morgan said triumphantly. ''There's only one problem.''

''What?''

Smiling, he held up the bataca bat. ''I broke the handle off this sucker.''

•   •   •

For several months Morgan and Jack worked around the edges of the deaths of Easy and Dave Bruckner.

''You're keeping them alive with your nightmares, Morgan,'' Jack said. ''You've got to let them go.''

''I can't,'' Morgan insisted.

''You mean you *won't*.''

''All right, I won't,'' Morgan said defiantly.

Jack sighed. ''Morg, what's your objection to letting them go?''

"If I don't remember them, who will?" Morgan said, his voice trembling.

"They're dead, Morg. Let the dead take care of themselves."

"I can't!" Morgan yelled.

"You won't."

"Fuck your can'ts and won'ts. I was the one who—" Morgan lowered his head and covered his face.

Jack waited a few seconds, then said, "You were the one who what, Morg?"

Morgan raised his head. His eyes reflected incredible pain. "I," he said in an emotion-choked voice, "was the one who loved them." His voice broke on the word "loved."

"You loved them," Jack said, his own voice tinged with emotion, "and now they're dead. They have peace. And if you say good-bye to them, you'll have peace."

Morgan rubbed his eyes. "If I say good-bye to them, I'll cry." He stood and made for the door.

"What's your objection to crying?" Jack asked.

Morgan stood in the doorway. "If I start crying, I won't ever be able to stop," he said shakily, and disappeared.

• • •

A week later, Morgan showed up for his therapy session with Jack.

"Hello, Morg. How are you?" Jack asked as the two men shook hands.

"I've been doing a lot of thinking," Morgan said, taking a seat.

"Come up with anything?"

"I'm ready."

"Ready for what?" Jack asked, lighting a cigaret.

"I'm ready to say good-bye to Dave and Easy."

Jack looked at Morgan appraisingly and ground out his cigaret. "You're sure?"

"It's time to get it over with. You just show me how."

"Well," Jack said, "what you do is imagine that your buddies are here in the room, and then you tell them whatever's in your heart."

"O.K.," Morgan said. He closed his eyes for a minute in heavy concentration, then opened them, cleared his throat, and began.

"I, ah, never had a chance to tell you guys what I really thought of you—what you really meant to me. I'm sorry that you had to . . . die, but I can't do anything about that." His voice grew tremulous. "I have to let you go so I can get on with my own life. I miss you guys so much that it hurts," he said, and finally years of held-back tears welled in Morgan's eyes and slipped down his cheeks. "I loved you," he cried.

"Morg," Jack said huskily, "tell them individually."

"Easy, I loved you. You were great." Tears dropped from his face onto his chest. "Dave," he quavered, "you were my brother. You were *more* than a brother. You took care of me in the hospital. I loved you so much."

"Now, say good-bye to them, Morg," Jack said gently.

Morgan's shoulders shook as he began sobbing. "Good-bye, Easy. Good-bye, Dave." The body-wracking sobbing continued. He looked at Jack with pleading eyes. "Good-bye . . . Dave."

"What, Morg?" asked Jack, his own eyes rimmed with red.

Morgan's lips trembled. He put out his arms. "Hold me." Jack got out of his chair and embraced Morgan. After a while Morgan's sobbing subsided to crying, which in turn gave way to sniffling. Jack released him. Morgan blew his nose into a Kleenex, and both men lit cigarets.

"Do you feel like it's over with Easy and Dave?" asked Jack.

"It all felt real. I could feel them in the room with me."

"Are they here now?"

"No. They're gone."

"How do you feel?"

"Drained. Beat. A little sad."

"Sounds normal. You've done a lot of good work."

Morgan looked at his watch. "We're into overtime." He stood up. Jack walked him to the door and said, "Two ghosts put to rest and one to go."

"Tam," said Morgan.

"Right."

"Not tonight. I'm all out of tears."

"Soon," Jack said. "When you're ready."

Morgan and Jack stood at the door and impulsively hugged each other.

"Take care," said Jack.

"You, too."

He drove home and told Rhonda about the session; they cried together and later made love.

He had a nightmare that night; his shout woke Rhonda. She rubbed his arm. "They're still with you, huh?"

Morgan wiped sweat off his face. "Just one," he said. "Dave and Easy are gone."

* * *

Therapy continued, but no matter what Morgan tried or said, Tam visited his dreams almost nightly, never saying anything, just torturing him with her sorrowful eyes.

Morgan grew impatient and frustrated. "What the hell does she want from me, Jack?" he asked one night after six weeks of fruitless work.

"Well," he began slowly, "she doesn't want you to forget her. Or else you don't want to forget her. After all, you're the one producing the dream."

"Ah, shit. Either way it's a bitch. Sometimes I feel like going out and getting drunk again."

"You know what that did to your marriage the last time. How are you and your wife doing now?"

Morgan smiled. "Ever since I said good-bye to Dave and Easy, we've been getting along a lot better. We're going out again and hitting the beach."

"Good," said Jack. "How's your sex life?"

"A hell of a lot better than when I was drinking."

Jack nodded, grinning. "Stick with the Coke, Morgan. It might be aphrodisiacal."

— 83 —

January 1971. Rhonda was watching the eleven o'clock news, and Morgan was sitting at the kitchen table looking at a Rand McNally Road Atlas. He got up and sat next to his wife.

"Honey," he said. "I've got to go to Arizona."

She raised her eyebrows. "For what?"

"Well, you remember the story I told you about Sergeant Bighorse and the white buffalo?"

"Yes."

"Look at this," he said, handing her the map and pointing with his finger. "Right here. See what it says? Buffalo refuge."

Rhonda studied the spot on the map and said,

"Morgan, you don't really believe there's such a thing as a white buffalo, do you? I mean, it's a nice story, but it's only a superstition."

"Sergeant Bighorse didn't think it was a superstition," Morgan said defensively. "And besides, I'll never know unless I go."

Rhonda sighed. "You've really got your mind set on this, haven't you?"

"Yep."

"What about work?" she asked.

"I already asked for a week off, and they gave it to me."

"When do you leave?" she said resignedly.

"Tomorrow morning."

"Well, you're your own person, and I know I can't talk you out of it, but . . ."

"But, what?"

"I don't think you're going to find a white buffalo, so I don't want you to be disappointed. Why don't you look at your trip as a vacation? There's a lot of pretty country out there."

"O.K.," he said, "I'm just going on a vacation."

"That's better," she said. "Just relax for a week."

"Right," he agreed.

Rhonda gave him a half-serious, half-playful look. "But if you mess around with any Indian girls, I'll scalp you."

"You're kinky," he said. "Want to take a shower together?"

• • •

Morgan left shortly after dawn. He stopped in Barstow for breakfast, then passed through Needles and crossed the Colorado River. He took his time and eventually climbed into the green plateau country of Arizona. That night he camped near Williams. Tam visited his dreams; Morgan's inevitable shout woke up several campers.

He ate breakfast in Flagstaff, then drove to the Wupatki Indian ruins and meditated for three hours in the main room of an eight-hundred-year-old ruin. As he meditated he heard or, rather, felt a voice within him. It said, "I am waiting."

Leaving the ruins, he reached the south rim of the Grand Canyon. For hours he admired the canyon's majestic beauty, and lingered on until the sun set. He drove to Cameron and rented a motel room. After dinner he bought a cold Coke and walked down to the banks of the Little Colorado where he sat and gazed northward. Somewhere out there, he thought, is what is waiting for me. He felt a mixture of excitement and apprehension, and when he turned in, he slept fitfully. Tam, of course, appeared right on schedule.

In the morning after breakfast Morgan stocked up on food, water, and firewood. He drove north for several hours, seeing nothing except an occasional roadrunner. He turned to the west, crossed Navajo Canyon Bridge, and continued on. A small herd of antelope bounded gracefully across the road, white tails flashing.

Thirty minutes later he spotted the small sign at the entrance to the buffalo refuge. He turned off the highway and drove slowly on a deeply rutted dirt road, the car's tires throwing up clouds of dust. After eight miles of traversing the primitive road, he came to a rise, reached its crest, and stopped.

Below him, ranged across an arid valley, were buffalo. Morgan felt a strange thrill course through him as he watched the shaggy-haired creatures. He estimated that the herd contained more than a hundred head. For an hour Morgan was content to stay where he was and simply watch the herd graze. Then he started the car, descended the hill, and entered their realm. The huge animals looked up as Morgan drove among them, their nostrils flaring as they made grunting piglike sounds. An old bull with a broken horn pawed at the ground ominously, then abruptly wheeled and lumbered away. A calf, hiding behind its mother, bawled piteously. The

mother turned and tongued her offspring's face; the calf
fell silent.

Morgan made a simple camp. He cleared brush and
stones from a small area and lay out his sleeping bag,
then dug a shallow hole to contain his cooking fire.
Finished, he drank from a canteen and watched the buffalo who continued to graze near him, totally aware of
his presence and completely unconcerned with it.

Darkness enveloped the valley; the night air grew
chilly. Morgan sat near the fire staring into the flames.
Smoking leisurely, he reviewed his simple plan for the
coming morning: he would follow the buffalo herd until
it led him to the Wakan Tonka.

He knew his plan was naive and probably foolish, but
he also knew that he had nothing to lose and, as he had
told Rhonda, he owed it to Sergeant Bighorse.

He stood and stretched, then drank his fill from the
canteen and walked a few yards from camp to relieve
himself. The night was so dark that he could not see any
of the buffalo, but he knew they were near. He walked
back to camp, stripped, and crawled into the sleeping
bag. Feeling alone but not lonely, he watched the
flickering fire until he became drowsy, then slept.

Morgan was not alone for long, however. Tam came
to him in his dreams, her eyes filled with more anguish
than ever before.

•   •   •

The next morning Morgan hurriedly finished breakfast, buckled the canteen belt around his waist, put on
his bush hat and sunglasses, and set out to follow the
herd which was about a half mile away. He hadn't gone
more than several hundred yards when he spotted a
small rattlesnake slithering across the hard ground. He
gave it a wide berth, and moved on.

When he was a hundred yards from the buffalo, he
stopped and squatted, waiting for them to move. Eventually they did, ambling onward for thirty or forty

yards, then stopping to graze. Morgan sighed in frustration at their slow movement but followed them resignedly.

Long before noon the sun baked the valley with stifling heat, and the air was so dry it drew perspiration from Morgan's pores. He had already finished off half his water supply. He found a smooth, flat pebble and put it on his tongue; it would stimulate the production of saliva.

The sun reached its zenith; the herd maintained its stop-and-go pace, with Morgan plodding along behind. The only thing he had discerned from being with the animals was the fact that the dominant bull led the herd while the flanks and rear were guarded by less assertive bulls. The subservient and sickly ones mingled with the cows and calves.

Shortly before dusk Morgan, exhausted, sunburnt, and dehydrated, admitted his folly. With a farewell wave to the beautiful animals, he turned and started for his camp. He reached it after nightfall and went directly to his water supply. Sipping slowly so as not to sicken himself, he consumed nearly a gallon of the sustaining liquid before his body was sated. Too worn out to eat or even to build a fire, he stripped off his salt-encrusted clothing and dropped onto the sleeping bag. He lit a cigaret and stared at the darkness, disconsolate. I didn't find the white buffalo, he thought grimly, but Tam will find me. He shuddered. It was a long time before sleep overtook him.

In his dream Morgan stood alone on the runway at Tan Son Nhut. He was the last American in Vietnam. All around him the kingdom of Annam lay burning and dying—the tragic legacy of thirty years of American involvement in a once-proud and beautiful land.

He looked at an abandoned hangar and spied a still figure standing just inside its smashed doors. He walked slowly to the hangar and halted in front of the figure.

She was a pretty Vietnamese girl dressed in white—

the Vietnamese color of mourning. The girl held a blood-red orchid in her delicate hands. A livid scar marked her cheek: It was Tam.

Morgan's voice cracked as he said, "I loved you, but now I must go. I'm sorry."

Tam looked at him for a long time, her eyes filled with immense sorrow. Finally she smiled sadly and whispered, "I forgive you, Morgan." She extended the orchid; their fingers touched fleetingly as Morgan accepted it. He looked into Tam's eyes for the last time and realized they mirrored his own; dark and pained. Yet, behind the pain he discerned a measure of courage which, although not invincible, was strong enough to endure the seemingly unendurable and, ultimately, to prevail.

Morgan touched Tam's scarred cheek lovingly, then turned and walked away, leaving her standing forever in the lengthening shadows of the broken hangar doors.

Morgan awoke from the dream and sat up. His cheeks were wet with tears. In the distance a coyote barked. He looked at the brilliant stars for a long time and allowed his tears to wash the pain from his body. When his weeping subsided he wiped his eyes. Focusing on a particularly bright star, he said softly, "Thank you, Tam."

His words triggered more tears, and when he was done he slept easily.

Shortly before dawn he experienced another dream. He was standing near the edge of the Grand Canyon, hot and tired and dirty after walking all day. He spotted a sinkhole half filled with water in the sandstone rocks. He stripped and entered the water, luxuriating in its coolness for a long time.

Revived, Morgan emerged from the sinkhole, water streaming off his naked body. Suddenly he was aware of an awesome presence. He turned slowly and came face to face with the Wakan Tonka.

The spirit-buffalo stood firmly on a raised outcropping of rock, its entire body a dazzling white. Its woolly head was massive, and its alabaster horns curved sharply.

The white buffalo benevolently regarded Morgan for an eternity encompassed in minutes, mere minutes in which Morgan was filled with inexpressible tranquility.

Then, fulfilling its purpose and no longer needed, the Wakan Tonka tossed his majestic head and disappeared.

The magnificent dream did not awaken Morgan, but he would remember it in the morning and realize that he had been graced, as Sergeant Bighorse had told him, although to Morgan grace was such an intangible quality that he did not know what form it would take.

Several hundred miles away, Rhonda Preston knew exactly what form the grace would take. She waited patiently for her husband's return.

When Morgan broke camp later that morning and departed the buffalo refuge, he left behind, nestled in a hollow and covered by a flat piece of sandstone, the bone amulet engraved with the buffalo head. Sergeant Bighorse's wish for Morgan had been fulfilled.

Morgan arrived home late on a Saturday night. Rhonda embraced him when he came through the door. Without preamble he began telling her what had happened in Arizona; both of their smiles broadened as the story unfolded.

When he was finished Rhonda kissed him. "I don't know what to say. I'm just glad that it happened, and I'm glad you're back. I've missed you."

"Let me get out of these raunchy clothes and take a shower, then I'll show you how much I missed you."

•   •   •

Morgan lay on his back after making love; Rhonda was propped up on one elbow, idly curling his chest hair. "There's something I've been waiting to tell you," she said.

"What's that?" Morgan murmured.

She moved closer to him and whispered in his ear. He bolted upright. "You're pregnant? How? When?"

Rhonda laughed. "You know how, you silly ass. As to the when, about six weeks ago. I saw my doctor yesterday, and he confirmed it."

"Jesus," said Morgan.

"Is that all you can say? Are you happy or upset, or what?"

He took her in his arms. "Hell, yes, I'm happy. I'm also scared."

"Why?"

"I've never been a father before."

"I'm a little scared, too," she admitted. "I've never been a mother."

Morgan patted her shoulder. "We'll work it out. Right now we need to celebrate. I'll get the Amaretto."

"Wait a minute, honey," Rhonda said. "You haven't had a drink in months, and I won't drink while I'm carrying the baby. Besides, I know a better way to celebrate."

"How?" he asked.

Her hand worked down his stomach and stroked him.

"Oh," he said, growing hard under her ministrations.

When they were finished, Morgan and Rhonda talked for more than an hour, discussing all the things that needed to be done before the baby's arrival. Eventually they grew tired and fell asleep in each other's arms. Rhonda slept soundly in the knowledge that a precious new being was growing in her womb. But it was Morgan who slept best—Tam was gone, her troubled spirit returned to its proper place: My Lai.

• • •

The months passed quickly. Morgan continued therapy sessions with Jack, working on smoothing some sharp psychic edges that caused him discomfort.

Rhonda continued working at the hospital, not telling

any of her friends that she was pregnant. When her growing belly gave her away, they gave her a baby shower.

Morgan came home one evening with a rocking chair. Rhonda fell in love with it and rocked by the hour as she knitted baby clothes.

The pregnancy advanced into its eighth month. Rhonda was not the type to complain about the pain in her enlarged breasts or the clumsiness induced by her swollen belly. And when the baby kicked, she reveled in its movements. To Morgan, she had never seemed so serene and beautiful.

•   •   •

Morgan lay on the bed on a Friday evening reading a novel. Rhonda came in and lay beside him.

"What's up?" he asked, still reading.

"Oh, nothing. I just felt like being with you," she said casually. He detected something different in her tone of voice. He put down the book and, looking at her, saw that she was focused inward. He took her hand. "Are you in labor?"

"Yes."

Morgan felt a thrill run through his body. "How far apart are the contractions?" he asked calmly; they had taken a Lamaze class during the seventh month of pregnancy.

"About ten minutes," she said.

"We've got a lot of time yet. Are you having much pain?"

She shrugged. "Nothing I can't handle."

"Is there anything I can do to make you feel better?"

"Just hold my hand, Morgan. That's all I need."

When the contractions came at three-minute intervals, Morgan helped his wife into the car and drove to the hospital.

Rhonda had been on the delivery table for forty-five

minutes. Morgan stood behind her, holding her in a sitting position.

"Push, Rhonda," urged Dr. Braghini, who sat on the stool between her stirruped legs.

"I can't," she gasped. "I don't have any strength left."

Dr. Braghini shrugged. "Then go home and wait nine more months. Come on, honey, push with the contraction." She pushed, her face beet-red and bathed in perspiration. A nurse gave her a whiff of oxygen.

"One more time, sweetie," Dr. Braghini cajoled. Rhonda gritted her teeth and pushed.

The doctor chuckled. "Your baby comes."

Morgan and Rhonda looked into a large mirror on the wall and watched their child's head emerge, then one shoulder. Dr. Braghini eased the other shoulder free of the birth canal, then with a deft movement he delivered the infant into the world. He suctioned out its mouth and held it aloft triumphantly. The baby was mottled red and blue, and wrinkled. Its eyes opened and shut, its little hands clenched and unclenched. It started to cry, a mewling which gradually grew in strength until its wails echoed off the delivery room's tiled walls.

It was a girl.

Dr. Braghini laid her on Rhonda's stomach. She and Morgan tentatively touched the child they had created, their love expanding to encompass her.

"She's pretty," said Dr. Braghini, "even if she is bald. What are you going to name her?"

Rhonda looked down at her daughter. "Megan," she said. "Megan Marie Preston."

— 84 —

The next morning Morgan walked into Rhonda's hospital room carrying a vase containing three yellow roses. Rhonda lay with her eyes closed, a tranquil smile on her face as Megan suckled her breast. Morgan thought that he had never seen anything that looked so natural and beautiful.

He crossed the room, set the flowers on the table, and kissed Rhonda on the cheek. She opened her eyes. "Hi," she said sleepily.

"Hi. How are you feeling?"

"Sore. Tired. Happy."

"How is she?" he asked, putting his hand on Megan's head and tracing the soft spot.

"She's a hungry little girl." Rhonda closed her eyes. Morgan moved to the window and stood looking down at the parking lot for a long time.

Rhonda woke up. "Morgan?"

He turned to her, his forehead wrinkled in thought, his face serious.

"What are you thinking?"

Calmly, he said, "I was thinking about where I've been and where I am. I've been hearing a lot of people say that Vietnam is a worthless cause, and in my head I know the war is senseless. Hell, the Vietnamese people don't care who rules them as long as they're allowed to work their fields and raise their families in peace. But if I admit the war is wrong, then I have to admit that my buddies were killed and wounded for nothing.

"I don't know if I'll ever be able to get my head together about this difference between what I think about the war and what I feel about my buddies who were wasted, but what I *do* know is that Vietnam created a brotherhood among us that anyone who wasn't there will never understand. We gave Vietnam everything we had and, right or wrong, we *believed* in what we were doing. Until 'sixty-eight, at least. Before then most Americans supported the war, but after the Tet Offensive they lost their will or became disillusioned. Then there's the 'survivor's guilt' that Jack talked about. I know there wasn't anything I could do to save Easy and Tam and Dave, but I'll never forget them.''

Morgan smiled sadly. "I volunteered for Vietnam and came home sick, and I was treated like a leper. I left my hometown to get away from the rumors, and because no one would hire me. The same thing is happening to a hell of a lot of other vets. We thought we were John Waynes, but what most of us really were was a bunch of eighteen- and nineteen-year-old kids who were scared but who learned to take care of each other and survive the best way we knew how.

"Vietnam has caused me a lot of pain, and because of it I've caused you pain, and I'm sorry. But even when I was getting drunk every night, I loved you. I've never known anyone as kind and understanding as you are.

"I'm babbling," he said, and stopped talking. He put a finger on Megan's miniature palm. Her tiny fingers curled around it.

Morgan looked at Rhonda again. "What I'm trying to say is that Vietnam has scarred me, along with thousands of other guys. I'll always feel pain to some degree or other, but I can live with it. What counts now is that I'm with you and our little girl. It's been a long trip, but here I am right where I belong.''

Tears spilled down Rhonda's cheeks, but she was smiling. She took her husband's hand in hers and squeezed it.

"Morgan?"

"Yes?"

"Welcome home."

MORE TITLES AVAILABLE FROM
HODDER AND STOUGHTON PAPERBACKS

	GORDON STEVENS	
☐ 36027 5	Spider	£2.95
	JAMES PATTERSON	
☐ 40226 6	Black Market	£2.95
	ROBERT MOSS	
☐ 37790 9	Moscow Rules	£2.95
	A J QUINNELL	
☐ 37179 X	Blood Ties	£2.95
☐ 40719 0	Siege of Silence	£2.95

All these books are available at your local bookshop or newsagent, or can be ordered direct from the publisher. Just tick the titles you want and fill in the form below.

Prices and availability subject to change without notice.

Hodder & Stoughton Paperbacks, P.O. Box 11, Falmouth, Cornwall.

Please send cheque or postal order, and allow the following for postage and packing:

U.K. – 55p for one book, plus 22p for the second book, and 14p for each additional book ordered up to a £1.75 maximum.

B.F.P.O. and EIRE – 55p for the first book, plus 22p for the second book, and 14p per copy for the next 7 books, 8p per book thereafter.

OTHER OVERSEAS CUSTOMERS – £1.00 for the first book, plus 25p per copy for each additional book.

Name ....

Address ....

....